REGIS COLLEGE LIBRARY
100 Wellesley Street West
Toronto, Ontario
Canada M5S 2Z5

Tissa Balasuriya

PLANETARY
THEOLOGY

BR
115
W6
B33
1984

ORBIS BOOKS
Maryknoll, New York 10545

91604

The Catholic Foreign Mission Society of America (Maryknoll) recruits and trains people for overseas missionary service. Through Orbis Books Maryknoll aims to foster the international dialogue that is essential to mission. The books published, however, reflect the opinions of their authors and are not meant to represent the official position of the society.

Bible quotations are from the Jerusalem Bible.

Copyright © 1984 Orbis Books, Maryknoll, NY 10545
All rights reserved
Manufactured in the United States of America

Manuscript Editor: William E. Jerman

Library of Congress Cataloging in Publication Data

Balasuriya, Tissa.
  Planetary theology.

  Includes index.
  1. Church and the world. 2. Christianity—20th century.
I. Title.
BR115.W6B33   1984   261.1   83-19339
ISBN 0-88344-400-3 (pbk.)

CONTENTS

ACRONYMS

ASEAN	Association of South East Asian Nations
CCA	Christian Conference of Asia
EEC	European Economic Community (Common Market)
FAO	Food and Agriculture Organization
FABC	Federation of Asian Bishops Conferences
GATT	General Agreement on Tariffs and Trade
GNP	Gross National Product
IBRD	International Bank for Reconstruction and Development (World Bank)
IMF	International Monetary Fund
MNC	Multinational Corporation
NIEO	New International Economic Order
OAU	Organization of African Unity
OPEC	Organization of Petroleum Exporting Countries
TCDC	Technical Cooperation among Developing Countries
UNCTAD	United Nations Conference on Trade and Development

Chapter 1

Why Planetary Theology?

It puzzles and saddens me that so many who call themselves Christian are so little concerned about the immense human misery and suffering in almost all parts of the world. Sometimes we are even the cause of this suffering and we seem not to realize it. Our going regularly to church and attending prayer services seem to leave us uninterested in the fate of our sisters and brothers. On the contrary, our being considered good Christians may be what makes us insensitive to them.

Why is it that most of the Christians who attend Sunday worship in the city of Colombo, Sri Lanka, hardly ever reflect seriously on the utterly inhuman conditions of the one hundred fifty thousand shantytowners who "live" in our beautiful city? The roof of their hovel cannot prevent the rain from drenching their one-room dwelling. The floor on which they sleep is damp. They have no clean water. There is one toilet for about every hundred persons. No schooling for children; no jobs for adults. They live in filthy conditions. Infant mortality is high; malnutrition is standard. And this continues from generation to generation; if anything, the situation worsens. The rich prosper, and many of them are Christians and consider themselves good Christians.

How was it possible for an American bishop to visit the U.S. forces in Vietnam at Christmas and encourage them to fight the poor Vietnamese . . . in the name of the Prince of Peace? Did he not know that more bombs were dropped by the U.S.A. on Vietnam than all the bombs dropped in World War II? How was it possible that Western missionaries could accompany European and American traders, gunboaters, and soldiers into China in the nineteenth century? How could good Christians allow themselves to be slave traders and slave owners in the New World, which they occupied after killing or driving away the aboriginal inhabitants?

These are not questions only of the past. How is it that good Christians in Europe and North America still are not aware that their countries have abundance partly at the expense of the poor of the Third World? How is it that $1 million is spent each minute on armaments by governments, mainly of countries that think of themselves as Christian, when over 500 billion human beings have not enough food to satisfy their hunger? Why is it that the urgent appeals of Popes John XXIII, Paul VI, and John Paul II for justice and sharing fall on deaf ears even among their own faithful? Why is it that the World Council of Churches' Program to Combat Racism in South Africa is not only unheeded by many Christians, but is even suspect by many of them?

A simple response to these questions would be to say that unfortunately persons and countries paid no attention to the Christian message, or that sin is a commonplace in human history. However, we can go a step further and ask whether *a world system of unjust relationships* has come to be set up in the past few centuries. And we can ask whether the teaching, motivations, and actions of organized Christian churches contributed toward it. Has a distorted social order in turn influenced the churches? Has the prevalent Christian theology lent a religious justification to unjust attitudes and approaches?

TRADITIONAL THEOLOGY

It seems to me that dominant groups—based on race, class, sex, or religion—were encouraged in their convictions of superiority by the theology that prevailed in the Christian churches during the five hundred years from about 1450 to about 1950. And similar theological perspectives still prevail, by and large, within the mainstream thinking of the churches, with some adaptation to modern times.

This is not a problem peculiar to theology. It seems to affect human knowledge as such. Our understanding of history, and even of right and wrong, is conditioned by our environment, interests, information, and field of awareness. I write mainly from a consciousness arising from an Asian context, though I have had the good fortune of having been in or visited very many other parts of the world.

Reflecting on these issues, I cannot escape the conclusion that the traditional Western theology, which claimed a certain universality, was very much determined by dominant world powers and groups. European—and later, North American—capitalist-oriented, adult, male, clerical groups determined the method, contentual boundaries, and application of theology. They read the gospel and human history in a manner suited to their dominant situation. Many of the concerns that preoccupied Western theologians over the centuries were irrelevant to Third World peoples or even detrimental. Instance divisions of North Atlantic Christians solidified into Catholic and Protestant positions on rather marginal issues and exported to rural villages in Bolivia, Sierra Leone, or the Philippines. The approach toward other religions also began with a Western prejudice against them—as if they could not be from God and salvific, unless they could somehow be considered "Christian in disguise." Again, the close link between Christian missionary activity and Western colonial expansion unduly affected both theology and pastoral practice all over the world. Following is a sketch of some of the major traits that traditional theology accrued from its North Atlantic conditioning.

A Culture-Bound Theology

Traditional Christian theology was in fact profoundly culture-bound throughout its development. It was implicitly ethnocentric: arising from and directed toward concerns of the West. It was a handmaid of Western expansion, an unwitting ally in the exploitation of peoples of other continents, first by Europeans and later by North Americans. The symbiosis of the "sacred duty" of civilizing, baptizing, and saving pagans and the North Atlantic quest for military, economic, political, and cultural domination was disastrous for Christianity itself. It not only made many aspects of Christian theology unacceptable to the rest of humankind, but it also dehu-

manized the content of Western theology and blinded its practi-
tioners to the cultural implications of what they—and others—were
creating.

The attitude of many Westerners toward nature is one aspect of
this cultural impact on Christian theology. African, Amerindian,
and Eastern peoples have had a respectful attitude toward nature,
almost to the point of overdoing it. Indian culture respects life in all
forms, including plants and animals. Chinese culture attaches a high
value to the harmony of all things: the heavens and the earth, nature
and humanity, society and the inner person. Western Christianity,
in its emphasis on possession and work, has largely neglected this
respect for nature. Nature becomes an appropriate object for human exploitation. Although this has fostered an extraordinary development of science and technology, it has been harmful for the
conservation of nature and the dignity of humankind. The quality
of human life has in fact been lowered in the process, and now nature itself is being irreparably damaged and threatened with global
devastation.

A Church-Centered Theology

Traditional theology has been very largely church-centered, tending to equate the universal kingdom of God and the common human good with the expansion of the church. The divine claims of the
church made all else seem faulty, in need of submission to and remediation by the church. The good of the church became the ultimate
value according to which other priorities were gauged and issues
resolved. The church was regarded as the indispensable vehicle of
salvation. The main focus of interest of theology was life within the
institutional churches. That life was very much dominated by the
more powerful Western churches, and among Catholics particularly
by the church in Rome.

A Male-Dominated Theology

The clergy teaching in seminaries and universities has maintained
a virtual monopoly over theology. Theological preoccupations were
very much those of persons within church institutions and depen-

dent on them. Thus theology pursued many interests of concern to
adult, male clerics and, in the case of Catholics, celibates. They
tended to read the Scriptures through an adult-male (celibate) lens.
They naturally were inclined to find in revelation many texts that
reinforced their authority, importance, and indispensability.

The rights of women did not figure in traditional theological
reflection. All rights seem to have been attributed *a priori* to males,
beginning in the garden of Eden, leaving women to struggle for their
rights by themselves, if at all. During the many centuries of male
domination, the churches, in particular the Catholic Church, saw
God on the side of the dominating male. Even now what changes
have been tolerated in the Catholic Church are reformist and
analgesic. Thus women are to be given functions such as the distribution of communion under exceptional circumstances. But there is
no acceptance of the fundamental equality of men and women in
the life of the church—and this in an age when there are female
heads of state, including elected prime ministers. Within the
churches, real power in matters both spiritual and temporal is kept
in the hands of males. The laity-clergy relationship is dominated by
the (male-dominated) clergy. The theology of marriage is such that
marriage is a bar to certain positions within the church. These may
be disciplinary, not doctrinal, norms, but they reflect the reigning
pattern of thought.

An Age-Dominated Theology

Traditional theology was also age-dominated, representing the
thought of those who had spent many years studying hefty tomes of
the past. The whole apparatus of church life is still age-dominated:
the higher the echelon of ecclesiastical authority, the more advanced
is the average age of those exercising it. The young are practically
excluded from having an impact on thought and action in the
churches. Even the most forward-looking changes give the young
only a subsidiary role. It is scarcely acknowledged that persons of
eighteen to twenty-five or so years of age can be mature human
beings, capable of making a significant contribution to the life of a
community. Yet what youth can contribute is vitality, dynamism,
freshness of approach, openness to the future, a keen sense of justice, and readiness to face risks.

A Procapitalist Theology

In its social orientation, traditional theology was procapitalist. Theological thought and ecclesiastical activity were influenced by the class composition of church personnel. The lifestyle of most theologians and churchmen was fashioned within the framework of Western capitalism, and they benefited from it. Consciously or unconsciously, they did not deal with issues that threatened their interests and positions. Thus traditional theology had little to do with the conditions of the working classes. Even today it is largely unrelated to the issues that concern the rural poor, who form the bulk of the population in the poorer countries of the world, or the many millions of the urban poor everywhere.

Where theology or church social teachings touched on these issues, the remedies they proposed were palliatives rather than fundamental reforms of social structures themselves. Economic power was to remain with the owners of capital—with a certain softening of the exploitative process through the sedatives of recreational facilities for workers, labor laws, profit-sharing, workers' councils, and trade unions. These are good in themselves, but there was no serious intention of fundamentally altering the social system so that workers would receive a just share of the benefits of their work. There was to be no basic change of the social order to end exploitation of person by person. The attitude of many Christians was even more conservative than were official church teachings.

An Anticommunist Theology

Now that the Western world is coming to a coexistence with the Soviet Union, Eastern Europe, and China, Christian thinkers are beginning to turn from condemnation to tolerance of communism. But in the early decades of the Russian, Chinese, and Vietnamese revolutions, the Christian churches took a strong condemnatory attitude toward the new Marxist regimes. The churches saw the negative aspects of communist dictatorship, but were slow to acknowledge their achievements for the people.

This caused conflicts with the revolutionary governments and a long estrangement with them, including the expulsion of missionaries from China. From about 1950 onward, Western theology turned a blind eye to the half of Asia that is China, which was going through one of the most significant revolutions in human history.

We thus are faced with the enigma of a theology that gives a positive acceptance and evaluation of colonialism and capitalism, and a fault-finding evaluation of socialist regimes, which have been in many areas and aspects the liberators of African and Asian peoples. Once again, culture-bound preferences of the West pass for Christian theological positions. Concerning traditional Christian theology Asians are therefore in a dilemma, much deeper than merely that of being asked to adopt Western languages, rituals, and thought-patterns. It concerns a whole worldview of human reality and human history.

A Nonrevolutionary Theology

A similar evaluation can be made of the traditional thinking among churchmen concerning development, justice, and peace. Development within the present world order, with the technology of the West and its financial and economic institutions, is presupposed as normal, or qualifiedly normal. The Western, urban technological model is implicitly accepted as the normal pattern of national development. The naked greed and insatiable thirst for profit central to this model are not seen as contrary to the spirit of the gospel. Christianity has come to terms with this legitimation of greed, neglecting nonmaterial incentives to build a just society and recast the common understanding of what the goals of human endeavor should be.

As yet the churches have not opted for a world system different from the prevailing capitalist, Western-dominated system. Except for some references in recent papal encyclicals, remedies suggested for problems are mere anodynes. The churches recommend reforms *within* the world system, such as economic cooperation through "aid," commodity agreements, currency reforms, deceleration of the arms race, and promotion of peace. These are good things in themselves, but utterly inadequate to transform a system in which 80 percent of the world's population has access to 20 percent of the world's resources. Poverty thus continues in the midst of plenty. Peace is understood as the preservation of the given status quo.

Yet, in view of the magnitude of Third World problems, totally different approaches are necessary. A revolutionary change in the

world system is needed. Revolutionary change does not necessarily
imply violence. It does, however, mean a radical and rapid change
in the world system—a change neither marginal nor quantitative,
but qualitative and all-pervasive. The world is meant for all and a
qualitative change in the relationships among peoples and resources
is required to ensure basic human rights to all.

Christianity lacks a revolutionary global theology. Even the Latin
American theology of liberation is articulated in terms of changes
within the world created by Western expansion since 1500.

A Theology Bereft of Social Analysis

Social analysis has not yet been accepted and incorporated as an
essential ingredient in theological reflection. For the most part,
traditional theology was drawn directly from scriptural sources;
inasmuch as data from other deposits of God's revelation were
largely ignored, that theology was heavily influenced by the prejudices, delusions, and preoccupations of the theologians, who were
mainly used to an urban bourgeois way of life. This is a further
point of methodology in need of radical remediation if there is to be
any meaningful consensus among the churches concerning Christian
action in society. The absence of socio-political power analysis lulls
the churches into complacency with the fact and the consequences
of the dominance of some over others.

Because a great deal of theological thinking is individualistic in
orientation, the social aspects of the kingdom of God, of sin, conversion, and salvation, have been neglected. Sometimes these social
aspects are considered "merely" human, humanitarian, horizontal,
"merely" natural—as if they were not related to the spiritual, to
God. Here too basic presuppositions must be overhauled to meet
the aspirations of contemporary men and women, and to be honest
about reality, with its absurd extremes of towering affluence and
abject poverty.

An Overly Theoretical Theology

Closely related to the absence of social analysis is the absence of
action-orientation in traditional theology. When theology is only
theoretical, it fails to take into account the exigencies of real situ-

ations and of the efforts required to change them. But only in action do the many dimensions of multifaceted problems become clear. When action is precluded from reflection, thought tends to be sterile, oriented to the status quo, and conservative. It is then possible to elaborate theology in a merely academic way, having but little relevance to the flow of events and forces as they develop in the world. An action-oriented theology, on the other hand, would have to assess the forces operative in a given situation, think of goals, strategies, and tactics, yields and risks, timing and alliances. All these require skills different from those of merely academic theologians. It will also have to develop a different spirituality, one that will not shun active participation in social change even in conflictual situations.

Churches have been action-oriented, mission-oriented, even when their theology was overbearingly speculative. But the action was largely church-centered in its missionary approach and conservative in its social aspirations. We need a theology that pays more attention to all aspects of the human person and is oriented toward justice in society. This demands an option in favor of the oppressed. Such a theology would also be more God-centered—that is, centered on God actively present in human history. Traditional theology neglected the dynamic nature of the kingdom of God and its impact on human history.

A theology that is action-oriented must take into account the dimension of time. Timing is of the essence. Awareness of the pace of events has to be included in the input for decision-making. There is not much use condemning the old colonialism today, except as regards Macao, Hong Kong, and the like. Today we have to deal with neocolonialism and new forms of exploitation, as in such nations as Malaysia, Chile, Afghanistan, and Poland. The churches—like so many civil governments— have generally sided with oppressors in power, but then with liberators once they are in power. This is sheer opportunism. Prophetic timing demands that we be with the oppressed in their struggles while they are engaged in them—not only after they are successful.

Such a theology would be continually in process, not static; it would endeavor to meet the problems posed by a fast-changing world. An action-oriented theology would also be largely lay, rather than clerical. The ministerial clergy, as such, would not necessarily provide leadership in a theology requiring the skills of sociopolitical analysis, decision-making, and risk-bearing. The young would play a significant role in the growth of such a theology: they have a greater penchant for being present where the action is than do older adults, especially patriarchal academics and clergymen.

Action-orientation also implies that theology be concerned with strategies of action for different places and environments. Traditional theology was largely concerned with intrachurch strategies and methods. The action called for today is very much in the field of public life. Hence the confluence of events, forces, and obstacles has to be evaluated and different strategies weighed and adopted. Risk-bearing in such situations is quite different from risk-bearing inside a cloister or in intrachurch or even interchurch issues.

A spirituality that faces up to conflict situations requires a reevaluation of the virtues of a Christian life and of progress in the spiritual life. Ascetic practice and mystical experience can and will have to evolve within the context of struggle against the wrongs of socio-political structures and the sacrifices and joys that struggle will entail. Spirituality will have to critically relate to politics, which is an essential target area for charity and justice. All these elements are only now beginning to be brought into Christian theology. They are indispensable for the building up of the kingdom of God in our world.

CONTEXTUAL THEOLOGIES

Though we may understand the traditional Western theologies of the past five centuries as being of one overall mold—from within the context of the North Atlantic quest for world domination—history shows many other examples of the contextualization of theology. Catholic theology has been very much conditioned by its West European and Roman matrix. The theologies of the Orthodox tradition arose from an oriental context in reaction against West European, particularly Roman, perspectives and authoritarianism. The Orthodox churches have always maintained a certain autonomy at the local level, while being linked in a wider federation. However, they have not often escaped the dominant influence of the political powers in their parts of the world.

The different schools of Protestant theology were also affirmations of an autonomy from Roman and Latin domination and related to national issues facing their peoples or political authorities. They retain differences with Catholicism and among themselves concerning matters such as the nature of grace and redemption, the sacraments, church ministry, and ecclesiastical authority. However, all of them that began in Europe or North America are within the general framework of white Western capitalist world domination.

After the Russian Revolution of 1917 and the establishment of socialist regimes throughout Eastern Europe, the Orthodox churches there have developed theological perspectives in line with a critique of capitalism and imperialism. They are developing theological orientations in keeping with the general ideological stance and social structure of their Marxist-dominated socialistic countries. They are supportive of the struggles of the oppressed peoples in other countries against capitalism and neocolonialism. But they are less energetic in articulating a theology that would voice a prophetic critique of their own societies.

The Chinese revolution compelled the Christian churches in China to rethink their own theologies without an ongoing contact with any other Christian churches. The Protestant churches in China have thus evolved their own way of Christian life guided by the principles of the Three-Self Patriotic Movement: self-government, self-support, self-propagation. They have reread the Scriptures from a postrevolutionary perspective and see many of the gospel values better realized under the new dispensation. The Catholic Church in China has set up the Catholic Patriotic Association and claims an autonomy for the church in managing its own affairs, especially in selecting its bishops. They too are supportive of the revolution. Both Protestants and Catholics affiliated with the Patriotic Association share in the public life of the country and endeavor to make a critical contribution to China's advance within the framework of the communist revolution. The Protestant churches are moving toward a postdenominational relationship among themselves: they have been on their own, cut off from denominational "mother churches," for over three decades. These experiences of the Chinese churches are very significant developments of Christian life and theology in an Asian context. They will doubtless influence Christian reflection in the future, especially inasmuch as they have to do with nearly a fourth of the human race.

With the setting up of the Vietnamese socialist government of the liberated zones from the early 1950s, most of the Christians—mainly Catholics—who remained there cooperated with the Marxist-led liberation movement. They faced together the trials of struggle and the horrors of war, especially after the United States came into the Vietnam war with over half a million soldiers and daily bombardment. After the defeat of the south and the U.S. withdrawal, in 1975, many of the Christian leaders in the south also gave critical support to the unified Vietnamese revolutionary regime. All this implied a Christian theological reflection in and through a revolutionary struggle. Christians in Vietnam are going through a difficult period, intensified by the continuing conflicts throughout the nation. The Catholic Church in Vietnam counts about 10 percent of the population. Its size and the evolution of both Christianity and Marxism may have helped to avoid such a sharp break as was experienced in China.

Contextual theologies are likewise being evolved in other Asian countries, such as South Korea in the face of a people's struggle against an oppressive dictatorial regime. Here the concept of the people—Minjung—as cared for by God receives special attention. In the Philippines Christians are theologizing in small groups from their experience of participation in national liberation from the procapitalist dictatorship. In India the concern for dialogue with other religions has been expressed in the ashramic movements and has led to a questioning of the major traditional theological positions of Christians concerning other religions. In India and Sri Lanka the two currents of concern for socioeconomic justice and religiocultural dialogue meet in a search for a more integral approach to liberation.

During the past decade Latin American theologians, using Marxist analytical methodology, have evolved a theology of liberation based on a critical study of their capitalistic society and a rereading of the gospel from their situation. They make a powerful critique of traditional theology and offer penetrating insights into the teaching of Jesus from the point of view of the poor and the oppressed. In more recent years they have developed an ecclesiology, related especially to grassroots Christian communities, and a spirituality in commitment to liberation even unto martyrdom. This Latin American theological evolution, clearly demanding a Christian option in favor of the oppressed in the harsh world of socioeconomic reality, is one of the most significant developments in theology in recent centuries.

The African Christian experience is quite varied from Ethiopia and Egypt to black peoples' liberation struggles in southern Africa. All these are providing a base for contextual theologies. African culture is seen as a basis for a people's integral approach to life, community, and God.

In the United States black theology and the theology of woman have been more strongly articulated during the past decade, and have influenced other continents as well.

The political theologies that are being developed in Europe, especially in West Germany and France, have the advantage of posing sociopolitical problems in the perspective of the ultimate goal of the church. They emphasize the eschatological nature of the kingdom of God. Yet few of them present a clear analysis of the contradictions of the capitalist form of society, on which the quest for Western dominance over the world has been built. They have not yet moved theology into the sphere of political conflict. These trends may develop as the process of politicization continues. The political change in France in favor of a prosocialist government had the support of many Christian reflection/action groups. In Portugal, Spain, and Italy there is now a more serious critique of the capitalist system, influenced by their intermediate position in world capitalism and by Latin American thinking.

THEOLOGY: CONTEXTUAL AND GLOBAL

Contextual theologies arise because the earlier theologies, which claimed universality, did not take local contexts seriously, and because they are articulations of insights from different situations. Contextual theologies arise from a new consciousness of groupings—a class, an ethnic kinship, a sex, a culture—or an overall social or religious environment. They are a valid and necessary contribution to the evolution of Christian life and theology. They can lead to deeper scriptural insights and a better understanding of the sufferings and aspirations of different groups.

Contextual theologies by their very nature tend to be partial, being rooted in local situations and experience. They may, however, have a permanent value insofar as a microhuman experience may embody a universal value. By deepening the analysis of a particular context, we can arrive at more universal perceptions. A contextual theology related to one group, nation, or region may be too narrow to respond to all the aspects of even a local problem. Thus, a black theology may not be open to the values of an Asian people, and so may not be able to analyze or absorb the significance of the Chinese revolution under Mao Tse-tung. A Latin American theology may neglect the problems of marginalized racial groups within that continent, as well as the issues relating Latin America to the whole world. Latin American theologians do not look upon Brazil and Argentina as vast underinhabited lands in a land-hungry world. They may not understand the tragedies caused by overpopulation in India and Bangladesh, and the impact of Latin American anti-Asian immigration laws on famine and starvation in other parts of the world. Hence even the best of contextual theologies, related to a limited group or region, must be counterbalanced by more universal perspectives relating to the world as a whole.

The action-orientation of contextual theologies may lead to liberation struggles that are necessary but only partial. They may sidestep the problems of global domination within the world. What is needed, therefore, is a dialectical interchange between local struggles and the world situation, between local theologies and a theology that tries to read the significance of global realities. Even local liberation struggles, such as those in El Salvador, Namibia, and Poland dare not be fought in isolation, for the enemies of human liberation are organized globally.

The universal approach will be very valuable in the development of a global strategy for bringing about social change. Only a universal approach can help us to respect human beings everywhere, whatever be their ethnic inheritance, color, creed, sex, or social class.

Rejection of the false universalisms of the past should not dissuade us from at least trying to evolve the general outlines of a truly universal theology grounded in the basic elements of the human condition and the overall world situation. Such a theology would recognize the global implications of many of our local or regional problems and proceed accordingly. Reflection on the Asian context seems especially recommendable in the search for a global theology inasmuch as Asia's population is more than half of the world population.

By extension, the whole planet earth, as an entirety, must also be seen as a context for theology. The human search for meaning and fulness of life takes place on this planet, with all its potentialities and limitations. Today the destinies of all peoples are closely interrelated and linked to the future of the earth: the land, the seas, the atmosphere, and outer space.

The world system that humankind has built up especially in the past few centuries is increasingly global in communications, economy, polity, culture, and way of life. The major power blocs would gladly have the whole world as the arena of their interests and operations. Some groupings based on class, color, sex, religion, ideology, and culture are also global in many aspects. The efforts of world bodies such as the United Nations further highlight planetary interdependence for peace, human rights, justice, the resolution of international conflicts—even food and employment.

REORIENTING THEOLOGY

Some of the approaches required to reorient theology are already being developed in the political theology of Europe, in the practical, issue-oriented theology of North America, in the theology of liberation in Latin America, and by the action/reflection dynamism evident in Asian and African churches, the Socialist countries, and women's movements. Their reflection would be broadened by a keener awareness of Asian contexts. It could lead to a sharpening of strategies, thanks to a better understanding of the demands of Asian revolutionary processes.

We have to take a fresh look at the central core of the Christian message. This requires a direct return to the sources of revelation— the Scriptures—especially to the person of Jesus Christ as we see him in the gospels. We must purify our minds of the restrictive Christendom-centered theologies that have blurred the universality of Jesus Christ. We must ask ourselves how we are to understand the gospels in our times.

Another point of departure must be socioeconomic and political reflection on the contemporary world in diverse contexts. We should try also to relate them to the basic yearnings of the human person for freedom and personal fulfillment. The de facto world system of order and disorder can be one starting point for the growth of a planetary theology, for the world system affects the life of each person and group within it. This impact grows rapidly as human global interdependence increases.

Chapter 2

The World System

A systematic analysis at the level of the whole planet earth, together with historical dimensioning, is necessary for us to understand how particular sectors and events in the world relate to each other. Without such a holistic perspective, we shall often not know the interconnection among issues and how some actions affect others—how even some actions, good in themselves, may cause havoc to others far away. The present world system of human relationships did not arise in a day or a generation. It is the result of a protracted historical evolution of the human race in its relationship to nature, of different peoples and cultures to one another, of the sexes to each other.

We all live on planet earth within one limited, interlinked, global ocean chain, one atmosphere, and one overall weather system. Depletion and disturbances in their ecological balance can seriously affect nature and human life. Human beings, by their intelligence, scientific skills, and manual labor, use and develop the resources of our planet. Advances in human civilization have been grounded on the steady progress in this millennial effort.

On the other hand the modern growth of science and technology without a corresponding development of concern for the rights of human beings and the care of nature is resulting in severe damage to humankind and nature. Pollution of the environment, soil erosion, the expansion of deserts, the "death" of lakes, the extinction of fish, bird, and mammal species, and the wastage of recyclable materials are some of the results of our reprehensible stewardship of the

17

planet's resources. The unrestrained urge for private, corporate, or national gain has often been the cause of such predatory conduct. Entire civilizations have been wiped out in the pursuit of profit and power.

The desire to dominate nature and persons has been a human characteristic throughout history, though some peoples have been more prone to it than others. Empires such as those of the Egyptians, Assyrians, Greeks, Romans, Moguls, and Mongols are examples. However, until the mid-fifteenth century the power of rulers depended on ancient means of warfare: the bow and arrow, the lance and sword. For thousands of years the fastest means of transportation and communication were horses and the ship with sails. The feudal system of economic and social life was organized around castles and feudal lords. Even powerful kings had to depend on the loyalty of numerous chieftains.

The modern era is characterized by the rise of nation-states, which brought many local lords and territories under the direct rule of national sovereigns. Technological advances in the methods of warfare were one on the main causes. Gunpowder, invented by the Chinese in the tenth century, was no respecter of castles or of the medieval laws of chivalry when knights fought each other in simple combat armed with lance or mace. Later on the steamship enabled much faster and more secure means of travel by water.

The fifteenth and sixteenth centuries saw the rise of national states under absolute monarchs, especially in Europe. It is important for our reflection to remember that it is only for about five centuries that the world has known sovereign nation-states. Prior to that there was feudalism and empires of greater or lesser centralization. In Europe the moral law flowing from the Scriptures and interpreted by the church was supposed to be binding on the Holy Roman Empire (which some have said was neither holy nor Roman nor an empire).

The rise of modern nation-states was related politically to the growth of power of absolute monarchs, economically to the development of mercantile capitalism and the enclosure movement in agriculture, culturally to the decline of the overarching Latin culture and the evolution of national languages, and religiously to the breakup of medieval Christendom due especially to the Protestant Reformation. The "discovery" of "new lands" that could be conquered for the European national monarchs and states was a further step to the disintegration of medieval Europe and the strengthening of the national kingdoms, which then became far-flung empires, beginning with the Spanish and the Portuguese.

There was a close relationship between territorial expansion and the modernization of the internal economies of the West European nations. The possibilities of travel expanded the sphere of trade and the availability of resources, and the enclosure movement in agriculture made more workers available for the industries growing up in the urban areas. This was also a period of rapid population increase after the devastation of the Black Death in the previous era. Mercantile capitalism dependent on trade later developed into industrial capitalism linked to the growth of colonies in the conquered lands. The empires provided living space for European peoples, cheap raw materials, lands for plantations with cheap labor, if not slaves, and markets for industrial products. These enabled the owners of capital in the European countries to increase their wealth from the surpluses accumulated both in the metropolitan countries and in the colonies. The working classes of both were exploited, but those of the European homelands were coopted to join in the exploitation of the colonies by being given a share of the spoils and a greater chance of upward social mobility in expanding empires and economies. Culturally they were made to feel that they were agents in the bringing of civilization and Christianity to poor, ignorant pagans.

The nation-states became the subject of rights in international relationships. Both within the nations and among them, the possession and use of physical power is the ultimate determinant of issues. National self-interest is the primary motivation.

The world system developed its structures for the strengthening of those who are already powerful. World relationships are relationships of domination and dependence. Powerful nations built the mechanism and trained the agents of this domination—economic, political, military, cultural.

The distribution of the earth's surface among the peoples of the world is a fundamental prerequisite for the understanding of the world system, as well as for the evaluation of its justice or injustice. In the general understanding of international relationships it is presupposed that the present world system or prevailing world order is just, and hence that we are all well off when there is peace and stability in the world. The status quo is given a high priority: the threat of its disturbance is something that must be prevented, and disequilibrium is something that must be remedied by a return to what prevailed before. Relationships among nations are discussed on this basis, unless the situation is drastically changed by physical force, as in the Middle East in 1967, or Bangladesh in 1971.

The assumption of the territorial rights of peoples based on the present distribution of land among them is so embedded in the contemporary mind, especially in Western countries, that there is little questioning of its justice and of the way it arose. Or perhaps there is a deep visceral awareness among dominant peoples that the present world system, from which they profit, was brought about unjustly by their forebears—and they prefer that it not be discussed. Because of an unarticulated guilt feeling and continued desire not to change the situation, these issues are not placed on the agenda for world discussion. This is a profound cultural conditioning that prevents world problems from being situated in their larger historical and geographical context.

Due to the enormous influence of the Western nations on the thinking of almost all the peoples of the world today, there has been a tendency to see history from the Western point of view. This is one factor in the cultural impact of power. The world system built up by the Western nations is given implicit approval. It is taken for granted that they have "developed" the world, and that the poor countries are "on the road to" development.

Language itself communicates this value pattern. The technologically advanced nations are considered "civilized." Their economic system is supposed to bring about "fair play" through the instrumentality of marketing (guided by the invisible hand of a kindly Providence, or by the "magic of the marketplace," as President Reagan once eulogized it). Their political forms are regarded as the highest such achievement of humanity. Their military exploits are extolled as extending the frontiers of human progress. Their religion is proposed as the highest form of human communion with the divine. Their culture is implicitly glorified as a supreme realization of human evolution.

All these biases contain an element of truth. Western peoples have undoubtedly contributed to the advancement of humanity in the past five centuries. Yet the normal assessment that is prevalent in Western and Western-oriented circles does not do justice to the real historical situation. It neglects the contributions of other peoples and their alternative possibilities, as Japan and China have demonstrated. It likewise neglects the large-scale damage done to countries by the imposition of a foreign dominance, and the damage done to the whole earth by the waste and misuse of its resources.

ORIGINS OF THE PRESENT WORLD SYSTEM

The present world order is mainly a result of the territorial and economic expansion of European peoples to other parts of the earth. From the point of view of the West, the past five hundred years were a period of great expansion and growth. For others, they were centuries of defeat, pillage, colonization, exploitation, and marginalization, in diverse forms.

The expansion of Europe in those centuries resulted in the European occupation of most of the habitable land of the earth. West Europeans occupied North, Central, and South America, Australia, New Zealand, and parts of Africa. They made colonies of the whole of Asia except China, Japan, and Thailand. The Russians, an East European people, expanded their empire to the Pacific and the borders of China. With superior technology, military forces, and economic power in their hands, they built the present world order to their own great advantage. They put in place economic, political, social, cultural, and religious structures and values to suit their domination over the rest of the world.

It is too easily forgotten that the Western colonial powers came to Asian countries because they had many riches that the more powerful Europeans wanted. This was also true of America and Africa. I would not say that the Asian peoples of the sixteenth century were underdeveloped, or that—even relatively—there was as much of a gap as there is now between them and the Western powers. Their technology was less advanced, and they were defeated militarily.

The result of the Western dominance over Asia was to disrupt the economic life of Asian peoples and make them dependent on their colonizers. The textile trade of India and its dissolution by the British in favor of their own industries is a classic example of the creation of dependence by imperial rulers. The Asian countries had traditionally been self-reliant and self-sufficient, though at a low level of subsistence. During centuries of colonial domination the colonizers raised the economic level of a collaborating small local elite while impoverishing the masses. They rendered the colonies economically dependent on the "mother country" for industrial goods in return for primary products in which the colonies had to specialize.

Due to the type of military, political, and economic dominance that the Western powers exercised over the rest of the world, the poorer countries actually gave economic aid to the colonial powers—Spain, Portugal, Britain, France, Holland, Germany, Belgium, the United States, and Russia—over a period of three to four centuries. This extorted aid assisted the Euro-American nations in building up their worldwide economic network.

Underdevelopment of Third World nations was a European creation:

> Europe, beginning with Columbus, did not go out and find "underdeveloped" countries; she created them. For example, the system of "mono-cultural production" (a one crop or mineral export economy), described by certain experts as the source of backwardness in the Third World, is not a system that dropped from heaven. It was brought and imposed by the Europeans on all their colonies in Asia, Africa, and Latin America.
>
> The sugar plant was brought by Columbus to the West Indies. Soon millions of slaves were brought from Africa to work the sugar plantations and cut the immensely profitable cane. Rubber was taken from Brazil to Southeast Asia, where Indians and Chinese provided cheap labor. Peanuts were brought from Brazil to West Africa and coffee from Arabia to Central and South America. The best lands, originally providing healthy diets for their inhabitants, were expropriated to produce cash crops for the European market. Malnutrition and starvation have been the lot of native peoples ever since. A particularly notorious example of this was the northeast of Brazil, originally one of the most fertile regions of South America. It was completely ruined by the ruthless exploitation of its soil by the Dutch and Portuguese sugar plantations of the seventeenth century.
>
> Even in the area of manufacturing, it was the East which first provided finished goods for the more primitive economy of Europe. India in the seventeenth and eighteenth centuries

had a large textile industry based on cottage-type organization. With the development of cottonopolis in Manchester, and the need to export its production, English political domination resulted in the *deindustrialization of India*. Between 1815 and 1832 cotton exports from India fell 13 times. British imports to India increased 16 times. The maiming of the hands of thousands of Bengal weavers by British soldiers is an apt symbol of the whole process.

From the conquest and the pillage of Mexico and Peru by the Spaniards, sacking of Indonesia by the Portuguese and the Dutch, and the exploitation of India by the British, the early history of capitalist development is an unbroken record of the international exploitation and consequent concentration of wealth in Western Europe [Eugene Toland, Thomas Fenton, and Lawrence McCulloch, "World Justice and Peace: A Radical Analysis for American Christians" in Thomas P. Fenton, ed., *Education for Justice: A Resource Manual* (Maryknoll, N.Y.: Orbis, 1975), pp. 102-3, 101].

These instances give an idea of the inhuman methods used by Euro-American powers to build the present world system. There are many books on history, economics, and even Christian missionary activity that hardly speak of such methods. Many generations of Westerners have been brought up to believe that their countries played a civilizing role in Asia, Africa, and the Americas. This is part of the Euro-American worldview. It overlooks the massive damage done to those countries during centuries of pillage, intrigue, exploitation, and overall military, political, economic, cultural, and religious domination. It may even seem brutal and ghoulish to remind ourselves of this. But it is necessary to do so because the prevailing world system cannot be understood in depth if this long history of the rape of the rest of the world by European peoples is ignored.

CHARACTERISTICS OF THE WORLD SYSTEM

Distribution of Land to Population

If the nation-state is the basic political structure of the world system, the control over a defined geographical territory gives the nation-state its first title to the resources it can use for its own purposes.

The ratio of land to population is, from country to country around the world, anything but uniform. When its population was increasing rapidly between 1500 and 1900, the West appropriated to itself most of the vast open spaces of the earth and built a world system aimed at perpetuating them for the Euro-American peoples.

Table 1
Worldwide Distribution of Land to Population

	Land (1,000 km²)	% of world	Population[a] (millions)	% of world
White-controlled areas				
Europe	4,929	3.632	523.6	12.4
U.S.S.R.	22,403	16.508	261.2	6.2
U.S.A.	9,363	6.899	218.4	5.2
Canada	9,976	7.351	23.6	.6
Latin America	20,553	15.146	347.2	8.2
Australia	7,687	5.664	14.4	.3
New Zealand	269	.198	3.2	.1
South Africa	2,045	1.507	27.7	.7
Israel	21	.015	3.7	.1
Total	77,245	56.925	1,423.0	33.8
Asian areas				
China	9,561	7.045	914.1	21.7
Southeast Asia[b]	1,718	1.276	161.3	3.8
India	3,268	2.408	643.9	15.3
Japan	370	.272	114.0	2.7
Indonesia	1,492	1.099	136.0	3.2
Other[c]	11,113	8.197	394.5	9.4
Total	27,522	20.297	2,363.9	56.1
Africa (less S. Africa)	28,179	20.764	422.5	10.0
Oceania (less New Zealand, **Indonesia**)	2,751	2.014	4.7	.1
Total	30,930	22.778	427.2	10.1
World total	135,697	100	4,214.1	100

Notes: (a) As of mid-1978. (b) Countries included: Vietnam, Philippines, Thailand, Malaysia, Laos, Singapore, Brunei. (c) Does not include figures for Kampuchea (Cambodia).
Source: *World Bank Atlas*, 1979.

The distribution of land is heavily weighted in favor of the white segment of the world population because whites were principally the ones who set the present national frontiers of the world. In that sense we can say that we have a white-racist world system. Today whites, who comprise about 34 percent of the world's population, control 57 percent of the land surface of the earth.

This grave primary imbalance can be illustrated by the following. The growing populations of India, China, and Japan have no room for expansion. With about 1.7 billion citizens they comprise 40 percent of the human race and yet are confined to 10 percent of the earth's surface. On the other hand, Canada, Australia, and New Zealand, with 41 million or 1 percent of the world population among them, control 13 percent of the earth's land.

The population in these three countries, by comparison, is growing slowly in spite of immigration. Brazil is only slightly smaller than China, but has 100 million persons compared to China's 900 million; Bolivia is three times the size of Japan but has 5 million persons compared to Japan's 115 million.

Bangladesh has a population twenty-five times that of New Zealand on half the land area. Bangladesh has twice the population of New Zealand, Australia, and Canada combined and 1/125 of their land surface. Australia, Canada, and New Zealand have 6.9 million square miles for 41 million persons. Yet it is doubtful whether even ten Bengalis were admitted to these three countries in 1971 when 10 million of them were displaced.

The U.S.S.R. has 16 percent of the world's land for 6.6 percent of the world population. The U.S.S.R. has more land than do India, China, Japan, Indonesia, and the rest of Southeast Asia combined—and they make up 47 percent of the world population. The rural areas of the Asian portion of the U.S.S.R. are very sparsely populated.

World Population Growth

This imbalance of population to land and the immigration policies of the underpopulated countries are among the most pernicious obstacles to human development and justice in the distribution of the world's resources. Even making allowance for the Australian desert and the Arctic north, the imbalance is very great. With the

exception of a few technicians of high caliber and some workers,
Asians are denied the right to migrate to any of the vast open spaces.
All the underpopulated countries—such as the U.S.A., the
U.S.S.R., Canada, Brazil, Argentina, Australia, and New
Zealand—have immigration laws that discriminate against Asians.
Some lands that are rather unsuitable for human habitation, such as
the Saudi Arabian desert or Siberia, have vast mineral reserves that
are utilized for the benefit of a very sparse population.

Table 2
Populations and Average Annual Growth Rates by Regions, 1750 to 1980

	Population[a] 1750	Growth[b]	Population 1800	Growth	Population 1850	Growth
World	791	.4	978	.5	1,262	.5
Africa	106	-0-	107	.1	111	.4
Latin America	16	.8	24	.9	38	1.3
North America	2	2.5	7	2.6	26	2.3
Asia (less U.S.S.R.)	498	.5	630	.5	801	.3
Europe	125	.4	152	.6	208	.7
U.S.S.R.	42	.6	56	.6	76	1.1
Oceania	2	-0-	2	-0-	2	2.2

	Population 1900	Growth	Population 1950	Growth	Population 1980
World	1,650	.8	2,513	1.9	4,415
Africa	133	1.0	219	2.5	469
Latin America	74	1.6	164	2.7	369
North America	82	1.4	166	1.3	246
Asia (less U.S.S.R.)	925	.8	1,379	2.1	2,558
Europe	296	.6	392	.7	483
U.S.S.R.	134	.6	180	1.3	267
Oceania	6	1.5	13	2.0	23

Notes: (a) In millions. (b) Exponential growth rates, annual average for the
50-year period between the two successive dates.

Sources: John Durand, "The Modern Expansion of World Population,"
Proceedings of the American Philosophical Society, 3/3 (June 1967) 137. Data for
1950 and 1980 are taken from: *Selected World Demographic Indicators by
Countries 1950-2000* (New York: United Nations, 1979).

On the other hand, Australia pays whites to emigrate to its
sparsely populated landmass. Those born of white parents have
almost the entire underinhabited world open to them in which to
settle down and reproduce their kind.

With time, the maldistribution of population to land (and there-

Table 3
Gap between Rich and Poor Countries in Terms of GNP (1978)

	Population (millions)	% of world	GNP ($ billion)	% of world
Developed countries				
Market economies				
U.S.A.	218.4	5.2	2,117.9	24.2
Canada	23.6	.6	216.1	2.5
Western Europe	391.6	9.3	2,319.8	26.7
Japan	114.0	2.7	836.2	9.6
Others[a]	49.2	1.	185.3	2.1
	796.7	18.9	5,675.3	65.1
Centrally planned economies				
U.S.S.R.	261.2	6.2	965.5	11.1
Eastern Europe	132.0	3.1	452.9	5.2
	393.2	9.3	1,418.4	16.3
Total	1,189.9	28.2	7,093.7	81.4
Underdeveloped countries				
Market economies				
Africa[b]	422.5	10.0	191.0	2.2
Asia	1,261.6	29.9	500.3	5.7
Latin America	337.6	8.0	474.2	5.4
Oceania[c]	4.7	.1	5.3	.1
	2,045.0	48.1	1,170.8	13.4
Centrally planned economies				
China	914.1	21.7	424.6	4.8
Other Asian[d]	74.1	1.8	23.2	.3
Cuba	9.6	.2	7.9	.1
	997.8	23.7	455.7	5.2
Total	3,024.2	71.8	1,626.5	18.6
World total	4,214.1	100	8,720.2	100

Notes: (a) Australia, New Zealand, Israel, S. Africa. (b) Less S. Africa. (c) Less Australia, New Zealand, and Indonesia. (d) Vietnam, N. Korea, Laos, and Mongolia; no data available for Kampuchea.

Source: *World Bank Atlas*, 1979.

fore to resources) is steadily worsening due to the increase in population in Asia. The population pressure in southern Asia is likely to cause more catastrophes and emergencies such as famines in Bihar and war in Bangladesh, unless the world finds rapid and radical solutions for it.

Hardly any international body that deals with the problems of world development considers this aspect of the question seriously. Development and underdevelopment are regarded merely in terms of gross national product (GNP) or industrialization. Only the factors of population, capital, and productivity are considered as variables. The present distribution of land is taken as an untouchable absolute.

This concept of development suits the big landowners of the world, who want to preserve the status quo. Even the United Nations has a history of being oriented to the status quo when it comes to maintaining the present territorial boundaries of nations.

Boundaries and laws defended by armed forces prevent idle land and untapped resources from being made available to hungry and unemployed millions. Development planning and discussion is vitiated by this bias in favor of the status quo. The present territorial structure of the world is basically unjust because it subordinates the human rights of many to the privileges of a few.

World Apartheid

There is almost universal disapproval of the policy of apartheid—separation of the races—followed by South Africa. Few stop to think, however, that the whole world system is based on a sort of apartheid. Each nation-state is confined to its present territorial limits and expected to develop within them. The different racial groupings of the one human race are allotted separate "preserves" in which they have to live. The yellow peoples have China, Japan, and the adjacent lands. The blacks have Africa. The brown peoples are allotted India, Pakistan, and Southeast Asia. The Arabs have North Africa and the Middle East. The rest of the world—Europe, North, Central and South America, Australia, New Zealand, South Africa and the U.S.S.R.—is largely reserved for whites. When black, yellow, and brown peoples have been free to migrate, it has generally been as slaves or as cheap labor for whites—for example, blacks in the Americas; Indians in Malaysia, Sri Lanka, and the West Indies; Koreans in Japan.

The resources and wealth of the Soviet Union and its East-bloc satellites are not evenly distributed among its many peoples and regions. Russia uses its own and their enormous resources for its own benefit and for the maintenance of its superpower status—with space flights and nuclear arms.

It is a striking fact that Marxists, who lay primary emphasis on the class nature of exploitation, hardly ever give much attention to this racist aspect of the world system, wherein exploiting racial classes dominate exploited racial classes. Within nations, classes tend to be the dominant units of social evolution. But among nations, race too has a profound impact, in spite of the international linkup of capitalist classes.

The division of the world by the Western powers has meant the availability of many more resources for them. The gold and diamonds of South Africa and the mineral harvest of Namibia are sent off to Western countries; the gold, diamonds, and other riches of Siberia benefit the Soviet Union.

Looking at the territorial structure of the world system, the ideological systems of capitalism and communism do not seem to be fundamentally opposed to each other. The land-rich capitalist countries are coming to terms with the land-rich socialist countries. The political détente between the capitalist and the communist superpowers is a corollary to their privileged position. That a socialist country can be in a privileged position internationally is a very important factor for the understanding of political forces in the world. The Marxist analysis based on class as the determinant of history seems inadequate inasmuch as it neglects the possibility that a working-class state could have a privileged position in the world. The 100 million cattle of the U.S.S.R. have today a much better chance of being fed during a situation of world food shortage than do the 75 million human beings in Bangladesh. Canada, Australia, and the U.S.A. will readily sell their grain surpluses to the U.S.S.R., which can pay higher prices than the poorer countries can. This happened during the food crisis of 1972.

As long as the nation-states maintain their present boundaries, it is unlikely that a just world order can be realized. In fact, the growing pressures on the land in the poor countries are likely to lead to phenomenal political explosions that could ultimately overthrow world territorial structures. We are perhaps at a stage in world history, as in the fourth and fifth, sixteenth and seventeenth centuries, when there will be mass population movements across countries and continents.

Table 4
Population and Percentage Distribution by Age Groups, 1960, 1980, and 2000

(Projection: medium variant)

		Total	0–14		15–29		30–44		45–64		65 & Over	
		(millions)	(millions)	(%)	(millions)	(%)	(millions)	(%)	(millions)	(%)	(millions)	(%)
World	1960	3026.5	1121.8	37.0	740.6	24.5	544.3	18.0	462.0	15.3	157.8	5.2
	1980	4415.0	1546.0	35.0	1206.4	27.3	759.3	17.2	645.8	14.7	257.5	5.8
	2000	6199.4	1957.8	31.6	1602.7	25.8	1265.0	20.4	978.0	15.8	395.9	6.4
More	1960	944.9	269.9	28.6	213.2	22.6	186.3	19.7	195.2	20.6	80.3	8.5
developed	1980	1130.7	260.2	23.0	281.4	24.9	225.8	20.0	234.7	20.7	128.6	11.4
regions[a]	2000	1272.3	273.8	21.5	261.2	20.	276.0	21.7	294.1	23.1	167.2	13.
Less	1960	2081.6	851.9	40.9	527.4	25.4	358.0	17.2	266.8	12.8	77.5	3.7
developed	1980	3284.3	1285.8	39.2	925.0	28.2	533.5	16.2	411.1	12.5	128.9	3.9
regions	2000	4927.1	1684.0	34.2	1341.5	27.2	989.0	20.1	683.9	13.9	228.7	4.6

Note: (a) North America, Europe, U.S.S.R., Australia, New Zealand, Japan.

Source: *Age-Sex Composition of Population by Countries* (New York: United Nations, 1979).

Inequities in the relationships of population to land will worsen in the coming decades, because the populations of the affluent countries are not growing at all, or not so rapidly as in the countries of Asia, Africa, and Latin America. Secondly, the white peoples or "more developed regions" have an aging population. According to UN projections, the "more developed" countries, including Japan, will have 13.2 percent of their population over 64 years of age and only 21.5 percent below 15 years. On the other hand the "less developed regions" will have only 4.6 percent above 64 years and 34.2 percent below 15 years.

Due to population increases in the poorer countries, there is less land available for the agricultural population—in spite of an increase in the total area under cultivation. On the other hand in the "developed regions" the decline in the agricultural population has led to an even more favorable land/worker ratio. In 1976 North America had 232 million hectares of agricultural land and a land/

worker ratio of 78.4 to 1. Whereas Asia and the Pacific, of the un-derdeveloped market economies, had 266 million hectares and a land/worker ratio of .98 to 1. The situation was worse in the Asian centrally planned economies, including China, with 141 million hectares of agricultural land and a land/worker ratio of .51 to 1.

Table 5
Agricultural Land Area and Corresponding Land/ Worker and Rural Population Ratios, 1970 and 1976

	Agricultural land[a] (millions of hectares)		Agricultural land/ worker ratio[b]		Agricultural land/ rural population ratio	
	1970	1976	1970	1976	1970	1976
Developed regions						
North America	234.0	232.0	59.97	74.83	25.23	32.96
Western Europe	99.9	96.1	4.42	5.09	1.80	2.10
Oceania	44.3	46.0	79.40	89.88	32.97	37.72
Eastern Europe & U.S.S.R.	279.5	278.5	5.66	6.48	3.32	6.48
Underdeveloped regions						
Africa	176.5	182.0	2.04	1.96	.85	.79
Latin America	133.0	143.6	3.71	3.79	1.16	1.18
Western Asia	78.5	81.1	2.42	2.36	.81	.77
Eastern Asia & Pacific	256.1	266.3	1.01	.98	.39	.37
Asian centrally planned economies	136.6	141.3	.51	.52	.24	.24

Notes: (a) Arable land and land under permanent crops. (b) Ratio of land area to agricultural work force.

Source: *World Population Trends and Policies, 1979 Report* (New York: United Nations, 1980).

This basic and growing inequality in agricultural land must be taken seriously by the "international community" (if there be such an entity) for it is one of the main causes of hunger and malnutrition in the world. These figures of course hide the hundreds of thousands of acres owned by Western and Japanese multinational corpora-tions in the poor countries.

The world cannot postpone this problem for long. Peoples without land and food are likely to reach out toward uninhabited or sparsely inhabited lands. This has been the broad historical trend over the centuries.

Since the end of World War II there have been significant politi-cal changes, such as the Chinese and Vietnamese revolutions, the

independence of former colonies, the expansion of Soviet power
into Eastern Europe, the formation of economic and political blocs
such as the EEC and ASEAN. However, the main political frontiers
remain substantially the same as they were when carved out by the
European colonial enterprise. The political balance of power has
shifted from European nations to the U.S.A. and the U.S.S.R.,
with Western Europe, China, Japan, and India being other major
forces on the international scene.

It is noteworthy that the poorer, exploited peoples of the world
have always had to struggle long and hard against the European
powers and the U.S.A. for any advance in their political or
economic freedom from the West. At each stage the major powers
have been opposed to freedom and liberation movements. Where
the U.S.A. supported a liberation struggle, as against Spain in the
Philippines and Latin America, it was only when the liberating
forces were on the verge of victory.

Many peoples have had to face the economic, political, and military interventions of the U.S.A. and Western Europe. The young
Soviet Union faced it soon after the 1917 revolution; the Chinese
prior to 1948. The African freedom movements had the power of
the West against them. They were considered rebels—guerrillas and
terrorists—until they won their struggles in country after country, as
in Ghana, Kenya, Angola, Mozambique, and Zimbabwe. U.S.
interventions in South and Central America have been numerous.
Vietnam is now a classic example of U.S. support for reactionary
Third World regimes. Iran and Ethiopia have further demonstrated
how the U.S.A. has supported repressive and exploitive rulers. The
Soviets have done likewise in Afghanistan and Poland.

The world has no effective political means of settling issues of
international justice and freedom in a peaceful manner. The main
obstacle is that posed by the beneficiaries of the status quo, the
Western powers and the Soviet Union. They maintain the world
political system set up by them during previous centuries. This is the
basic challenge to world justice in the political sphere. Unfortunately, it is not recognized as such by the vast majority of Europeans and North Americans, be they capitalistic or socialistic. The
weaker Third World countries can do little about this, in spite of
such alliances as the Non-Aligned Conference and the Group of 77.

The contracting world economy, the growing economic exploitation of the poor, along with the absence of any major political changes in the world system in favor of the poor is leading to heightened tensions almost everywhere. In the countries of the Third World military dictatorship is more and more the norm. Most of Latin America, Africa, and southern Asia have such regimes. "Democracy" there is often a manipulated process of rigged elections and controlled public opinion. The local elites of poor countries and the world superpowers do not allow the poor countries to work out an economy to the benefit of the masses.

The socialist countries have attempted to escape the web of control of the rich capitalist Western powers. The Soviet Union, whatever its other deficiencies, has generally helped the struggling poor countries against capitalist domination. This may be in the Soviet Union's self-interest. All the same, these countries have demonstrated that a socialist economy is a viable economic proposition and have helped other countries opting for such a course.

Socialist regimes have, however, their own different approaches and even conflicts. China adopted a more Asian and participative approach to economic reorganization under Mao Tse-tung. Problems between socialist powers, such as the Sino-Soviet and the Chinese-Vietnamese conflicts, and the problems in Eastern Europe, especially Poland, show that the adoption of a socialist regime or economic model is not by itself a final solution to the basic human dilemmas of our time. The reconciliation of the exigencies of economic development, technological modernization, social justice, freedom, and popular participation in economic and political life are not easy or settled once and for all in any given society. The massive upsurge of workers under the banner of Solidarity in Poland also points a way toward mass economic and political action where injustice is rampant due to corruption and false priorities in socialistic planning. All the same the socialist economies have on the whole met their peoples' basic needs for food and other essentials in a more egalitarian manner.

WORLD ECONOMIC STRUCTURES

The structure of the global economy is based on the distribution of land and natural resources among the peoples of the world, the accumulation of capital, skills developed by diverse peoples, trade relationships among nations, and the use to which all of these are put by the decision-making officials or agencies in the world.

The original inequity in land is further strengthened by the disproportionate relationships in incomes, capital, technology, trade, business organization, and the use of resources. During the past five centuries, the world system has grown in such a way that there are financial and economic centers served by peripheral groups of nations. These economic centers or metropolises are the U.S.A., Western Europe, the U.S.S.R., Japan, and now the newly rich oil-producing countries.

The world economy is so organized that the principal benefits of economic activity are derived by the metropolitan countries, and within them by the rich entrepreneurs and owners of capital. Those at the periphery work hard but share little of the fruits of their labor.

Likewise, there is a widespread system of domination of poorer economies by richer ones. This is a continuation of the economic aspects of colonization even after colonies have become politically independent. The domination is many-sided. It relates to factors such as ownership of capital, type of goods produced, the technology in use, and the international monetary system.

The economies of the poor countries have been fashioned to fit into the needs of the rich ones. Capital has been accumulated by wealthy individuals, families, companies, and countries by centuries of hard work, business acumen, technological superiority, and large-scale exploitation and pillage. Today vast decision-making powers are concentrated in powerful multinational corporations and government agencies, including those of socialist countries.

The world economic system is built on the basis of profit maximization. Here the worst evils of the capitalist system have almost free rein: there are few checks on the use of economic power to one's own advantage. Changes in the price of crude oil show how power ultimately determines economic variables. In their quasi monopoly, the oil-rich countries can set prices and profits. The big oil-refining companies, too, were able to make high profits in spite of the increase in all oil prices by producers.

At the apex of this capitalist world order is the U.S.A., controlling about a third of world productivity. Within the U.S.A. a few multinational corporations dominate the economy. These corporations in turn are controlled by a few multimillionaire families with interlocking relationships among themselves. The Rockefellers, Mellons, Du Ponts, and Fords, along with similar enterprises and families in Western Europe, the U.S.S.R., and Japan, dominate the world economy. Poor Americans, Europeans, Russians, and Japanese are also exploited by these firms and families. However, they reap a larger share of world productivity as a reward for their participation in the exploitation of the rest of the world. They so far have shown little sympathy for the more exploited peoples of Asian, African, and Latin American countries.

The maintenance of a global status quo is the highest priority of these powers. For this they use agencies such as the World Bank, the International Monetary Fund (IMF), and the General Agreement on Trade and Tariffs (GATT). Recently the oil-rich states have joined other nations in global power. But the poorer classes of these countries, such as Saudi Arabia, Iraq, and Iran, are meted out only a miniscule percentage of this new wealth.

When Asian and African colonies became politically independent, their economic relationships with the exploiting countries were not substantially changed, except where there were Marxist-led revolutionary takeovers, as in China, North Korea, and North Vietnam. The advantage to the colonizers in "granting" political independence without waiting for a total revolution was that they could transfer power to a collaborating local elite who would maintain the capitalist economic system. Thus the advantages of the colonial system continued to accrue to the colonizers.

In the old colonial system the colony supplied the raw materials for the industries of the exploiting country, which manufactured finished products from them. The terms of trade were consistently to the disadvantage of the colonies. Technology developed in the colonizing country, whereas the earlier skills of manufacture were neglected and gradually exterminated in the colonized country. The metropolitan center grew at the expense of the peripheral colonies.

In India, for instance, the British policy of deindustrializing the colonies changed the percentage of the population dependent on agriculture from 60 percent in 1893 to 84 percent in 1947. The pressure on the land reduced its output per person and increased the indebtedness of small farmers to wealthy landlords and moneylenders.

The lands of a colonized people were taken by foreign companies for plantations of rubber, tea, coffee, sugar, and the like. Foreign companies took over the marketing, processing, insurance, shipping, banking, and sales operations for these primary products. Foreign companies also established themselves as either producers of consumer goods or as wholesale agents for imports from the metropolitan country. Local production of consumer goods dwindled in good measure in favor of imports. Thus the population was reduced to primary agricultural work on plantations and clerical and administrative work for the rulers. Even the production of basic food commodities was neglected unless it helped the exploiters.

During the past three decades—since "independence" of the former colonies—the system of domination has built up new modes of continuing and even strengthening exploitation. Due to the dependence of the former colonies on markets for their products, they have not been able to liberate themselves from their economic stranglehold. This is particularly true of small countries. When they have tried to take over the land possessed by foreign companies or by foreign banks and insurance companies, there has been retaliation in various forms. For fear of reprisals, governments of dependent countries are forced to respect the dominant position of foreign economic interests.

Governments that welcomed further foreign investments have been supported by the Western powers. This foreign investment has led to some economic development, as in Malaysia and Singapore, but it has also increased the dependence on foreign companies. They extort tax exemptions, restrict trade-union rights, keep wages low, and in general influence government policies in their favor. Banking, insurance, shipping, and even aspects of distribution are still in the hands of foreign companies.

MECHANISMS OF ECONOMIC DOMINATION

Aid and Trade

What is called "aid" to underdeveloped countries has been another means of increasing their dependence and tying the poor countries to the economies of the rich ones. Aid is generally in the form of loans for buying equipment or raw materials and consumer goods from the aiding country, or to pay for technicians, who generally give advice on how the developing countries can fit into the developed countries' economic system. Such "aid" generally becomes a burden to recipient countries. The proportion of the poor countries' export earnings required to pay off aid debts has also been rising and has now reached critical levels in some countries.

The effects of this system have been disastrous for the poor countries. They have had to produce more and more in order to earn less and less. In 1960 Malaysia exchanged four tons of rubber for one jeep; in 1970 it cost ten tons. The transfer of real resources from the poor nations to the rich has more than outweighed the total aid given by the West.

Multinational Corporations

Today some of the major agents of economic exploitation are the giant multinational corporations (MNCs) that have their headquarters in the rich countries, especially North America and Europe. The MNCs have vast financial and technological power that enables them to draw on the advantages of the worldwide interdependence of economies. Their presence in the poor countries tends to marginalize the rural populations. Agriculture itself is made dependent on their requirements. Capital flows tend to be from the poor to the rich countries. The MNCs help create unemployment and economic dependence in the poor countries. They manipulate the prices of goods on world markets.

The International Monetary System

The international monetary system also works in favor of the rich countries, especially the United States. During the 1950s and '60s, when the U.S. dollar was accepted as an international currency, the United States was able to earn nearly $3 billion annually and obtain real resources from other countries in return for its paper money. This was one of the highest forms of aid from the rest of the world to the United States.

THE WORLD ECONOMIC STRUCTURE IN CRISIS

Since the mid-1970s the world economic structure has been in severe crisis. Among the symptoms are acute food shortages; the monetary crisis; the energy crisis; massive unemployment even in the developed capitalist countries; the growing income, wealth, and technological gaps between the affluent and the poor; the pollution of the environment; the depletion of certain nonrenewable natural resources.

The world faces a crisis that is endemic to the capitalist system itself. For the international economic system is based on the capitalist principle of profit maximization. Even the socialist regimes in the U.S.S.R., China, Eastern Europe, and elsewhere generally operate, in international economic affairs, within the capitalistic world market.

The modern world economic system has been built on the basis that might is right, that profits can be maximized regardless of the effects on others, that productivity is for profit rather than needs, that persons can do what they want with the resources of nature for their own advantage, and, ultimately, that ethical norms have no role in economic activity.

Organization of the world economy based on such principles is bound to bring about injustice and suffering to the poor, the weak, and the marginalized. Over the centuries the worst of these evils have been partly kept in check within nation-states by social reforms and particularly the establishment of socialist regimes. The Keynesian recommendation that public authorities determine demand by appropriate fiscal and budgetary policies, such as public expenditure during periods of low economic activity, was able to ensure almost full employment in the developed countries during the 1940s, '50s, and '60s.

However, in the international sphere there have been no effective mitigating forces to check the economic exploitation of poorer peoples and countries. Instead there has been an unending transfer of resources and wealth from the poor to the rich countries.

With the world now so economically interlinked, an economic recession in the rich countries has to be met by creating a demand for their commodities in the world markets. But the poor peoples and countries, due to their lack of purchasing power, are unable to buy even the food they need. The world inflationary trends and their own economic problems compel them to reduce their imports.

To remedy this, there would have to be a massive transfer of funds to the poor countries for the creation of an effective demand among them for the goods produced by the farms and industries of the developed countries. But this is precisely what the rich world has not done and is unwilling to do. The total aid given after World War II was less than 1 percent of the GNP of the rich countries. This, too, was often in terms of loans or payment for military equipment and infrastructures.

No solution is yet in sight for the grave problem of mass unemployment in the advanced capitalistic countries. The contradictions between enormous production capacity and mass unemployment, uncultivated lands and large-scale world malnutrition, the search for security and unprecedented phenomenal expenditure on armaments are so blatant that many think that humanity is on its way to inevitable planetary catastrophe. The poor countries are so exasperated at the callousness of the rich, especially the United States and Britain, that there is hardly any hope in international negotiations. Within the rich countries themselves the policy of cutting subsidies for the poor and favoring the rich in the hope of increasing investment and employment—as presently followed in Britain and the United States—is leading to grave social discontent and dislocations.

That there are unlimited resources has always been an assumption of capitalist economies. But the growth of population and, even more, the rate of resource consumption in rich countries are straining these resources—which are not unlimited.

This very situation shows that healthy and sustained economic development cannot take place in the world as a whole if the distribution of the fruits of economic growth continues to be neglected. Unshared affluence will make it impossible for the capitalist system to maintain a self-sustaining, long-term growth process in the capitalist world—let alone in the whole world:

> A unit of population today in the developed world consists of
> a human being wrapped in tons of steel, copper, aluminum,
> lead, tin, zinc, and plastics, each day gobbling up sixty pounds

of raw steel and many pounds of other minerals. Far from getting these things in his homeland, he ranges abroad much as a hunter and more often than not in the poorer countries. His energy need instead of being equivalent to a single 100-watt lamp is equivalent to ten 1,000-watt radiators continuously burning. According to a U.S. Senate report, the American people consumed, in the decade 1958–1968, more of the resources of the world than all the people of the earth consumed in all previous history. If all the peoples of the world were to consume resources at the American rate they would use up in six years all the known petroleum reserves. Their annual consumption of iron, copper, sulphur, timber, and water would exceed the present available store of these resources. Of the 100 minerals most important to U.S. industry, it possesses within its borders adequate supplies of only twelve [*Ecumenical Review* (Geneva: World Council of Churches), Jan. 1973, pp. 29–30].

Definite limits must be placed on the global expenditure of natural resources, taking into account the present level of technology. This requires a rational planning and a world authority capable of dealing effectively with such issues.

There has been hardly any serious effort toward significant change in the fundamental economic relationships or the political map of the world. The most favorable recommendations of the United Nations are for the transfer of resources, the cancellation or rescheduling of debts, the creation of international liquidity to help poor countries, and the moral support for exploited countries in their efforts to regain control over their resources.

But the world system, which is unjust in its whole orientation and division of land and resources, will not be changed by such piecemeal efforts. They are only palliatives within a worsening overall framework. Immigration laws are, if anything, being tightened against the poor countries. The terms of trade are worsening. Population pressures are growing in the poor countries. Imperialism of the neocolonial type is becoming more voracious, more sophisticated, more impervious to analysis, and hence more difficult to combat.

How long can such a world order be maintained militarily and

through the exercise of national sovereignty of individual states
against the just demands of their peoples? What are the means, if
any, for the liberation of peoples through political measures? Can
the political power of the masses overcome or control the economic,
legal, and military power of the national elites and world superpowers?

GLOBAL CULTURAL DOMINATION

The world system is maintained not only by control over wealth
and the use of political and military power, but also by influencing
the mentalities, values, and habits of persons everywhere. There is a
kind of cultural ambience into which citizens are fitted in different
societies. In capitalist countries, this cultural setting legitimizes the
exploitation of the weak by the strong. In the Soviet Union and
Eastern Europe there is likewise a strong cultural conditioning that
justifies their socialist societies and their present coming to terms
with the capitalist world system. Mao's China had another pattern
of cultural orientation that was more revolutionary and encouraged
self-criticism. This has now been changed in favor of a more accom-
modating approach toward the West as part of the price to be paid
for China's modernization and desire to catch up with the rich capitalist powers.

Today, cultural domination is exercised by many means: mass-
media communication, the educational system, the official ideologies of governments and political parties, the religious and social
customs and values of peoples. Through these the dominated are
made to accept and internalize the values, attitudes, and priorities of
dominant groups, and to accept the roles assigned to them by the
more powerful. During the long centuries of colonial domination,
Western rulers used cultural means such as education, social values,
the legal system, and religion to subordinate the minds of the colonized peoples.

The Legal System, the Mass Media, the Schools

The Western powers changed the system of law, especially concerning property, in order to favor their economic activities. In
precolonial times, property was held as a collective trust in almost

every Asian country. The system of registration of land was not the same as in Western individualist societies. The colonial powers changed the legislation in favor of private individual holdings or company ownership of land. Lands that did not have such titles were regarded as state property. They were allotted to foreigners and foreign companies for small sums of money. Thus the people's right to land was taken away and given in perpetuity to foreign companies and agencies. The legal system was made to suit the interests of the economically dominant rulers.

In many countries the law is still administered by persons trained in the individualist tradition. Although this may favor the defense of some human rights, it is not conducive to bringing about peaceful changes in the legal system in favor of a more just distribution and a more communitarian ownership of property. This in turn influences the pattern of development, which tends to be on a capitalist basis; this further deepens inequalities in society. Thus the legal profession, the legal system, and the judiciary, which are much respected by the social system, are bulwarks of the prevailing economic system.

The mass media are also dominated by foreign agencies and the same local elites. In some Asian regions—Thailand, Malaysia, Hong Kong, Singapore—the newspapers are owned by foreigners, generally British and American multimillionaires. Day after day, they present to the people a view of life and culture that is alienated and alienating. They do not help the people make a critical analysis of society. On the contrary, they feed the people the myths of the neocapitalist society that is being built up in many of the poor countries.

The school system was one of the main agents of the cultural subversion of colonized peoples. The schools further encouraged a system of values and relationships that were individualist, competitive, and subservient to foreign interests. Under the individualist system, the traditional communitarian life of the country was disrupted. The element of sharing in the economy was thus greatly reduced. The new elite was encouraged to seek employment in the services of the colonial government or of the foreign-based companies. This further strengthened the breakdown of the self-reliant, community-oriented economic system and social life that generally prevailed earlier in Afro-Asian societies.

The values of private enterprise, efficiency, consumerism, profit maximization, militarization of the economy, and rugged individualism were integrated into these societies through the mediation of local elites.

Cultural Myths

The cultural domination of the world by Western peoples has foisted on others a number of myths that help perpetuate the notion of Western supremacy.

The teaching of subjects such as history, geography, economics, politics, and law is largely dominated by the Euro-American worldview. History is presented as the story of the "discovery" and "development" of the world by Westerners. Many aspects of the despoliation of nature by colonial enterprises are not taken into account. The misuse of the resources of the world by the wealthy nations in the form of waste, pollution, and armaments is implicitly justified or accepted by not being questioned.

Western colonizers are said to have brought democracy and freedom to underdeveloped peoples—while keeping them in political, economic, and cultural subjection. Today these same powerful nations show that they are happier with Asian dictatorships in favor of the privileged classes than they are with progress toward democratic participation in government and power.

THE MYTH OF AID

It is a myth that, with the attainment of political freedom, a poor people becomes master of its own economy. Both during and after the colonial period, the flow of resources and funds in the world has always been from the poor to the rich. On balance it is the poor countries that contribute to the economic advancement of the rich countries.

Belgium received more from Zaire than it gave Zaire; likewise Holland from Indonesia, Britain from India, France from French Africa, Spain from Latin America, Portugal from Brazil, Angola, and Mozambique, the United States from the Philippines, and Japan from South Korea. At the end of the period of political colonialism, the colonial powers were rich and the masses in the colonized regions were impoverished.

Since political independence, "aid" to Third World nations has always, in the long run, been to the advantage of the "donor" countries. In addition, such aid is a form of cultural genocide by which the dignity of a people is destroyed and its self-image twisted into that of a beggar. And the populations of the rich countries are kept ignorant of the facts. Complacency is inevitable.

THE MYTH OF ANTICOMMUNISM

Another myth of this century has been that of anticommunism. It was traditionally argued that the Western powers had a responsibility to save the world from communism, regarded as the worst evil on earth. For this cause the Western powers maintained military bases in the poor countries and undertook counterinsurgency activities to brainwash the peoples of the so-called free world. Today these same Western powers are moving closer toward alliance and détente with communist regimes in order to maintain their spheres of influence in the world.

The free-world countries, unlike communist countries, were said to offer religion an appropriate framework. The capitalist way of life was more pleasing to God than was the communist way of life. Now we see organized religion decaying under the permissive materialism of the West more than under the materialist socialism of Marxist countries. The role of religion in such a traditionally Catholic country as Italy is some indication that religion does not necessarily flourish better under Western materialist capitalism.

THE MYTH OF POPULATION CONTROL

Overpopulation is a fact and a serious problem, especially in the Third World. Some form of population control is necessary in the world. But the population problem results, at least partially, from the maldistribution of population to land and resources. Hence it is wrong to use all manner of pressures for reducing the population growth rate of the poor countries without at the same time reducing the waste of resources by the rich countries.

If we compare the living standards of diverse peoples, we see, for example, that 120 million Indonesians and 75 million Bengalis can live on one-fortieth of what 200 million North Americans consume. Even if their population multiplies forty times in the near future, at their present level of consumption Indonesians and Bengalis will not use as much energy as North Americans use today. A dog in the United States probably consumes more natural resources than does a child in Bengal.

The unspoken fear is that the poor, if they continue to grow in numbers as they have in recent decades, will be a threat to white capitalist world supremacy. The well-off are afraid of losing their possessions and privileged position. (The Soviet Union too can follow the capitalist line in international issues of this nature.) Rather than change the present world system, they would tailor the world population to fit the present distribution and use of resources. The International Population Year (1974) sponsored by the United Nations hardly dealt with these aspects of the problem, though UN agencies spend much on family planning in poor nations. Some rich countries such as France now encourage and subsidize larger families.

Distractive Mechanisms

The mental conditioning of peoples can be so great that they are oftentimes unaware of the real forces that oppress them. In Malaysia very many think that the most important question affecting the country is the racial issue, because of the economic superiority of the Chinese and the political power of the Malays. But it is forgotten that 62 percent of Malaysian industrial and commercial undertakings are in the hands of neither Malays nor Chinese, but of foreigners: British, American, Japanese. Malaysia is becoming increasingly dependent on foreign capital, consumer goods, and even foreign ideas. Yet the media successfully distract the attention of the people from the real issues. The policy of "divide and conquer" works effectively in favor of the dominant powers of the present world order.

A large-scale intellectual subjugation has thus developed, helping to reinforce the economic, political, and military domination by foreign powers in league with local elites.

COLOR, CLASS, SEX, AND THE WORLD SYSTEM

The world system, in its social aspects, has many interrelated lines of affinity and division based on color, class, and sex. They are global, as well as local and personal. An understanding of them and their interrelationships is essential for the cause of integral human liberation.

Sex is, by its nature, biological, not determined by us, not (easily) changeable. Color is also by birth and is historical in origin. Class is changeable, dependent on education, employment, wealth, and status. Sex is primarily of a person; race and class are very much of groups. All three have widespread political implications.

Sexism, racism, and classism are of human social making. We seek liberation from sexism, not from sex; from racism, not from race. Class, however, is in itself undesirable. A classless society would be preferable. We must recognize biological, historical, cultural, and functional differences, but they should not be allowed to make for inequality of persons or groups. In this the weak, the poor, and the dominated can heighten the consciousness of others through their struggles for identity, dignity, and equality.

Similarities

A common feature of sexism, racism, and classism is the tendency to regard the other, not as a free, responsible person or human community, but as an object, something to be used for one's pleasure, power, or profit. The other is used, dominated, manipulated, domesticated physically and psychologically, as under slavery, in capitalism, or in totalitarian socialist regimes. Such oppression dehumanizes both the oppressed and the oppressor.

The dominated are made to exist for and in function of the dominant. Even psychologically, the dominated are made to accept the values, goals, priorities, and social preferences of the oppressor. Relationships and roles in society and terms of trade in economy are determined by the more powerful. Power is used to maintain the privileges of the powerful.

The privileged status quo of the powerful is given the sanction of law, morality, culture, civilization, religion, and public acclaim. The dominated are deprived of power; if they oppose their subjection, retaliatory repression can be psychological or even physical and violent. The powerful may give "aid" to the weaker, who are regarded as handicapped and unfortunate. But the underlying relationships of superiority and inferiority are maintained. They are buttressed by the ideology, myths, and even theology expounded by the dominant. The oppressed do not know one another internationally. They are kept ignorant, weak, and divided. Consequently there is an enormous thwarting of the human potential of the weaker sex, the weaker racial groupings, the weaker classes—and a human impoverishment of the dominant themselves.

SEXISM

In cultures around the world, men tend to determine the purposes, roles, and values of women's lives. In a male-dominated society, women are thought of more as helpmates. A woman's personality is made to seek fulfillment in relation to a man. Man is the norm; woman is the "other." The work of the male is considered more productive and is better paid for. Child-caring is considered so much a concomitant of child-bearing that the father leaves almost the totality of it to the mother. Yet women's household work is not considered to have an economic value.

Women have generally had less opportunity for education than have males. This had its impact on employment. Women's freedom of movement is much more circumscribed than is that of men.

Politics is considered normal for men and abnormal for women, except where they have been born to high rank. Politics decides many issues of public life, and it is men who decide—and they decide according to their perceptions and interests. Public institutions and work relationships are thus organized to take into account the masculine point of view. Women's needs are considered secondary in economic, political, and social life. Holding public office is more difficult for women. Because child care and domestic work are still mostly done by women, they have less access to social life during the child-rearing years of their lives. Further, inasmuch as women have often been excluded from the decision-making processes, they are generally less aware of the ramifications and consequences of economic and social policies. We have to recognize that we have long been and still are in a male-dominated world system.

RACISM

Racism is an attitude that considers one racial grouping superior in rights and dignity to another and leads, as a consequence, to the oppression of one group by another. Racism can surface at a rather universal level, centering on the color groups of humankind: black, white, yellow, brown. Or it can be at local levels in the interrelationships of like-skinned groups: the Sinhala and Tamil in Sri Lanka, the English and Welsh in Britain. The latter variety of racism is more closely related to geography, language, history, religion, and culture.

Racial identity is a powerful social bond. Marriages are generally within the same racial group. Nationalism and patriotism are closely linked to race. The passions of racial enmity are often aroused in times of war or even in democratic elections. The survival of a racial group is a major cause that evokes human loyalties and sacrifices. Here women and men cooperate; they do also in warfare.

A dominant racial group tends to build political, economic, and social institutions and cultural traditions to serve its interests and maintain domination over subject or marginalized racial groupings. Religion too is invoked to legitimize domination.

Politically the world system has been built up by white expansionism. There have been large-scale exterminations of peoples due to racial intolerance, as in the advance of white peoples into the Americas, Australia, and New Zealand. The violence of more powerful racial groups has been a major driving force in history. Once they establish their power over a people and a place, they consolidate it by legal and constitutional maneuvers and by the imposition of one-sided economic relationships. Marginalized racial groups have to struggle to maintain their identity, to affirm their rights, or even simply to survive. There is a close affinity between racial and economic domination.

Women and men in a dominant racial group often cooperate in the exploitation of minority groups. The common interests of women and men who benefit from such a process generally outweigh the differences between them as women and men. In the interests of families, clans, tribes, and castes, racial injustices are perpetuated by both women and men.

Color, class, and sex can combine to pursue discrimination against different groups of persons. The continuity of the racial group is ensured by relationships of sex and family. Women and men can be equally racist and classist. Sexual assault on women by men of another racial group can be an expression of racial affirmation. Sometimes races and classes combine to maintain male domination.

On the other hand, color and sex can also come together in the process of liberation. The revolutionary cause is stronger when women and men join forces for a common objective. Freedom fighters are often motivated to take risks to their own lives in order to make life better for their families and descendants. Participation of women in the struggles of liberation of peoples and classes can help in developing the strength and rights of women—though it is often the case that women are subjected to traditional forms of oppression once the struggle is over.

Another positive achievement would be for women and men to relate across racial frontiers to identify with sisters and brothers of another racial group, especially an oppressed group. Would not sisterhood be a potent force for liberative alliances, due to the common interests of women as such? Would not the evils of patriarchy be overcome by women and men working together across racial lines? This is a question women of oppressed racial groups ask of their sisters in oppressor racial groups.

CLASSISM

A class is a group of persons having the same socioeconomic status. Differences in classes are intensified by income and the consequent access to opportunities in education and employment. Influence and power in most societies depend very much on one's class position.

As in sex and color, a dominant class tends to form the social institutions, mentalities, myths, customs, and traditions to suit its own needs and advancement. The affluent class generally controls the means of influencing opinion—namely, education, mass media, institutions for maintaining law and order, and the like.

State power within a country is generally controlled by the powerful—a class. Political democracy is ineffective without a large measure of economic democracy. State power can thus become a means of perpetuating the domination of the wealthy class. The poor are unable to sway the use of state power because of their lack of consciousness of their internal divisions, their lack of organization, their lack of fixed and shared purpose. In a word, their powerlessness. They therefore continue to be poor.

The social system, however, offers some opportunities, often more symbolic than real, for upward class mobility. This gives the poor some hope of advance, even though it turns out to be illusory for the majority.

In economic activity the relationships among the classes are such that the poorest derive the lowest income for the work they contribute to the productive process. Terms of trade are unfavorable to the poorer classes and, in general, to women—all of whom are relegated less remunerative functions. In starker terms, these groups depreciate in value. The price mechanism is a means by which certain privileges are retained by the privileged, behind the myth of the "magic of the marketplace."

In addition, class consciousness is a deeply ingrained characteristic, especially in capitalistic societies. It is manifested in one's mentality as well as in one's possessions and demeanor. Social intercourse is mostly among persons of the same class. Lifestyles, neighborhoods, means of transportation, recreational facilities—all help to maintain class differences.

The class system also influences families. Marriages most often take place among members of the same race and broad socioeconomic class. Social relationships too are influenced by levels of income and degrees of wealth. In terms of educational opportunities, children in free enterprise countries are much more dependent on class than on personal abilities or color or race.

Within given nations class is the main dividing line, the major contradiction in society. Sex and color differences are often less important than economic divisions—unless of course color itself implies economic discrimination, as between blacks and whites in South Africa.

At the international level racial groupings tend to act together in global politics. Here the economic interests of whites are linked with the world system built up by them. Even poor whites generally wish to maintain this system against attacks by the black, yellow, and brown races.

The system of social classes is generally seen as operative within a given nation. Generally a small percentage—10 to 15 percent—of the population of capitalist countries (or market economies) appropriates 60 to 70 percent of the total income. Class conflicts explain much of the political, social, and cultural dynamics within countries. Liberation movements too have a class character; they may be geared toward the transfer of power either to a class that is economically well-off or to the working class. National liberation struggles that did not lead to a transfer of power to the working class and the setting up of socialist economies have generally been coopted into the prevailing world system of dominant capitalism. Unless a process of liberation genuinely transfers economic power to the vast majority of the people or to the working class, it is not likely to reduce class discrimination within a country. We can therefore evaluate the achievements of social movements and political parties by their practical action toward a removal of these disparities.

Dissimilarities

Awareness of persons as sexual beings develops primarily in terms of individual women and men.Everyone has links of love and common lifestyle with some members of the other sex: spouse, parent, sibling, child, relative, colleague.

A racial grouping or a class is a moral or legal entity. It is not a physical person. The experiences and memory of racial groupings and classes are collective and historical, and their aspirations go beyond the lives of given individuals. Questions concerning the sexes are first personal and only secondly externalized in the social sphere, such as education, employment, and wages. Issues of color and class are first collective and structural, and secondly personal and internalized. There are only two sexes, whereas classes and racial groups are many. The sexes are strongly attracted toward each other; there is generally a closeness and identification that racial groupings and classes as collectivities cannot achieve. Women and men as sexual partners can reproduce human beings, whereas classes relate to each other in the production of goods and services. The reciprocity of the sexes is much more intimate than the complementarity of color or class collaboration in economic life. Racial groups can do without each other, at least on their own terms, but one sex cannot do without the other. Classes compete; racial groups coexist; the sexes cohabit.

Considerations of sex tend to personalize issues, whereas those of color and class take us outside ourselves to a wider group. When dealing with women and men we encounter individual persons—bodies, minds, wills, emotions—a psychophysical whole; hence sexual exploitation affects persons at a very intimate and deep level. In color and class we encounter a collective psyche. Racial and class domination affect us more from the outside. It also entails a common entity or community shared by many, and is hence more bearable. Sexual domination has a much more personal character. Rape is a physical intrusion into another's being.

Sex, has, all the same, a strong economic, political, social, and cultural character. Sexual domination can be and is socialized and expressed in the relationships of women and men in society.

In racial and class issues the demand is for justice and dignity. In the personal relationships of women and men more is demanded: understanding, sharing, love. There is an intimate natural, biological, and psychological link between female and male in which one accepts sacrifice for the other in a way that cannot be explained except by calling it love. This is a phenomenon basically different from the interactions of classes or racial groups.

The nature of the basic relationships of female and male are fundamentally different from group relationships, be they of color, class, caste, tribe, or religion. Women and men, it would seem, are made for each other. The liberation and fulfillment of one is inextricably linked to the liberation and fulfillment of the other.

These dissimilarities make sexual domination and the movements for women's liberation a different kind of complexity from those concerning color and class.

The struggles of classes, racial groups, and the sexes cannot therefore be reduced one to the other. It is necessary to defend the autonomy of these struggles. But it is also necessary that these struggles not be isolated from one another. The forces of exploitation gain by dividing their victims. There should be togetherness in going ahead though the force of domination may be seen and contested from different vantage points. Diverse forms of oppression often are linked together and are cumulative. A poor black woman is oppressed in her class, her color, and her sex. Liberation, to be genuine, has to be integral. The growth of human consciousness from more than one intuition of human rights makes the quest for liberation fuller, more challenging, and more extensive. These different movements must understand their own identities within the overall planetary human search for fulfillment on this one earth that we all have for our home.

Strengths and Weaknesses of Marxism

Marxism has contributed valuable insights to the understanding of human relationships, social processes, national histories, and international developments. It has helped explode myths that served to cover up exploitation. It has also been the most powerful revolutionary force during the twentieth century. Over a third of the world's population now has regimes that call themselves Marxist.

Marxism has, however, some difficulties in explaining the relationships of race at an international level. Thus the white working class of Britain does not make common cause with the black workers of South Africa. The growth of capitalism to an imperialist stage has led the working classes of the superpowers to identify more with their capitalist compatriots than with their exploited colleagues of the periphery. In addition, rapid advances in technology—as in the computerizing of production and business transactions—have reduced the role of labor. The silicon chip gives much more productive capacity to capital. This and continued large-scale unemployment have decreased the power of labor in the social bargaining process.

Marxism also may have some difficulty in appreciating adequately the movements for women's liberation. A socialist society will be more liberating for women insofar as the conditions of economic life will be altered to enable all women to participate in the productive process. However, not all the goals of women's struggle for identity, equality, and dignity can be achieved by the mere transformation of the relationships of production.

All these raise issues as to how far the relationships of class, following upon the relationships of production, are a motive force for social change. Have not the working classes of the power centers been co-opted to the side of their dominant classes as against the exploited classes of the periphery? On the other hand, local elites of the Third World are often readily bought over to support the world's rich companies and families.

Here we see a crisscrossing of loyalties and conflicts. Internationally the economic interests of a nation seem to be a greater factor of cohesion than those of a given class with its counterpart in another country. Similarly the loyalties of sex do not usually extend from one nation to another in a conflict of classes or racial groups. In personal relationships the women's movement makes a valuable contribution that has a fairly universal validity. But the movement has not yet expressed itself strongly on the liberation of even other women from the structures of economic or racial domination in other countries. Antisexism alone does not have the dynamism of liberation from class and racial domination. The same is true of other struggles. The emancipation of workers or of an oppressed racial group does not necessarily mean a triumph over male domination. Hence there is a need for integral human liberation that will help individuals understand and give direction to the liberational dynamics of each oppressed group.

Chapter 3

Asia

The Third World has long been paying the price for the prosperity of the First World, which has fashioned the world system to suit its interests. The Second World has tried to escape bearing this cost and endeavors to go its own way, or even build its own centers and peripheries. Third World peoples are finding it increasingly difficult to pay the heavy price in cheap raw materials and cheap labor and to provide markets for the "developed," "advanced" countries. They are posing challenges to the whole system, its way of thinking, its values and structures. The First World is particularly sensitive to this challenge and, led by the United States, wants to maintain the status quo.

Within this overall challenge from the Third World, Asia presents a variety of issues that profoundly question the world system. During the past four centuries Asia has been at the mercy of the merciless Western exploitive system. During the present century Asia has been awakening from its long slumber. During the twenty-first century Asia is bound to make its mark on world society—if it survives.

Asia, with 85 to 90 percent of the world's poor, is a continent of large and growing populations. Over 40 percent of all Asians are below fifteen years of age and only 5 percent above sixty years. The average rate of population growth is 2.1 percent per year in Asia as a whole; China has a low rate of 1.2 percent.

Birth control programs have been encouraged almost everywhere. The rapid increase in population puts severe pressures on these countries. When European populations increased rapidly in the eighteenth and nineteenth centuries, they had almost the whole world as an area for resettling their excess populations, temporarily or permanently.

The gravity of the problem may be grasped from the fact that India has to provide each year for a population growth about equal to the entire population of Australia—14 to 15 million. To adequately house, care for, and educate these children, India would have to build ten thousand housing units, one thousand new classrooms, and one thousand new hospital wards every day for the next twenty-five years.

Africa and Latin America too will face similar problems in the coming decades. The advance of science and technology, especially medicine, has contributed to the problems by reducing the high infant mortality rate and lengthening life expectancy.

During the next fifty years, if present trends continue, there will be a remarkable change in the population balance in the world. The rich First World countries, including Japan, will have a much lower population growth than will the rest of the world and a higher median age. The Asian population will continue to increase at a more rapid rate, though slower than in the 1970s and '80s.

At the beginning of this century Europe was a continent of relatively large national populations. The Asian countries, other than China and India, were relatively smaller in population. Even in 1950 Europe had 392 million, East Asia had 673 million, and South Asia 706 million. But by the year 2000, Europe is expected to have 520 million whereas East Asia will have 1.4 billion and South Asia 2.2 billion.

The pressures of an ever growing population have to be faced by the Asian countries—and the rest of the world. The rise of repressive Asian regimes is partly due to the inability of governments to respond to their peoples' needs within the limited land and resource base available to them and the burden of providing a high lifestyle for local elites and an even more costly support for the foreign companies that operate there.

The Sino-Soviet conflict has also to be understood, in part, by the land-population disproportions in their immense 4,500-mile common border region. There are millions on the Chinese side and empty spaces in Soviet Asia, some of which the Chinese claim were wrested from Chinese possession by Russian czars. This border is likely to be an internationally explosive issue in the coming decades. There are also population pressures on the less inhabited regions of Southeast Asia and Oceania.

Table 6
Estimates and Projections of Asian Populations, 1981 and 2000

	1981 (millions)	2000 (millions)
China	968	1,189
India	700	1,036
Indonesia	155	221
Japan	117	128
Bangladesh	91	153
Pakistan	85	147
Korea	57	78
Vietnam	53	79
Philippines	52	83
Thailand	50	76
Turkey	46	69
Iran	39	65
Burma	36	55
Afghanistan	22	37

Source: *World Population Trends and Prospects by Country, 1950–2000* (New York: United Nations, 1979).

These population problems also present serious challenges to the racism of the present world system, which has been built basically to support the expansionism of white nations. The question before the planetary society is whether it will be able to find a peaceful remedy to the horrendous contradiction in our world between an aging, relatively stable white population occupying empty, fertile land-masses and the young increasing population of yellow and brown peoples. Africa is vast and may cope with the increase in black peoples for quite some decades.

ASIA AND THE WORLD POLITICO-ECONOMIC SYSTEM

During the greater part of this century Asian peoples have been trying to liberate themselves from or in some way deal with the world politico-economic system. They have adopted different ap-

proaches, with varying degrees of success. The Japanese have
proved that they can beat the West militarily—as they did in the
1905 war against Russia—and economically—as they are doing now
at the global level. The Japanese opted for a long period of isolation
from the dominant West, while learning from it, before opening
their doors to contact with outsiders. Now the Japanese government supports industry and foreign trade. The big Japanese MNCs
guarantee lifelong employment and social services to their employees. They combine small-scale enterprises with the largest business
enterprises in the world. Combining the Japanese cultural values of
care for persons with efficiency in business, they have ensured
greater harmony in industrial relations. Unemployment is not a
serious issue there in spite of modernization.

On the other hand Japanese business success has been built at the
expense of the exploitation of other countries, especially in Asia.
The Japanese import raw materials at cheap prices, operate
pollution-intensive industries in poor countries, pillage the forests
of Southeast Asian countries, and share in setting up free trade
zones, as in Taiwan, South Korea, and the Philippines. Japan be-
haves in the rest of Asia just as do the Western imperial powers,
though perhaps in a more low-keyed and nonmilitaristic manner
after its defeat in World War II. But the armaments industry is a
major element in its economy.

Japan has met its problem of land and resource shortages by population control, rapid economic development based on up-to-date
technical competence, competitive marketing, hard work, and the
Japanese tradition of humane industrial relations. However, this
success does not offer a model to other Asian countries: it depends
heavily on the ruthless exploitation of foreign countries and support
of dictatorial regimes, especially in the Far East and Southeast Asia.

Two Socialist Giants

SOVIET CONSOLIDATION

The U.S.S.R. spreads over 8,707,870 square miles in Europe and
Asia. It occupies one-sixth of the planet's land surface and 42 per-
cent of the surface of the Eurasian continent. The Asian part of the
U.S.S.R. covers about 40 percent of Asia's land surface.

In the first half of the sixteenth century Russia was a small state
confined to the Upper Volga region. During the century after 1550

Russian explorers and conquerors penetrated eastward into Asia to the Pacific Ocean. During the nineteenth century, Russia expanded into central Asia. Thus it is only within the past four hundred years that Russia developed into the largest country in the world. The Russians have incorporated most of this vast expanse within their political and cultural orbit, with certain rights being guaranteed to racial and religious minorities. Presently, only about 20 percent of the Soviet population is Asian (Georgians, Armenians, Uzbeks, Tartars, and others). If the present population trends continue, the proportion of Asians will grow to about 40 percent by the year 2020.

Although most European colonies have become independent and European powers have had to withdraw from Asia and Africa (except for Australia, New Zealand, and South Africa), Russia has consolidated itself as an Asian power. The territory of the U.S.S.R. has the advantage of being compact and spatially contiguous, like those of other continental powers: the United States, Australia, Canada, Brazil. The far northern region, sparsely populated, is rich in coal, oil, natural gas, diamonds, and gold. Half the world's coal is said to lie in the Siberian regions of the U.S.S.R.

About 70 percent of the U.S.S.R. population lives west of the Urals, Russian migration eastward from Europe having been slow and limited. Presently about 176 million, or 65 percent, of the 270 million inhabitants of the U.S.S.R. dwell in urban areas, and 94 million in rural areas. By the year 2000, however, 76 percent are expected to be living in urban areas. As migration to the cities continues, Russia will be facing problems in developing the vast reserves of natural resources in its eastern and far eastern empire. The U.S.S.R. repudiated czarist rule and capitalism but retained the territorial gains of czarist imperialism.

The U.S.S.R. has established a socialist regime over one-sixth of the globe. Because Soviet socialism is socialism within one country, it is geared to the maximization of benefits for its dominant groups. Just because the U.S.S.R. is socialist does not therefore necessarily mean that there is a just distribution of the natural resources within its territory for the benefit of all its people.

In a sense, European Russia has been the most successful colonial power in Asia. It has occupied territory that might otherwise have been an area for the expansion of the rapidly growing populations of the Far East, especially China and Japan.

When the U.S.S.R. has been unable to develop by itself the resources of Siberian regions, it has made use of West European, Japanese, and American capital, in spite of its socialist ideology.

The United States, the U.S.S.R., and Western Europe reap advantages in maintaining the status quo against the demands of the poorer peoples of the world. Understandable too is the rift between the U.S.S.R. and communist China: nationalist aspirations and territorial claims are often more important determinants of policy than are the ideologies of capitalism or socialism.

CHINA: AN ALTERNATIVE SOCIALIST PATH

Prior to the communist revolution, China, like most of Asia, was feudal, subject to foreign exploitation and the ravages of nature. Local warlords and landlords dominated peasants and workers. Famine, disease, and floods caused millions of untimely deaths. Females were particularly exploited from childhood on. Foreign powers forced unequal trade treaties on China and tried to capture the Chinese markets for their goods. Following the 1949 revolution, China was boycotted by the capitalist powers. After 1961 even the U.S.S.R. ended its technical assistance to China. China thus went through a quarter-century of isolation from the international community. This helped in the evolution of its own strategy of revolution and growth. China under Mao Tse-tung went through a long period of deep travail in order to implement its own socialist program. A basic aspect of this program was the change in mentality that had to be effected among the people. "Serve the people" was a constant public exhortation toward this end. A process of self-criticism and self-revolutionizing was begun, with emphasis on the virtues of dedication, self-denial, frugality, hard work, temperance, honesty, self-purification, and service. This was to be a corrective to the evils of the centralization and technocratic control of the Soviet model of socialism.

Educational reforms were carried out to communicate the values of service and make the Chinese people self-reliant in rebuilding their country. Education was reformed to break down the barriers between manual and intellectual work, village and city, peasant and worker, practice and theory, poor and rich, education and socialist construction. Education became an instrument of the revolutionary process. Culture and the arts were also at the service of the people and the revolution. Individualism and capitalist motivation were to be combated mainly by persuasion.

The Chinese revolution was largely a peasant movement. Villages were reconstructed into large communes where production and distribution were on a communitarian basis. The communes were designed to be new centers of life in which agriculture, industry, trade, culture, and even military needs would be provided. This communal reorganization of agriculture in China can be credited with carrying through a massive socialist revolution involving several hundred million rural poor.

The rebuilding of China through self-reliance in all ways was the ideal of the revolution. China thus had to be self-reliant in raw materials and markets. This very process helped to stimulate the creative potentialities of the people. New technologies were evolved, especially on a short-term basis, in order to cope with the shortage of capital and surplus of workers. Droves of Chinese were employed to remake the face of China, building roads and dams, schools, hospitals, and factories, and tilling the soil. Education too was geared to work; students had to contribute to the increase in productivity.

The revolution also fostered a growing industry geared to the needs of the people. As in agriculture, the goal was not profit but the satisfaction of the urgent needs of all. Administrative cadres, technical experts, and experienced workers cooperated to develop both communal and Chinese industry, especially after the withdrawal of the Russians. Technology was developed to make the best use possible of the raw materials and skills available in China. The high level of specialization was even capable of producing an atomic bomb.

Changes also occurred in health services, in which the ancient Chinese medical system was revived in conjunction with modern Western medicine. The intermediate medical practitioner (the "barefoot doctor") was trained to meet the needs of the villages. Dependence on foreign imports was given up, and the brain drain of doctors to the West was stopped. Medicine would serve the people and not be a means of profit for the doctor.

Three decades of this socialist effort produced a China self-sufficient in its basic needs. The nation has been able to hold its own against the major evils that affect capitalist countries: unemployment, inflation, gross inequalities, energy crises, and famine.

It is true that there is not political democracy in China. Nor is there freedom for Chinese to overthrow the socialist system or leave the country at will. But there is a measure of participation in the construction of a socialist society. The excesses of the "cultural revolution," which was begun as a corrective to bureaucratism, did much harm to the revolution both in China and abroad. Chinese foreign policy tends to be nationalistic rather than attuned to issues of international justice.

What China achieved in so short a time is extraordinary by any human standards. The Chinese people had to pay a high price in self-discipline and hard work. But for the first time in their modern history this one-fifth of the human race can look after itself. Although the changes since the death of Mao Tse-tung and Chou En-lai have somewhat altered the course of the revolution in favor of rapid modernization, the Chinese example is a definite challenge and trailblazer for other peoples. It provides a feasible alternative to capitalistic "development," especially for poor countries with high unemployment, although many problems of socialism still remain unresolved. (For an interesting and insightful examination of the less commendable aspects of the Maoist regime, see Bao Rua-Want, *Prisoner of Mao* [New York: Coward-McCann, 1973].)

Ideological Conflict: Korea and Vietnam

During the past four decades ideological conflict has been acute in many Asian communities with Marxists and procapitalists vying for power. The ideological battle was fought out militarily in Korea and Vietnam. Korea remains divided. Vietnam is unified under Marxist rule.

North Vietnam demonstrated under Ho Chi Minh how a small country could both win a war against the major imperialist powers and carry through a socialist reorganization of the country. In more recent years the situation in Indochina, involving Vietnam, Kampuchea, Laos, and China, is far from satisfactory or exemplary. Marxist powers have been at war with each other, thus not only impoverishing themselves but also discrediting their regimes and ideology.

In terms of a global analysis the historical experience of Marxist regimes in Asia and Eastern Europe reveals that they tend to be motivated more by national interests than by world justice, and worse still by internal party and personal lust for power. The Vietnam war is very important in the impact it had on the United States, which absorbed its first military defeat. This superpower was not only humiliated but the people of North America in large measure had their eyes opened to the myths of their power as well as of their history. It will not be easy in the future for the United States to mount a similar operation, due to the unwillingness of its youth to fight in such wars for the benefit of the U.S. ruling elite.

Afghanistan is another country involved in civil war and occupation by Soviet armed forces. The Soviet Union claims it is helping in a people's liberation struggle, but others see in its intervention another instance of the centuries-old expansionist policy of Russia, this time toward the Persian Gulf and the Indian Ocean. The resistance of Afghan guerrillas may make this the Soviet Union's Vietnam.

The refugee problem in Asia is very much aggravated by the troubles in Afghanistan and Indochina. Millions of persons are now refugees in many nearby lands, especially Thailand and Pakistan. The world refugee problem is another deep wound that affects the countries of Asia, Africa, and Latin America. Tens of millions of human beings are on the move as vagrants in our "civilized" world. This is one more indication of the importance of land-population relationships in global perspectives.

West Asia

During the past decade the Arab countries of West Asia and the Middle East have become a vigorous presence on the world scene. By nationalizing their oil enterprises and cooperating with other oil producers to form the OPEC oil cartel, they have demonstrated to the world another way in which primary producers can change their terms of trade and economic fortunes. Until OPEC showed the world that the rich countries needed the resources of the hitherto poor countries, it used to be argued that the poor were poor because they did not work hard. It was maintained that the market economy gave them their due. OPEC has shown how world prices of commodities can depend on national interests. The hundreds of billions of dollars now being accumulated to the credit of the oil producers also shows how much they were deprived of during the decades when foreign companies controlled the whole process of oil extraction, refining, and marketing.

The big multinational oil companies, on the other hand, are still glutting themselves with enormous profits. The oil-cost revolution has disrupted the economies of many non-oil-producing poor countries, as well as the industries of rich countries.

The West Asian countries use their oil income to develop their economies. This has also triggered a large-scale migration of Asian workers to the Middle East. They are among the best paid but most exploited workers in Asia. They have no trade union, or civic, or political rights. Women are subjected to cruel treatment and sexual harassment. This has prompted India, Pakistan, and the Philippines to enact legislation barring female citizens from migrating to the Middle East. Once again money power leads to human exploitation.

The oil-rich countries have political systems that are monarchical or dictatorial. The majority of their peoples are badly off, especially in the more populous countries, such as Iran. It is a tragedy that in many oil-rich countries the local rulers and elites waste their newly acquired wealth while keeping the masses poor. Nigeria, Indonesia, and Venezuela are examples of massive residual poverty in spite of oil wealth.

The Middle East has been the scene of many wars since 1945. Iran and Iraq started their most recent war in 1980. The superpowers sell arms to both sides. Oil profits thus return to armament producers. The tragedy takes on a cynical hue when the U.S.A. promises to keep both Saudi Arabia and Israel equally well armed. The world armaments industry, amassing $500 billion per year, is maintained by armed conflicts in the Third World. Since 1945 there has been peace in Europe and North America. The battlegrounds of armed conflict today are Asia, Africa, and South and Central America.

All the world's major problems are compounded in this region. The founding of Israel and the Palestinian struggle for a homeland have raised religious and racial tensions enmeshed in ideological and military global conflicts. The resurgence of Islam with a militant fundamentalist thrust, popular struggles for freedom and participation, foreign intervention, the emancipation of women, and coping with a desert environment are all major issues here. All these make the Middle East a new center of the planetary economic, political, military, cultural, and religious trends of the coming decades.

Southeast Asian Countries with Capitalist Regimes

South Korea, Taiwan, Hong Kong, the Philippines, Indonesia, Singapore, Malaysia, and Thailand have governments that have oriented their countries along pro-Western capitalist lines of development. Certain characteristics common to these areas are clearly discernible:

1) Priority is given to the growth of economic productivity measured by the gross national product, which has risen considerably in the 1970s and '80.

2) Social justice and an equitable distribution of wealth and incomes take second place. Care of the environment is neglected, especially under the pressure of foreign companies.

3) Foreign investments are welcomed under quite favorable terms and are guaranteed by governments. The foreign firms undertake development of the skills of the local population, use local materials, encourage exports, and import substitute materials. Sometimes they establish subsidiaries of the big multinational corporations; at times these are joint ventures with the participation of local capital and management. All the same, foreign indebtedness is growing; balance of payments problems make export orientation a high priority.

4) Trade with Western powers and Japan is encouraged. Growth of production in Southeast Asian countries now poses a threat to employment in Western countries, though not necessarily threatening the profits of multinational corporations that operate in both areas.

5) A rather strict control of labor and trade unions rights is maintained, on the pretext of "national security" requirements. Wages are kept low; capital (including foreign capital) receives the lion's share of profits. Working conditions are poor. Workers can be hired and fired at will by employers, who are generally favored by the law; large-scale unemployment allows employers to manipulate workers by threatening to dismiss them.

6) Development takes place mainly in and around urban areas. The urban elite are the main decision-makers. Industries are generally located around the big cities, and much of government spending is for industrial plants and amenities for the urban elite. Rural areas are often neglected. The enormous growth of the Bangkok-

Thomburi region and the neglect of rural areas in Thailand is an example.

7) Tourism is given a high priority. Prostitution is growing fast and affecting the moral and cultural values of the people. Women are particularly exploited in the free trade zones and as migrant workers in the Middle East.

8) The economic growth process is engineered by the local elite; the process in turn helps this elite rather than the workers and peasants. The managerial class is rewarded with better—First World-level—housing, transportation, and educational facilities. Discontent of the masses has often led to protests and uprisings, which have so far been crushed, often harshly.

9) The educational system is geared toward development of the skills required for the administration of the country and the servicing of the industrial companies. The values stressed by the schools and universities are individualist, competitive, and examination-oriented. In certain countries—India, for example—corruption has beset the educational system, especially in admissions to schools of higher education and in examination processes. Through control of education, governments and the ruling classes communicate their own values and those of the capitalist ethic to the next generation.

10) The mass media in these countries are owned and controlled either by the governments or by the very rich. Foreign millionaires control some of the main newspapers in Thailand, Malaysia, Singapore, and Hong Kong. They propagate capitalist views and values. Advertising orients consumer tastes toward luxuries, increasing the imbalance in the economy and the general disequilibrium throughout the nation.

11) Enormous expenditure is made on arms and the defense forces. As inequality grows, tensions grow within the country. In order to maintain the status quo, it is necessary to have a strong repressive force. In the process, a military elite is being developed in many of these countries. Even large sectors of the administration of some countries are controlled by the military, as in Indonesia and Thailand.

12) The constitutions and legal systems of these countries are being changed in order to increase governmental power. In certain instances this ploy has been used to prolong and perpetuate the tenure and powers of rulers, as in the Philippines and South Korea.

Emergency laws and internal security acts severely repress individual rights. Military dictatorships rule most of these countries. They are becoming "national security states," similar to the Latin American dictatorship pattern.

South Asia

The countries of the Indian subcontinent—India, Bangladesh, Sri Lanka, Nepal, and Pakistan—present a somewhat different set of values and strategies in the development process. They are basically within the capitalist sector of the world economy, and their economies are still largely based on private enterprise.

However, there is or has been an effort to modify the operation of capitalism by developing a socialist sector of production and implementing far-reaching social services. India and Sri Lanka still retain a democratic system of government, at least with changes of government by general elections.

This region too is coming increasingly under the capitalistic dominion of foreign companies and collaborating local elites. Pakistan and Bangladesh are virtual military dictatorships. Sri Lanka, since 1977, has taken an out-and-out capitalist course, heavily dependent on foreign investment. India alone seems capable of a somewhat independent stance, because its own capitalistic sector is strong enough to defend the national interests of the ruling class and the big companies. India is a major industrial power in the world, with a high level of science and technology. Indian capital is now reaching multinational status through its foreign investments. However, the Indian masses are among the worst off in the world, in large measure due to the inadequacy of social reforms.

South Asia's progress toward an egalitarian society has been halting and piecemeal when compared with countries under Marxist revolutionary regimes. Countries of South Asia have given a prominent place to the dominant religious traditions: Hinduism, Islam, and Buddhism. As a result, the values emphasized are less production-oriented than in communist countries or under the capitalist regimes of Southeast Asia. The South Asian countries present an interesting, though ambivalent, search for the harmonizing of such values as economic growth with social justice, political freedom, and a religion-oriented culture. Although materially poorer than most of the rest of Asia, they have much to contribute to humankind's search for meaning and harmony in life.

Burma, under General Ne Win, is a unique example of a Buddhist socialist military dictatorship. Burma is self-reliant and more egalitarian than other noncommunist countries. Though it has not yet enjoyed much economic growth, it is an interesting experiment that can teach other Asian countries lessons in self-reliance—at a price. After twenty years of this effort, Burma is now hesitatingly opening itself to Western "aid."

The South Asian countries are among the poorest and most hard pressed in the world. With 941 million inhabitants, they constitute 22 percent of the human race. By the year 2000 they are expected to have 1.5 billion inhabitants. Their effort at preserving democratic institutions and a socialist trend is under severe strain. We may expect volcanic social eruptions in this region in the coming decades.

Throughout Asia political dictatorships are becoming the norm, whether the economy be capitalist or socialist. India and Sri Lanka are exceptional in changing governments on the basis of free general elections. Elsewhere the repression of political opposition is common; imprisonment without trial and even torture are widespread. Corruption is a universal phenomenon in the free enterprise Asian countries at almost all levels of society. All these lead to deep frustration among the young who are unemployed and cannot bring about changes in their societies. Students who are more conscious of their situation are in many places the main force that expresses the discontent of younger persons, as in South Korea since 1961, Thailand in 1973, Indonesia in 1965, Sri Lanka in 1971, and in India in the campaigns of Jaya Prakash Narayan against corruption in 1974.

The free enterprise countries in Asia are most susceptible to local and international conflicts owing to their importance in the global strategy of nations. War has been waged in one or another Asian region continuously since 1945. There have been anticolonial wars, communist-inspired insurrections, the Korean war, the Indochina wars, conflicts in the Middle East, and the wars of India with China, India with Pakistan, Iran with Iraq, China with Vietnam.

If these countries pass into the Marxist camp or adopt policies of economic self-sufficiency and nationalize foreign investments, the capitalist countries will be badly hurt. They will be forced to lower their standard of living. They may call it "economic strangulation." Indeed, this was the accusation of President Gerald Ford and U.S. Secretary of State Henry Kissinger against the policies of the OPEC countries. The Western nations have for centuries benefited from the exploitation of Asia, and they will not give it up without a struggle. The Vietnam war, the Soviet presence in Afghanistan, and the U.S. readiness to support right-wing dictatorships in Asia are indications of the importance of this region.

Asia's Rural Populations and Elites

Rural Asians are exploited by the remaining vestiges of feudal oppression and the diversion of agriculture to suit foreign markets for cash crops. The big multinational corporations are penetrating the remotest Asian villages to sell their products, obtain cheap raw materials, and even buy land for large-scale cash crops.

The typical Asian village has its rich elite, who receive the main benefit from the economic enterprises of the villagers. Middlemen buy the produce, often in advance, and extend credit at very high rates of interest. Sometimes the capital stock belongs to them, with transportation facilities also under their control. Village laborers receive about half the value of their produce. Income from the village goes to the landlords, who generally live in the cities or in country mansions.

Population growth, mechanization of agriculture, fragmentation of peasant holdings, concentration of land ownership in bigger units, elimination of handcrafts—all combine to make the condition of the rural poor precarious. Their poverty, landlessness, and unemployment often lead them into debt because the new money economy makes no provision for credit on reasonable terms. Feudal landlords, local traders, and moneylenders all charge exorbitant rates of interest (often over 120 percent per annum). The immense poverty thus engendered, together with malnutrition and the other ills of an impoverished people, lead to a lack of vigor, vitality, and initiative—which are the generally cited shortcomings of Asian labor. By the turn of the century there will be 2.15 billion persons in Asia's rural areas, with about 1.4 billion of them outside China and Japan, which provide better for their villages. Asia's rural unrest cannot be contained. This is potentially the world's most revolutionary situation—a billion peasants demanding land and the means to cultivate it. Unfortunately Asian elites refuse to carry out the land reforms needed to avert catastrophe.

An elite is a group that has some special advantage or privilege and stands apart from the mass in any population. In the Asian countries, elites enjoy diverse forms of advantage: wealth, social prestige, political power, cultural advancement, military might, religious privilege, hereditary rank.

Their power varies with the nature of their elitism. The wealthy are well off materially. Their incomes are generally about ten times that of the average working-class family. At the top of the income and wealth pyramid is a very small percentage of highly privileged persons, generally millionaires in places such as India, Thailand, Singapore, Hong Kong, Taiwan, Korea, and Pakistan. Affluent families live almost as well as upper middle-class families in the rich Western capitalist countries. The political elite may be poorer, to begin with, but with time they too tend to acquire economic power. Patronage and corruption help in the process. The military elite today are inclined to seek political power and, in the process of exercising it, gain economic advantages as well. The cultural and religious elite do not *per se* have financial power. But they are tempted to conform to the values of the ruling political and economic elites, and those who do so acquire the benefits of wealth and power. The intellectual elite may not have wealth, but in molding a people's thought, they can exert great influence on the masses. They, too, are often co-opted to the service of the prevailing system by money and position.

These elites have evolved from the leadership groups of both the traditional and the modernized sectors. The traditionally well off families were the first to be recruited by colonial powers. To them were added those who emerged through the educational process. The modern elite emerged in symbiosis with the Western presence in government, plantations, industry, commerce, education, and the military. Foreign-based companies offered them employment at upper management levels. They acquired the skills necessary for such work. They were thus able to take over from foreigners the running of such enterprises, including the administration of the country. For this they had often to contest the foreign presence. But in the free enterprise countries of Asia, the transfer of political power to the local elite did not mean a fundamental break in the socioeconomic system, as happened in the Marxist countries of Asia. Japan and Thailand have gone through a somewhat different process of modernization, but they too have been integrated within the world system through the mediation of local elites.

There is also a subgrouping of westernized elites that champion Marxism or democratic socialism. In social life, both groups live a rather sophisticated style more in keeping with capitalist-oriented consumerism. This is true of socialists and Marxists in India, Sri Lanka, Japan, and Singapore. Only those involved in armed struggle for a socialist society try to identify with the masses in their way of living. This is part of the strength of leaders such as Mao Tse-tung and Ho Chi Minh, who lived in close association with the poorer masses during a long period of struggle. The alienation of both the capitalist and Marxist-oriented westernized elites from the actual sufferings of the poorer masses is part of the tragedy of the free Asian peoples, and one cause of the ineffectiveness of even Marxist elites.

Besides the Western-educated, modernized elites there are leader-ship groups that are closer to the people in their language and way of life, even though they may be economically better off. In rural Asia, leadership is still held by more traditional elites. They may distinguish themselves from the masses in wealth, hereditary status, or religious positions, but they generally feel socially inferior to westernized elites. They can be quite exploitive of their poorer neighbors.

In some countries this leadership is asserting itself in terms of a return to the traditional languages, cultures, and religions. Some-times these groups are right-wing and socially conservative, such as the Jan Sangh in India and extreme Islamic groups in Pakistan and Indonesia. In general, the more westernized, modernized elites dominate. But traditional elites still have great political influence, especially among the rural masses.

There is a strong tendency for alliances to be formed among the various elites. Rural elites tend to take up residence in the cities; urban elites like to buy property in the countryside, thus becoming absentee landlords. Politicians seek the support of businessmen, and vice versa. Military leadership seeks allies and friends among politicians, professionals, business magnates, and landlords. Marriage, friendship, sharing in power, partnership in good works and in corruption—all tend to bring them together. Although family and party differences divide them, self-interest tends to bring elites together on more fundamental issues.

Economic planning at the level of central government is generally in the hands of the elites. Economists, planners, university professors, journalists, mass media executives, and officials of planning departments usually look out for their own interests. Even where the vast majority of the people is extremely poor, national planning has ensured the continued economic growth of the elites—social services are provided for the poor. The limited resources within the country and foreign exchange reserves are used to ensure the wants of the elites in such areas as housing, clothing, health, communications, education, transportation, and energy resources.

The business elite help companies to set up "joint ventures," thus giving them a national flavor and tax advantages. The political elite is open to influence and "commissions" from these companies. The prevailing planning priorities often help the multinational firms to obtain a firm base and a national image within these countries, especially in Southeast Asia.

Thus the ruling elites, generally westernized, are one of the greatest obstacles to the realization of social justice in Asian countries. They are reluctant to change a system in which they receive the main advantages: enrichment and political power. They further strengthen the forces of conservatism by appeals to democracy, anticommunism, and religious values. At the international level, they are not in favor of radical changes, even if their rhetoric is radical. They are in favor of conserving the Western capitalist world system from which they benefit.

On the other hand, one elite spearheads radical changes in national life—the cultural elite. Artists, writers, and academicians are among the more sensitive of the elites. A section of the political elite, especially those who have been influenced by Marxist analysis and values, are aware of the need for radical changes. Among the religious leadership, small groups are becoming more seriously concerned with the egalitarian message of the world religions. Even among military leaders, the encounter with deep poverty and starvation raises issues concerning the values of society. Thus the elites are an important element in the movement of Asian societies, even though the working classes and rural poor must bear the main burden of crusading for radical changes.

The tragedy of the Asian elites is that they could be the liberators of the masses instead of being their oppressors and betrayers. But this would demand enormous sacrifices of them. They have skills required for the rapid development of the peoples, but they lack the humanity and the political will to implement changes that would be radical enough to reverse the trends toward inequality and injustice.

The Asian elites resemble in many ways the local elites in the African and Latin American countries. Understanding the role of local elites is extremely important for any attempt at justice within poor countries or at the world level. They are the extension of the dominant world system into the poor countries—the principal local agents and collaborators of the central powers.

DISCRIMINATION IN ASIAN SOCIETY

Discrimination against Women

A traditional aspect of Asian societies is the unfair treatment of women, even though there is a certain respect for females and motherhood. From birth, girls are less wanted and, in a certain way, less cared for. Boys are welcome; the family is proud of them and looks forward to their becoming breadwinners. In education, there has been an almost universal neglect of girls in favor of boys. This is particularly true of Islamic countries; the proportion of literate females is low.

Throughout life there is a strong conditioning of females to their assigned domestic roles. They are not permitted to go about alone. Fear is instilled. They become physically and psychologically dependent on males. This situation is changing somewhat in urban areas and among the educated classes.

As girls grow up there is pressure on them to get married and "settle down." Parents are thereby absolved of any responsibility to look after their daughters. In many Asian countries, marriages, especially in rural areas, are arranged by the parents and elders. Sometimes girls are hardly able to choose a partner freely. The married state is an honor, whereas there is little acceptance of the single woman (apart from a religious dedication). Widowhood is considered a misfortune and divorce a disgrace for the woman. The same stigma is not attached to the widower or the divorced man.

There is discrimination against women in the field of employment also. Women are not encouraged or expected to take up regular employment outside their homes. When they are employed, they are often paid less than are males for the same type of work. Jobs available to women are generally of a less responsible and respectable type. Women are largely employed as unskilled laborers; those in administrative and supervisory positions are far outnumbered by men. Women are also exploited in the new free trade zones in hotels, restaurants, and tourist centers, sometimes through prostitution, especially when they are unemployed and their families are in need.

Women have little responsibility in social and political life. The example of female prime ministers—in Sri Lanka, India, Israel—is still the exception. By and large, there is little confidence in the ability of women to administer any area beyond the home.

The main root of this discrimination is a deep-seated psychological conditioning to male dominance and female dependence. Sometimes women seem to prefer the role of helplessness, in which they feel cared for, and the role of mother and nurse, in which their tenderness finds expression and warm reception. The mass media, in their consumer orientation, stress the sex image of women. And some women are as responsible as men in the downgrading of other women. The woman of high estate looks down on the woman of poorer condition. The caste and class systems are maintained as much by women as by men.

The religions in Asia share a good measure of responsibility for the subjection of women. Today, however, changes are taking place through modernizing trends, secularization, and socialist movements. The example of China is particularly attractive to women of other Asian countries. We begin to see increasing numbers of women taking responsibilities in social and public life and, in a sense, giving effect to the implicit undercurrent of female power that pervades many Asian cultures. Yet the full emancipation of women in Asia is still a long way off and many struggles will have to be undertaken before the Asian woman is accepted and accepts herself as a complete human person in all areas of life.

Racial, Minority, and Caste Discrimination

Problems of minorities, racial groupings, and castes are evident in every Asian country, from the Arab-Israeli conflict in West Asia to the racial discrimination in Taiwan. Pakistan has the problem of the Baluchis; the Bengalis caused the splitting up of Pakistan into two countries. India is a mosaic of diverse peoples and languages. Sri Lanka has the problem of the Tamils and their rights. Racial differences are a sensitive issue in Burma, Indonesia, Malaysia, and the whole of Indochina. In the Philippines the secessionist drive of the Muslims in Mindanao has a racial and religious element.

All over Asia, race is an important factor in politics. In the eagerness and rush to create national unity, the rights of minorities were swept aside. Whole peoples were marginalized and are now treated as second-class citizens. The borders of nation-states were carved out arbitrarily, along lines set by colonial rule—Malaysia and Indonesia, for example.

Caste, a system of rigid social stratification characterized by hereditary status, endogamy, and social barriers sanctioned by custom, law, or religion, is another form of discrimination in Asian society. It is particularly marked in the Indian subcontinent. In India the upper classes are also the higher castes. The lower castes, together with the poorer tribes and more disadvantaged classes, constitute about a fifth of the total population. These 130 million persons form the base of the social pyramid. In spite of constitutional provisions, the adoption of a socialist way of life, and the pledges of political parties to eradicate poverty, the lower castes continue to the be most exploited groupings in India.

The lower castes are mostly landless laborers. In rural areas social standing depends very much on land ownership, and in this the lower castes are always badly off in spite of land-reform legislation.

MULTINATIONAL CORPORATIONS IN ASIA

Today the main agent of the economic exploitation of the poor, postcolonial Asian countries in favor of the rich, former colonial centers is the multinational corporation (MNC).

The MNCs have captured many local markets for consumer goods all over free enterprise Asia. Nestle's, Unilever, Coca-Cola,

Pepsi, Maxwell's, Rothman's, I.C. Bayer, Johnson and Johnson, Bates, Singer, Hertz, Kodak, Philips, Sony, ITT, Mitsuibishi, Sanyo, First National City Bank, Western-based airlines, hotel chains, motor firms, and oil companies can be found in almost all Asian countries. Sometimes they have local names and native directors.

Mitsuibishi of Japan is an example of a giant Asian MNC conducting different lines of business in many other parts of the world. In the early 1970s it channeled 10 percent of Japan's exports and 13 percent of its imports. Its gross sales in 1972 amounted to $50.7 billion, just $2 billion less than the budget of the Japanese government. The livelihood of perhaps a quarter of Japan's citizens may be tied to the Mitsuibishi group of firms.

The giant MNCs today control much of the know-how in fields such as electronics, electrical machinery, aircraft manufacture, armaments, pharmaceuticals, and other chemical and scientific products. Their power depends on an oligopoly of technology and a worldwide control over markets and resources. They can virtually dictate terms to countries that want their products or their investments.

These corporations are a means of integrating the poor countries of the world into the international economic order. Asian countries that are open to capitalistic penetration by foreign countries find their production and consumption made to fit the interests of the MNCs. A particularly egregious example was the multinational promotion of bottle-feeding and formula food for infants that was linked to increased malnutrition and infant mortality.

The MNCs claim that they develop the economies of poor countries by using raw materials, bringing in capital, and creating employment. Is this true? Often they do not make a serious effort to use local raw materials until they are compelled to do so by economic and political pressures. The expansion of the Coca-Cola Company in India, Malaysia, and Indonesia has not included the purchasing of local fruits for soft drinks. These countries produce abundant crops of oranges, limes, mangoes, pineapple, jak, guavas, bananas, and such fruits. But Coca-Cola does not use them. Instead it imports powders and essences from the United States. Asians become accustomed to drinking imported mineral waters. Local technology is not developed. Local skills are not encouraged. Capital flows out of the country.

The same is true in the case of pharmaceutical firms. They import patent medicines to Asia. But they neglect native herbs, oils, and other medicines.

The MNCs claim that they bring capital to poor countries—and this is true in the initial stages. But they demand such high returns on capital, charge such exorbitant prices for their technology and services, make such unconscionable profits from sales to poor countries and by the sale of products from them that soon the flow of funds is from the poor countries to the MNCs. Countries that receive "aid" and foreign investments are heavily indebted and have huge balance of payment deficits. South Korea and the Philippines have large foreign debts due to such "aid."

The MNCs claim to create employment in poor countries. The total employment created is often small compared to the numbers unemployed. The type of jobs created do not provide workers with skills they could use elsewhere. Workers have low job security and are subject to rigid discipline, often enforced by local governments. The wages they receive are very unfair in relation to the companies' profits. Thus a shirt sold for $10 in America is paid for as if its selling price were $2 or $3 in an Asian market. Laborers are paid a dollar or two per day, whereas the same company may pay $60 per day to a worker in Europe. The garments produced by both are sold in the same markets, subject to tariff.

The creation of employment depends on a heavy capital investment by the host country, which has to provide the infrastructure of roads, power, water supply, communications, security, and even housing and recreational facilities for foreign investors. Although some employment is generated, certain other lines of employment are destroyed or not developed. The villages are often at a disadvantage because industries are located in and around the big cities. A few companies can supply all the consumer needs of a whole country or region. Almost every Asian village helps the big corporations by buying their goods. In return, the poor villagers have no outlet for their productivity. Their traditional arts and crafts are neglected and die out. Their skills go unused. All this leads to the impoverishment of the village. There is little that a village can produce other than cereals, vegetables, handicrafts, and curios, once the MNCs capture its nation's markets.

The "aid" that Asian countries have accepted from the First and Second Worlds has not only not solved their problems of food shortages and unemployment, but has drawn them into the wider problem area of world inflation, recession, pollution, and energy crisis. The poor are becoming more and more conscious of their situation of exploitation even in countries such as South Korea, which has witnessed a kind of economic miracle—because the advantages of growth do not accrue to the masses but to local elites and the foreign interests that supply "aid."

ASIAN CULTURES AND RELIGIONS

Two other aspects of Asian reality of relevance to the world system are the Asian cultures and religions. Through colonial contacts and particularly the closer linkage of the world by trade there has come to be an unprecedented imposition of Western science and culture on Asian peoples. This has been taking place gradually over the past few centuries and today is almost universal and has reached a point of no return. This is true not only as regards capitalism and Marxist socialism—both of which originated in the West—but also the modern scientific approach. Modern Western science developed in isolation from religious or spiritual values. It has been heavily mechanistic in its understanding of reality, not concerning itself with the spiritual and the numinous in human relationships and the cosmos, devoid of care for the human person and for nature.

Combined with triumphant capitalism, Western science has been used in a manner that has been harmful in many ways to the dignity of the human person, to social intercourse, and to nature itself. Thus in spite of its stupendous achievements Western civilization itself is in acute crisis. Its social fabric is breaking up due to the voracity of individuals and groups for maximum profit and pleasure.

Western religion—Christianity, largely—has been unable to inspire and cope with the advances of science. Hence there is a dichotomy in Western society between humanistic secular science and Christian thought. The dissonances of the scientific and religious approaches that characterize modern Europe have not yet been brought into harmony, though both are now more aware of and open to each other.

Blending Western science and culture with the Asian way of life entails bridging even deeper chasms. Asian cultures enshrine many values that are quite different from those of Western capitalism. In general Asia is still rural, agrarian, and feudal in its interpersonal relationships. Traditional family life is closely knit, based on respect for elders and concern for all family members. The sense of community is very strong, even to the extent of excluding other communities or castes.

The Asian approach to life is not so materialistic as is the Western. Personal relationships and lifestyles are simpler. Asian religions have had a profound influence in making their followers less acquisitive and more open to human values. This is within a wider attitude of closeness to and respect for nature and all forms of life. Another facet of this approach is tolerance of others' views, including their religious beliefs and practices. A sense of moderation and harmony predominates, especially in the Chinese tradition. Buddhism too emphasizes the middle path of tolerance.

Religion pervades the life of most Asian peoples. The creedal content of the religions differs, but there is a basic religiousness common to all. It is even related to forms of belief that antedated the intellectual synthesis of the great Asian religions—a profound animism and ritualism is found in the substratum of Asian societies.

Contact with the West has provoked a variety of cultural and religious reactions. Some Asians are thoroughly westernized and capitalistic in spirit and life. Others have accepted Marxism as their personal belief and political ideology. Still others have become more secularist and humanistic. But the traditional religions are also experiencing a revival. For some it takes the form of a militant fundamentalism, insisting on a rigid loyalty to traditional doctrines, as in some Islamic countries. Others are rethinking their religious traditions in the light of modern science and a study of their sacred scriptures.

The vast changes going on today pose to Asian cultures and religions the question: How long will they continue to be the inspiration of Asian peoples? Will they be renewed in the process of change? Will they be the inspiration for the liberation struggles of the Asian masses of tomorrow—the proletariat of the world? Will they combine personal and social liberation? Will they be virile enough in their impact to withstand the individualism and selfishness of capitalism? What will be their interaction with Christianity? Will all the religions be able to converge to provide a meaningful, contemporary explanation of human, social, and cosmic reality to the majority of humanity that is Asia today?

Chapter 4

Need of a New World Order: Vision and Goals

Consideration of the world system and of Asia's role within it shows that there is a deep, widespread crisis affecting the meaning of personal life, the harmonious evolution of social life, and the future of the earth itself. Wasteful modes of production and consumption, pollution of nature, and the arms race threaten the very earth from which humanity draws its sustenance. Malnutrition, ignorance, disease, the weakening of family ties, unshared affluence, the subordination of women and men to the pursuit of pleasure, power, and profit by the powerful and the rich have cheapened and brutalized human life, draining it of meaning.

At the same time, because of the integration of the whole world by the communications media and economic interdependence, this is the first generation in human history that can really think of a coordinated global approach to human problems. It is therefore incumbent on us to search for a vision of human life and the whole cosmos that can inspire all peoples to work toward world communion in justice and understanding. We need a vision that respects the dignity of each and every woman and man, of all races, peoples, cultures, religions, and walks of life.

The European peoples had a sense of global mission from about the sixteenth century onward. They had a sense of historic global destiny, although it was understood differently by different groups among them. Scientists and explorers were searching for an understanding of the universe, of the earth, and of human life, through the means of modern science and principally in terms of quantitative measurement. They built on the patrimony of human science and made the great voyages of exploration possible. Merchants and industrialists were intent on building their economic empires unhampered by any considerations of morality, culture, or respect for other persons' rights or even lives. Colonizers and administrators joined them in empire building. In their economic and political activity they had a sense of freedom from the ethical constraints that medieval Christianity placed on the social and economic life of believers.

Christian missionaries joined the bandwagon of empire building inspired by a zeal for the salvation of the souls of the millions who had never known Christ. They made no critical assessment of the development and use of science and technology, or of the economic and political activities of their compatriots. Hence in spite of enormous efforts by religiously motivated persons, there was no positive moral directioning in the European enterprise that constructed the present world system. The paths taken by colonizers and missionaries did not converge to ensure the common good of all humanity. In effect the captains of commerce and industry, along with the political rulers of the newly emerging nation-states, took the helm in practical life.

The net result was that the present world order is in disarray and incapable of meeting even the minimal needs of billions of human beings. Capitalism is incapable in principle of bringing about a just society because its guiding motivation is profit maximization for private individuals and companies. Marxist socialism, though it advocates care for the needs of all, is at present oriented toward the national common good of individual countries rather than toward the achievement of international social justice.

Neither capitalism nor Marxism has been open to the fundamental inspirations of the world religions. Capitalism is materialistic, though it claims to defend religion. Marxism is atheistic, though it advocates justice in social relationships. Both have yet to dialogue with the great world religions, which inspired the civilizations of the world or at least the vast majority of humankind for millennia.

The MNCs of the capitalist world cannot bring about an equitable world integration. They are not concerned with meeting the needs of all; much less are they concerned with social justice or care of the earth. They are effective in promoting science and technology and in increasing productivity, but they are among the principal agents of the unjust distribution of the goods of the world. What is needed is a vision of the world that sees it in a different perspective and public authority that can socially orient these giant enterprises—if they are to continue in existence.

Dissociation from the dominant capitalist world powers may in the present situation be a necessary phase of the economic, political, and cultural reorganization of the poor countries. However, it is not the ideal for all times. We must envisage the peaceful development of all peoples within a harmoniously evolving global society.

A just world order would be one in which (1) every human person is insured the basic essentials of life and is respected as a person, without discrimination; (2) each society is able to provide the basic amenities for the good life of its members and for its own cultural development; (3) the planet earth is cared for and not treated in such a way that it would become an unsuitable home for present or future humanity.

A NEW VALUE ORIENTATION

For the practical realization of a world order based on such objectives it is necessary that there be a change in the values by which human beings are inspired and motivated. Such a world order demands respect for the human person and for all human persons regardless of sex, color, creed, nationality, social function, or age. This may seem easy to some, but it is one of the most difficult conversions that most human beings have to go through in real life. It is a challenge to transcend, effectively and on a continuing long-term basis, the limits of the narrowness imposed by racism, classism, sexism, and national interests that may be damaging other nations. There are enough essential goods and resources in the world for every human being, including the needs in the coming century. The challenge is a judicious use of resources and a just distribution of their yield.

It may be asked whether such a vision is not too idealistic and utopian, inasmuch as human beings tend to be very selfish. It will not be an easy task, but it is a historical necessity today, a condition *sine qua non* of survival and civilized existence. During the Middle Ages cities had their own armies and fought each other. So did feudal lords. There was no national loyalty as such. But as the nation-states evolved in modern times, they took control over armaments, and many cities formed one nation with a national loyalty. Today we tend to think of them as absolutes. But can we not mature as human beings to recognize our higher loyalty to the human race and to mother earth, whence we derive our being and sustenance? Certain movements, such as those for the nonproliferation of nuclear weapons and the release of political prisoners, are already at work, across national and even continental frontiers, and across the frontiers of conflicting ideologies.

Increasingly we are being made aware that if we do not reverence human life and the earth, we are hurting ourselves; for we are all one human community sharing one earth. This is the greatest educational challenge to our generation. It also represents the highest growth point in the history of human consciousness.

The noblest inspirations of the world's great religions are in the direction of such a vision. The best in the Western way of life is democratic and egalitarian, the excesses of capitalism being a deviation from the Western ideal of freedom and justice. The Marxist vision of a classless, stateless society is also in the tradition of the apocalyptic vision of the prophets of Judaism. In the depths of every human heart there is an urge toward concern for others. Does not every spiritual tradition recognize that care for others is respect for the numinous in every person, as well as a manifestation of the divine within the one who cares?

GOALS FOR A NEW WORLD ORDER

Changes in National Policies

Efforts must be made to implement patterns of development that provide the basic essentials for all—especially food, housing, health services, and education—without an increase in pollution, expenditure on armaments, foreign indebtedness, and dependence on the international power centers. For some countries this may entail regaining control of natural resources and industrial and economic activities from foreign companies.

Such policies should be geared toward a growing equality within the country, in incomes, wealth, opportunities, and facilities. Imbalances between racial groups, between women and men, social classes, types of work, and regions must be reduced. The goal should be greater economic and political democracy—that is, a genuine participation of the people in decision-making in daily work and in civic affairs. Land reforms and policies of resettling citizens in rural areas and the less populated areas of a country could help both to increase production and provide living space for growing populations. China and Vietnam have sponsored such programs. Indonesia is sponsoring a "transmigration" of Indonesians, especially from crowded Java to less populous islands.

Each country must do what it can to look after its population. This should include a more rational planning of its population in view of its natural resources, paying regard to the capacity of natural systems to sustain its population. Nature should be cared for to achieve and maintain optimum sustainable productivity, but not in such a way as to endanger the integrity of the eco-systems and organisms that are an integral part of it.

A major challenge to Third World nations is that of utilizing the achievements of Western science and technological advance without incorporating the evils of its social injustice based on the selfish pursuit of maximum private profit without care for others. Western development has increased productivity immensely, and this is a definite advantage. What is needed is the harnessing of this productive potentiality to serve all humanity, present and future, instead of only the minority living today in unprecedented affluence.

Production in Third World countries must be geared to the urgent needs of the poorer classes for food, housing, clothing, education, and transportation, rather than to the demands of foreign markets or the affluent local elites.

Income distribution must be such that disparities are reduced and all wage earners can cover their basic requirements from their income. Imbalances between urban and rural areas, between intellectuals and manual workers, between the sexes, and between regions have to be drastically reduced.

Such goals require a different pattern of agriculture. The Third World is still largely agricultural and rural. It is here that most attention is needed. Those who work the land must receive a fair share of the benefits of their work. Agriculture must be so organized that the advantages of modernization can be realized without the evils of large-scale private ownership. Agriculture must be transformed to raise productivity and expand employment through revised technologies, complementary mechanization, integrated public works programs, land redistribution, product diversification, and promotion of agro-industries. The size of farming units must be large enough to permit such lines of development. Some form of reorganization of the structure of landownership and cultivation is essential. Communes are one such method. The Chinese communes have been successful in achieving mass participation in both cultivation and its benefits.

REORGANIZATION OF RURAL AREAS

Agriculture and rural populations present one of the biggest challenges to Asian countries. The free enterprise countries among them want to move quickly to industrialization and urbanization. This is partly due to the example of the West and of the Russian revolution. The first generation of leaders of independent Asia was enamored of the successes of the U.S.S.R. in modernizing itself. Japan, too, developed through industry. But the West had its colonial markets, and the U.S.S.R. had its immense territories. And the Russian revolution also carried through an agricultural reorganization that included collectivization and modernization. Japan had a lead in industry, with the world's markets for its products. The other Asian countries are in somewhat different circumstances. They do not easily reach outside markets, their problems of food are enormous, their populations are increasing, and inflation adds to their burdens.

These Asian countries cannot develop satisfactorily without reversing the trend of neglecting the countryside. Organization of the economy according to the values of Western, technological, urban consumerism will not provide a means of livelihood for the majority of their peoples. On the other hand, there will be no return to traditional rural values unless the rural way of life is made attractive and satisfying.

One approach would be to redevelop agriculture within a small-unit system. If villagers have the use of land to be worked by them in small units with appropriate assistance from larger agricultural units, rural workers would have meaningful employment and a full life. There would be no alien exploiters benefiting from their hard work. If several villages could plan, operate, and enjoy the fruits of their labor together, the advantages would be still greater. If to this were added small-scale agro-industries based on local raw materials and skills, the self-sufficiency of the villages would grow. It would also be a means of easing out the MNCs with their mass-produced consumer goods, fertilizers, and the like. In this way, some of the amenities of modern life would also be provided in the rural areas— for example, electrification, transportation, education, health services, and recreational facilities. The people could be provided an institutional framework for their self-regeneration in all aspects of life.

Such changes cannot be effected without a reorientation of the priorities in planning. Land reforms of a radical nature are essential. So far they are inadequate in all the Asian free enterprise countries. Even Japan has not reversed the trend toward undue and unhealthy urbanization, although its land reforms have many advantages. The Asian landlord class that is generally absentee and takes a disproportionate share of the fruits of the land must be reformed. But it is here that most Asian governments falter, for they are themselves tied to the landlord class. A revolutionary change is required for the reconstruction of the villages of Asia. The elites, which need the rural areas as a base of their economic and social power, will resist all reforms. So will the world economic oligarchies and their multinational firms, for they will lose one of their largest sources of raw materials and markets for the sale of their goods. The supply of cheap labor for urban industries will decrease if rural areas are made self-sufficient and employment-generating. At present, most of the approaches to rural development are a piecemeal and patchwork muddle; they dissolve in the face of vested interests and the lack of enthusiasm on the part of the masses.

INDUSTRIAL REFORMS

The experience of decades of industrialization shows that there is a need for heavy industry, but the patterns of industrialization must be related to the present and foreseeable conditions of these countries.

There is a growing consensus that although modernization is

necessary the technology suited to these Asian countries must emphasize the intermediate, the small-scale. So far as possible, needed machinery should be manufactured within the same countries, or at least within the wider regional economic area. Production processes should be developed according to the availability of raw materials and the skills of workers. This is a goal different from that emphasized by the planning elites during the 1950s and '60s. Technological self-reliance is a major challenge to the Asian countries, which can be met only through the hard process of learning by doing, of learning through trial and error—an approach that requires patience and determination.

The type of goods produced will have to be determined according to the human needs of all rather than by a minority's willingness to pay for them. This would lead in the direction of adequate food, clothing, low-cost housing, transportation, education, and medical facilities within the reach of all and under public control. The present privileges of the elite classes will have to be eliminated. Price mechanisms governing production and consumption will have to be altered.

Strong governmental action must induce and even compel a dispersive siting of industry, so that it is not overconcentrated in urban areas. This will involve a diversification of products, the use of local raw materials, and provision for employment in rural areas.

An even more fundamental problem is that of the decentralization or socialization of industrial ownership. We have noted the strong trend toward the formation of powerful oligarchies at the world level and within individual countries. The free enterprise form of social organization lends itself to this process of concentration of wealth and power in the hands of a few. Asian countries, as well as Western countries, have laws against monopolies, trusts, and restrictive practices. Yet the key MNCs have grown to unprecedented levels since the early 1950s. Radical changes are necessary if the trend is to be reversed. It is not enough to curb their activities a bit here and there or appoint parliamentary committees of inquiry. These big combines must be nationalized or socialized, or somehow put under social controls. Their ownership must be within the national community. Their goal must be service to all, not profits to an elite.

INTERNATIONAL TRADE

Commerce is another sector that needs complete overhauling if social justice is to be assured. Middlemen exploit the Asian peoples, especially the rural poor and urban workers. Producers get low prices for their output, but consumers pay much higher prices, owing to the manipulation of markets by traders. Trade has come to be concentrated in the hands of big companies. The major problems of international trade—high prices for the imports into poor countries and low prices for their exports—stem largely from the trading companies, the shipping lines, and the power of the richer countries. The oil-producing countries have demonstrated how important a factor trade is in the determination of the economic welfare of a people.

Trade can benefit the masses only if they have an effective control over it. Cooperative enterprises are one way. The socialization of trade by state control is another approach. Trade in essential goods, such as food, should be in the hands of a public or community authority, with the necessary safeguards against abuses, if there is to be an end to exploitation.

EDUCATIONAL REFORMS

Reform of society is not possible without reorienting the educational system. At present, education in free enterprise Asia is mainly an agency for the perpetuation of the established class structures and the communication of competitive, individualist, capitalist values. Educational reform must be geared to the generation of a new person with a spirit of service to the community and a sense of social justice. It must awaken the critical and cooperative spirit in the young. It must be a life-long process, not one that ends with the years spent in an academic institution.

Education must attempt to remove the gap between intellectual and manual work, which has been sanctioned by centuries of downgrading physical labor. The Mandarin class has been held in high honor in Asian countries. Colonial education further reinforced this gap, giving a high status to the Western-educated administrator and clerk. There are now trends toward incorporating work experience into the educational curriculum, modeled after the revolutionary Chinese experience.

The provision of equality of opportunity in education is another modification needed in all capitalist societies. Inequalities in this field operate as a disadvantage to poorer children from their earliest years. An equalizing process is needed so that every child has a fair chance for an education. Can this be realized if education is under the control of private agencies that run the institutions either for profit or for the benefit of only one sector of the population? It is generally the affluent who have the advantage of the prestigious schools in the capitalist countries. Unless there is community control over the whole field of education, it becomes a bulwark of the privileged classes. State control or ownership does not automatically eliminate the dangers of elitism, bureaucratism, and political favoritism. There must be a vigilant public opinion that watches over the orientation of education, particularly its orientation toward service of the whole people. The mass media and other channels of communication, such as the arts, should also be purveyors of the values of unselfishness and service to the people. This is unlikely to happen if the mass media are controlled by a few very rich groups or by advertisers.

Changes in International Policies

Policies must be oriented toward combating the evils of worldwide imbalances by such means as the following:

1) Fairer terms of trade. The terms of international trade should be determined by considerations of human values and needs, and not merely by the market interplay of supply and demand in a context of the MNCs and other monopolies or oligopolies. There should be an international authority to ensure fairer prices for primary products. UNCTAD has proposed a common fund, internationally controlled buffer stocks, indexation of prices, and organization of research and development to help those in greater need.

2) Organizations of producers to ensure fairer trade, with a common strategy. OPEC gives an idea of the possibilities in this direction, as well as its limits and drawbacks.

3) Greater regional cooperation in economic life—such as South-South Cooperation (an organization of Third World countries) and

Technical Cooperation among Developing Countries (TCDC)—to promote complementarities in production and trade among them or regionally, and cooperation in financial transactions. All these can help limit the power of the MNCs in marketing, banking, research and development, and control over industry.

4) Resource transfers from rich to poor countries—without strings attached.

5) An international income tax paid by nations on the basis of their GNP, or of their per capita income, or land base in relation to population, or on the nonuse of land for agricultural production, or on the production and sale of armaments or luxury goods, on waste, pollution of waterways and air, or on the use of the resources of the seas. Revenues from such taxes could be utilized for a redistribution of resources to poor peoples—as a matter of justice and a right, not as "aid" or charity. There could be subsidies to countries more severely affected by policies such as oil price increases.

6) An international authority to foster the common good of nations and peoples by controlling the activities of the MNCs. This could be done by establishing public agencies for the management of world responsibilities such as care of the environment, supervision of monetary policies and migration policies, regulation of shipping and insurance, maintenance of the seas. The use of natural resources should be controlled so as to maintain nature's powers of regeneration. Reasonable restraints should be applied to the consumption of nonrenewable resources.

These changes will require a strengthening of United Nations agencies so that their decision-making will not depend on the wealth of nations but on the needs of peoples. Control over bodies such as the IMF and the IBRD (World Bank) should be taken away from the rich nations, as poorer nations have already begun to demand.

7) Compensation for past and present injustices and exploitation; debt renegotiation or cancellation. The entire problem of debt repayment should be reevaluated in a long-term perspective of history, which should include the centuries of the kind of "aid" imposed by the powerful on the weak.

8) Measures to maintain or enhance soil productivity, prevent erosion, and, where possible, rehabilitate areas ravaged by human abuse.

Changes in the World System

A WORLD AUTHORITY

The sovereignty of nation-states is a major impediment to world justice. They are a threat to the earth and to the human race itself due to their control over nuclear arms. On the other hand the nation-states now cannot control the giant MNCs that dominate much of the economic process and the information, communication, and research networks. Today's weaponry and communications do not respect national frontiers.

The United Nations, inaugurated after World War II, is a good point of departure, but it is too weak vis-à-vis the major powers that set it up. They retained controlling or veto powers on important issues. The world today needs a global authority that can act for the common good of humanity as such. It should have powers of legislation and decision-making on issues affecting the whole human race and the future of our planet earth. Worldwide control over armaments should be in its hands.

The nations of the world will have to surrender their sovereignty to a world authority for guaranteeing justice and survival for all. This may seem unimaginable today. Yet the smaller powers have already lost much of their sovereignty vis-à-vis the superpowers. Five hundred years ago few would have thought that the cities, feudal lords, and smaller kingdoms would abdicate their rights to national states, or that burghers and villagers would develop such loyalties. Today the whole human race is per force called to build up a world authority: there is no other practical alternative.

Such a world authority would be better able to carry out the types of functions mentioned above than is the present system of nation-states. They of course will continue, but will not be sovereign in matters affecting the whole of humanity. Control over and directioning of international trade, finance, communications, natural resources, transfer of technology, care of the environment, supervision of armaments will have to be with such a world authority.

It is therefore extremely important that this body be truly motivated by the common good of all, and that the structures of decision-making be formed accordingly. We can proceed to this goal only by a process of trial and error, and with a heightening of the consciousness of our planetary togetherness among more and more persons, groups, and nations in the world.

POPULATION RESETTLEMENT

As noted earlier, one of the main defects and injustices of the present world system is the unequal distribution of land among the world's peoples. This is the most basic source of our inequalities. A world authority should be empowered to bring about a planned and peaceful reallocation of land to peoples. White peoples now control most of the unused land of the world. Their numbers are not increasing whereas the peoples of the Third World, especially of Asia, are increasing rapidly in lands that are already overpopulated. Other solutions—population planning, hard work, land reform, technological advancement, disfranchisement of local elites—should also be carried out; there is no reason why the distribution of land to population too should not be on the world agenda. It is one way in which the creative growth of humanity can be related to the use and transformation of the earth. It need not increase pollution and waste, for Third World peoples have long traditions of care for the earth, unlike the present occupants of North America and Australia.

There is no reason why European expansionism from 1500 to 1950 should set the pattern of land distribution for the entire future of the human race. Empires have come and gone for the past four millennia. The U.S.A. and the U.S.S.R. seem to think that nuclear saber-rattling will resolve world problems or at least ensure their own dominance. The superpowers' wastage on armaments derives basically from their determination to preserve their own interests, which come down to the "territorial integrity" on which their power is built.

The main orientation of global policy should be that, with existing populations ensured their rights, persons without land should have planned access to land without persons. There should be settlement policies and programs for moving excess populations to scantily populated areas such as Canada, Australia, the West of the United States, areas of Latin America—in addition to migration within existing national borders. In this connection we can call these vast landmasses "underdeveloped" areas. For they support few inhabitants, even if they produce much food. The terms "developed" and "underdeveloped" are used today in terms of technological advance. They could also be understood in relation to the actual number of persons supported by a landmass. Bangladesh, with 55,000 square miles, supports 90 million persons, whereas New Zealand supports only 3.3 million on 104,000 square miles. Which land is more developed?

Population resettlement on underdeveloped lands is necessary because of the present dynamics of population growth: the only alternative is gross injustice or future catastrophes. The world refugee problem is not unrelated to overpopulation.

Population resettlement is one way of compensating for the plundering of the resources of poor peoples by the MNCs and for inequities in international trade. It could put an end to the nonplanting or destruction of crops in order to keep prices high for U.S. or Australian farmers. It could reduce malnutrition, which now affects over 500 million human beings. It could increase employment in the land-rich countries. In the final analysis, large-scale unemployment in the U.S.A., Canada, and Australia is not due to overpopulation but to underpopulation and a poor use of resources. A larger population would mean more children, and hence a greater demand for schools, teachers, books, transportation, and so forth. These are much better purposes for which to spend North American or Australian wealth than are armaments. If there were a more open policy on resettling immigrants to the U.S.A., it would not have to spend billions of dollars on armaments. More inhabitants would mean more demand, more employment, more dynamism in the economy. This is one reason why the U.S.A. has grown much faster than Canada, though both were settled by whites at about the same time.

At present the world system is in acute crisis because there is not an equal increase in demand among the sectors of the world with increasing populations. A new approach to land and population would also lead to a reevaluation of agricultural methods, technology, and urbanization. All these could be positive gains for the whole of humanity. There would be enhanced possibilities for a better life, for employment, productivity, and creativity for the whole human race.

Planned resettlement of millions of persons per year in the underdeveloped areas of the world is a feasible proposal today; the question is whether we have the political will to carry it out. Hundreds of millions cross national frontiers and the oceans each year as tourists. World refugees number in the tens of millions. In fact such resettlement might be politically easier than even sharing resources across nations. It would not mean reducing Australia, Canada, or the U.S.A. in size, but increasing the number of Americans, Canadians, and Australians at a much faster rate than at present. This would increase national wealth, given the immense land base. The same would apply also to such countries as Argentina, Bolivia, and Brazil.

The main barrier, however, would seem to be that these countries—in fact, all countries—do not really consider all human beings equal in rights and dignity. Australia advertises to get whites to relocate there. It will take in 250,000 whites from Zimbabwe, but only begrudgingly accept 25,000 Asians—with skills and financial backing. No land-rich country will admit that racism is its basic objection to world population resettlement. All manner of other arguments are alleged, from the point of view of culture to the lifeboat theory of triage and survival of the fittest. All these need to be discussed in detail. But my intention here is only to place this issue on the agenda for planetary discussion.

If the world community wanted to reallocate resources and lands to population quotas, the expenditure on space flights or one day's expenditure on armaments—$1.5 billion—would be enough to resettle a million persons in a new homeland. It is not the technical capability that we lack. Our own inhumanity to other humans is the major obstacle to world justice.

The argument of cultural incompatibility is not without some practical validity. Persons of different cultures do not easily mingle as equals. They mingle as unequals—as when the United States and Brazil imported blacks as slaves—to the benefit of the stronger. Because culture is a problem, the process of the reallocation of lands and populations would have to include other provisions—for example, that all the whites in New Zealand would move to Australia over two decades, to allow New Zealand to be settled by Bengalis, with just provision made for the Maoris living there. West Canadians could easily be settled in the U.S. West and the area from Alaska to Vancouver and east to Winnipeg could absorb several tens of millions of Chinese, who would doubtless make better use of the land. Fair provision would have to be made for the Amerindians in those regions. These are merely suggestions to foster imaginative approaches to this issue. The old paradigm of the world system built on nation-states to suit white peoples is inadequate to meet the challenges of today and tomorrow. Humanity must find peaceful and just means of adopting a new paradigm in which human beings are more important than are national frontiers.

We are all called on to transcend our narrow particularities in order to arrive at a higher, wider, and deeper level of sharing among all human beings. This calls for a transformation of ourselves from within our innermost being to accept all others as sisters and brothers. Our growth to a planetary dimension is an invitation to spiritual deepening, a purification from selfishness to a more universal communion in real life, to our own humanization. Insofar as we do so, we shall become more truly civilized, approach the ideals of the best in all our religions and cultures, and pursue the the deepest and best aspiration of every human heart and mind.

Chapter 5

Strategies for Worldwide Transformations

An overall vision of a better world order and an awareness of realistic goals to be pursued in order to embody that vision are helpful in motivating us toward integral human liberation. But we must also try to understand clearly how human selfishness is structured into society in opposition to such goals and ideals.

We have to try to identify in the real world who are our allies and who are our enemies. We can then have common goals and strategies. We live in a capitalistic world system dominated by the Western powers. By and large capitalism as a system of economic relationships based on profit maximization for private interests has been and is the principal enemy of economic development and social justice in the Third World.

I am not saying that Western culture or the Western democratic way of life or even the mere principle of private enterprise as such is the enemy of world justice. In principle these have much good to their credit. But the whole system of economic life and social organization in which profit maximization is regarded as *the* goal has contributed to the exploitation of the poor and the weak everywhere.

Socialism as a political system is not oriented toward private profit. Historically socialist countries have helped colonized peoples fight for their independence from imperialism, although socialist superpowers can be imperialistic, as in Eastern Europe and Afghanistan. We have to be realistic. There can be no question of seeking comfort in neutrality. We have to deal with exploitive powers where we meet them.

Inasmuch as structured selfishness is the real enemy, remedial measures will have to be taken in the direction of contesting selfishness and changing unjust structures at all levels. The task, simply put, is twofold: transformation of persons and radical change of structures.

The type of strategies adopted will depend on the deployment of the enemy forces. International capitalism is a most calculating, callous, and determined power. It is brutal when it deems violence is required for the preservation and growth of its power, as in Vietnam and Chile.

For the purposes of our analysis we can distinguish levels and stages of struggle and the means of struggle. I use the word "struggle" here because I take it as axiomatic that some form of conflict of interests is necessarily involved in this process. If we want justice at any level against organized injustice, some type of active combat against injustice is required. For no one gives up power unless persuaded or compelled to do so. Such action may be either legal or illegal, peaceful or forceful, as circumstances may determine and demand.

LEVELS OF STRUGGLE

Local

Although we have a global vision, action has to be taken at the local level. Organization for action has to be grounded at the level of the down-to-earth places where persons live or work. But national and global perspectives can also be seen even in local issues, for the world is so interconnected. Thus if we deal with housing in a slum in Bombay or Lima or Harlem, we can reflect on why there are such extremes of affluent and substandard housing in a city. We may then relate differences in personal incomes to national and international factors.

It is at this point that alliances must be sought with others struggling against injustice on another type of issue. It may be a woman's liberation movement, or a marginalized youth group, or a racial minority. The ability to get together and help each other in different issues arising from similar or related injustices is a prerequisite for the success of oppressed groups. If they are divided they are likely to long continue to be victims of oppression.

A three-stage actional schema recommends itself for local alliances: (1) a solid understanding of each issue and respect for the persons involved; (2) a cross-fertilization in the understanding of different issues; and (3) a coalition for a greater common good. The same can apply to national and international levels, and to mass movements. Successful leadership will be able to bring and hold these three stages together in their interrelatedness, maintaining communion in diversity within a focus on jointly accepted larger objectives and values.

National

At the present time this is the primary practical area for liberation struggles to take place, due to the general acceptance of the principle of national sovereignty. Working only at local levels can be inadequate, and concentrating on the international level can be idealistic. So long as those exercising power at the national level are capitalistic or procapitalistic, no global strategy is likely to be successful. This is also the lesson of the global negotiations that have been taking place during the past decade around such agenda as those of the NIEO (New International Economic Order), UNCTAD, the World Food Conference, and the Law of the Seas. The superpowers can refuse to cooperate. The representatives of Third World countries may be mesmerized by rhetoric for a NIEO without any real changes in the structures of domination.

Today, as yet, it is mainly at the national level that there are institutional bases for grappling with the market power of the MNCs or with the consumeristic tendencies of a given people. Even in the case of military intervention by foreign powers, the issue has to be dealt with nationally: a resolution may be passed at the General Assembly of the United Nations concerning the desirability of peace, but the UN is incapable of controlling the big powers.

For a nation to actively promote world justice, political power must be in the hands of rulers who genuinely desire to satisfy their people's needs. Otherwise they will not ask for the short-term sacrifices needed for making a country self-reliant and resistive to the pressures and allurements of the world's wealthy and powerful. Unfortunately today many Third World rulers succumb to the blandishments of capitalism for themselves and their supporting elites.

A necessary strategy for the poor countries is, therefore, an area-by-area liberation from the control of world capitalism. The methods for this may vary. It may come as a result of a revolution as in Mozambique and Angola, or a government may attempt it more peacefully as in Tanzania. In any case it is necessary to develop an alternative to integration within the world capitalist economic system. More and more countries are now turning in this direction. In Africa several nations are exploring a more socialistic path. The future course of Angola, Mozambique, Zimbabwe, Madagascar, Ethiopia, and South Yemen will be important in this perspective. In Latin America, Nicaragua is following a noncapitalist route to progress. Struggles are going on in El Salvador and Guatemala for the same purpose.

As more countries escape the hold of the capitalist power blocs, there will be fewer areas available for them as resource bases and markets for finished products. This is a fear of the world capitalist establishment. It is well aware that many more peoples want to be self-reliant, or cooperate among themselves, and not be subject to foreign exploitation. This is one of the reasons for U.S. counter-insurgency activity almost everywhere in the Third World. The capitalist powers also infiltrate deeply into the poor countries that are open to them through their MNCs, free trade zones, IMF loans, and package deals with local elites.

In most Third World countries the struggle for justice is a struggle for national self-determination and liberation from foreign exploitation. It is, however, unlikely to be successful if a local procapitalistic governing elite is not replaced by persons dedicated to serve genuinely the people and pay the price of a long and hard struggle. At this level too an understanding of other movements in the country, their cross-fertilization, and alliance for common goals is necessary for a successful struggle against injustice.

Within the socialist bloc too national struggles for self-determination against a socialist dominator can be necessary. The struggle of the Solidarity trade union movement in Poland is very significant in this connection. It was the first time that a popular movement was able to stand up to a dictatorial socialist regime that had the support of a neighboring socialist superpower. Earlier efforts in Hungary and Czechoslovakia at democratizing East European socialism failed totally. The Polish example shows at least that a nonviolent mass movement, even without the supports of a free enterprise economy, can bring powerful pressure on a dictatorial regime. The development of models for popular participation within socialist regimes is a sign of hope for the peoples of the world: the dictatorial nature of the de facto experiments with socialism has been a major disincentive to the socialist form of socioeconomic life.

International

At this level there are strategies that national governments and voluntary organizations can adopt. Some of them have already been mentioned under goals for global reorganization. Building solidarity among groups of countries can be a strategy for strengthening themselves against economic domination by rich countries or MNCs. Regional alliances such as OAU (the Organization of African Unity), South-South Cooperation, TCDC, the Non-Aligned Movement, the Group of 77, and OPEC are examples of such efforts at solidarity. The poor countries must build up institutions that can defend their interests against the organized power of the rich. The Trilateral Commission of business magnates, academics, and their supporters from the U.S.A., Western Europe, and Japan is an example of cooperation among the rich to foster their own interests by influencing their respective national policies.

A danger for Third World economic cooperation organizations is that the MNCs can infiltrate and benefit from them. Thus the MNCs entrenched in Singapore, Malaysia, and the Philippines can profit from the policies of ASEAN (Association of South East Asian Nations) to expand and consolidate their markets in a larger zone. They can then sway ASEAN leaders to political policies that are not necessarily for the good of their peoples.

Third World countries can work for the strengthening of international agencies and for a greater decision-making power for themselves within them. The UN General Assembly has been a forum for the Third World. UNCTAD has tried to foster their economic interests. Third World governments must work toward changing the power base of the GATT, IMF, and IBRD—three world agencies that influence national policies through their control of funds. At the Cancún (Mexico) conference of world leaders in October 1981 the U.S.A., Britain, and West Germany were not prepared to agree to a weakening of the position of the rich countries in the IMF, IBRD, and GATT.

Much can also be done by voluntary bodies all over the world to bring their influence to bear on world public opinion and on their own governments.

GOALS AND METHODS

Unless methods are effectively related to goals there will be a gap between intention and execution, aspiration and implementation, radical ideas and conservative foot-dragging.

The methods used by a group are also an indication of what it really intends. Methods disclose the difference between mere goodwill and serious commitment to a goal. Thus, in many Asian countries governments speak of social justice, but the means undertaken by them hardly lead to a better redistribution of fruits of national productivity. Parlor socialism can hold hands with galloping capitalism.

Methods are not neutral. They determine the use of our limited resources and time. If we do not make an intelligent choice regarding the methods we use, we may get bogged down in nonessentials. Some methods are diversions or distractions from serious goals and serve only to keep a group busy.

Methods can be changed as goals are reached or expanded. Critical evaluation of methods must be a basic strategy taking into account the de facto situation, the personnel, and the resources available. Practical judgment must be brought to bear.

Given the diversity of situations and personalities, we can expect a wide variety of methods or strategies all looking toward the same goal. They may vary in the intensity and rapidity with which they reach a goal. Different methods can be used by a movement at different times or at the same time, provided they all tend toward the same goal.

The social-service orientation, despite some advantages and its suitability for persons of certain temperaments, has grave inadequacies when its scope is limited to social service as such. It fails to effect a fundamental change in the social structures and relationships within a society. In certain areas in Sri Lanka, for instance, social-service units have visited the slums and given alms and medical aid for thirty years, and yet the condition of the slum dwellers is, if anything, worse than when they began. The rich grow richer and the poor have a few crumbs given to them by social-service workers.

Social service does not bring about a meaningful redistribution of wealth or of economic and political power in a society. It can even strengthen and perpetuate the existing system of inequalities and injustices. The system that exploits the poor is not challenged, and hence it is implicitly accepted. Have voluntary social services ever brought about a liberation movement in an exploited area? The affluent, moreover, are abetted in their complacency when they give contributions to such "charities."

A project orientation, in terms of building schools and productive units, is much better than social service, but this too is inadequate to bring about a reform of society in a reasonably brief period of time. Project orientation helps increase inequalities in developing societies unless the projects undertaken create a keen sense of critical awareness.

MEANS OF STRUGGLE

For justice in the world more radical and revolutionary changes are required. But mention of revolution usually triggers the fear of violence. Revolution, however, is not necessarily violent. Revolution is a radical change in mentalities and social structures. It is much better when this can be brought about by peaceful, democratic, and legal means. But often it is impossible; the oppressed will resort to violence against their government when their situation becomes unbearable, as the UN Declaration of Human Rights mentions. Or, as John F. Kennedy once said, "Those who make peaceful evolution impossible make violent revolution inevitable."

Violence

Given the nature, depth, and extent of the evils confronting humankind, a radical struggle is absolutely essential for the human race to survive, let alone prosper. Power never gives up its privileges without a struggle. Capitalism cannot be overcome unless a superior power replaces it at all levels within a country and at the global level. Ultimately, power must pass to the masses for the decisions of political authority to be for the benefit of all. This power may be transferred through the takeover of state agencies by representatives of the masses. But this is not enough, for the final arbiter in the struggles of capitalism has always been the local armed forces. Unless physical force backs radical reformers, the armed forces can overthrow revolutionary forces. Revolutions have failed when they lacked the backing of the military, as in the defeat of Salvador Allende in Chile, the failure of the French students in May 1968, the overthrow of Alexander Dubček in Czechoslovakia in August 1968, and the crushing of the insurrection in Sri Lanka in April 1971.

Consolidation of the transfer of power to the masses must include the transfer of military power to groups sympathetic to the masses. It is possible to envisage this happening without much violence if a constitutional revolution is carried out and the armed forces support it. Generally, however, the armed forces and the police are not politically neutral. They are usually on the side of the privileged classes. In most poor countries the military dominates the masses and benefits from the exploitation of the many by the few.

Violence is a daily reality in all the countries of the world. The use of physical force by those in power to dominate and exploit the others is the first violence. Ultimately, the sanction behind the authority of the state is its ability to coerce its citizens to conform to its dictates. Where and when it fails to do so, it falls from power, as did Emperor Haile Selassie of Ethiopia in 1974, and the shah of Iran in 1979. It is vitally important that we recognize the existence and use of force by the powers that be for controlling the others. We must realize that the problem of violence is not one that is started by those who promote radical social changes for justice. On the contrary, violence is first imposed by the powerful in their defense of the status quo.

There are enemies with guns and enemies without guns, as Mao Tse-tung says in *The Little Red Book*. Struggle must be two-fold: against organized armed force and against the subtle but powerful influence of the capitalist mentality on almost all the peoples of the world—even after a socialist revolution. Greed dies hard.

A Multiplicity of Strategies

Worldwide revolutionary transformation cannot be achieved by any single strategy, such as armed force or nonviolence. In the last resort the might of the military must be turned in favor of the oppressed masses; until then no social revolution of a political nature is secure. This can sometimes be done by persuading some of the armed forces to take the side of justice and by their overcoming others who are likely to oppose them. This is the way the battle against imperialism was won in some countries, such as Mozambique, Angola, and Guinea-Bissau. But this strategy may fail, as in the uprisings in Malaysia in the late 1940s and early 1950s and the victory of the right-wing generals in Indonesia in September 1965.

Global nuclear wars of liberation or of imperialist expansion are most unlikely, due to the threat of enormous destruction of human life on all sides. Small national wars of liberation are still possible today, in spite of the nuclear force of the big powers, or rather, due to their "balance of terror."

What must be highlighted more is the need for nonviolent strategies that can either replace or complement armed conflict. But it must be understood that the call for nonviolence does not necessarily derive from a philosophical opposition to violence. Sometimes violence may be the only way out of slavery. In other situations, violence may lead to defeat and a worse form of tyranny. Where no other remedies exist, where the consequences are not worse than the evil to be eliminated, and where there is a reasonable hope of success, violence is justified for a just cause.

Nonviolent Contestation of Capitalism

The forms of contesting capitalism vary according to the varying situations of persons and relationships. Some may contest by arms; they have to opt out of their nonsocialistically organized society. Mao Tse-tung and his followers adopted this strategy when they withdrew to the Yenan Mountains and built up their military base from there. They were operating at a time of confusion in China, and they were also able to rally compatriots to the nationalist cause of resisting Japanese invasion in the 1930s.

Some may contest by opting out of the forms of employment offered within capitalist society, in private companies or in government agencies. Communes may be set up in which a direct civil contestation of the capitalist system is undertaken. Today there are quite a few who make such options. For them the struggle encompasses a new lifestyle, a way of life according to the values of an alternative society. Such a search should not be a mere opting out of the mainstream of social life; it should be combined with participation in action for radical social change.

However, most persons are obliged to work and earn their living within the framework of capitalist or socialist societies. They have no realistic alternative. Their family responsibilities compel them to take up such employment. Nonetheless, even in that situation contestation with capitalism is essential and binding on the human conscience. It is wrong to cooperate with, participate in, and profit from exploitation at any level. The needs, much less the luxuries, of one's family cannot justify it. If there were no willing collaborators at all the levels of exploitation, capitalist enterprise will fail.

Cooperation in building capitalism may be well intentioned, but this does not justify it. Unfortunately, most of our societies live on exploitation in different degrees and levels. This continual benefiting from evil has had so deep an influence on most persons' thoughts that they are immunized against the inhumanity of their own situations. They take it for granted that they are entitled to extract so much from world enterprise and industry. One of the most important changes that has to be brought about in the world, especially among the rich countries and families, is the broadening and deepening of an awareness of the exploitation in which each one participates.

When someone becomes aware of exploitation, justice demands opposition to it, even though the demands of survival may sometimes require a certain external conformity. The more important question, however, is the standard of living actually required by a family, class, or country. What justification is there for a group to have a high level of luxury at the price of hunger for many others?

A mental contestation of an exploitive system is the first step that individuals must take. They should then try to form a group with others who may be similarly involved and concerned about the issue, for isolated individuals can do little against the consolidated power of a firm or industry and the pressures of society. Groups need to collect data about a given situation to see whether they are on solid ground and to convince others of their position.

Those convinced that a certain company is guilty of exploitation should go beyond mere dialogue with the management where this is not effective. They must work positively to contest the exploitation. Initially they can campaign for measures that would help Third World countries—publicizing, for example that Coca-Cola is wiping out small Asian soft-drink industries, throwing out of employment the vendors of fruit drinks, and reducing the demand for the products of Asian farmers.

If persuasion fails, they will have to resort to more effective measures of contestation to counteract the worldwide exploitation of the poor by U.S. MNCs. They may publicize some of the injustices committed by the MNCs through the type of values projected in their advertising. They can throw light on the economic battles in which MNCs compete with smaller local producers, buy them up, or send them into bankruptcy. That they sometimes enter into collusion with dictatorial regimes, help to overthrow popular socialist governments, or spy for the U.S. government (as in Chile) needs to be exposed and publicly castigated.

The contestation is even more necessary in the case of armament production and research. The peace movement in the United States has grasped the need for such contestation, regarded by the government as subversion. The American soldiers who refused to fight in Vietnam, the conscientious objectors to military service, and the millions who contested the Vietnam war were doing their duty to humanity in refusing to participate in that war.

After the U.S. withdrawal from Vietnam, popular pressure against the military and the government unfortunately decreased. But U.S. armaments and military "aid" are still involved in the destruction of life and property in many parts of the world—Latin America, for example. The publication of the *Pentagon Papers,* the exposures by the *New York Times* and the *Washington Post* of the intrusions of the CIA and FBI in Chile, China, the Philippines, and elsewhere, are good examples of the type of nonviolent contestation that can render valuable service to the cause of world justice.

American rank-and-file opposition to the Vietnam war had a chastening effect on U.S. foreign policy: it may now be much more difficult for that country to interfere in the internal affairs of other countries. Most American Catholic bishops are now openly opposing nuclear arms production. It would be well for the citizens of other countries to develop similar methods of peaceful opposition to their government's recourse to or toleration of injustice. The growing opposition to nuclear armaments in Western Europe is a healthy phenomenon that needs to be extended to armaments in general. The socialist countries too need similar movements.

There can be no effective contestation of the present worldwide exploitation unless the rich in all countries and even workers in the rich countries accept lowering their standard of living. It might be that social reforms in the rich countries would soften the need for the reduction of the incomes of the working class. At any rate, there must be a reduction in the quantum of goods and services that the rich take from the present world output.

Will the peoples of Britain, Canada, Australia, or Japan, for example, be prepared to scale down their lifestyles? Unless those of good will in the rich countries are prepared to do something effective against injustice at the international level, there can be no hope of a peaceful ending to the worldwide exploitation that prevails at present. The rich of all countries and the working classes of the rich countries must carry out a profound transformation of their values in order to remedy injustice. If they are unable or unwilling to do so, revolutionary violence may be the only road left for justice in the world.

Exploitation is so woven into the texture of modern society that there is a need for internal contestation within all countries. Presently some groups, in universities and research centers, for example, are aware of the need for such contestation. But this awareness must be extended in scope and depth. In Switzerland, for example, there must be a radical change in the banks that hold foreign accounts, including those of corrupt Third World rulers and elites. Swiss nationals benefit from this organized, legalized plundering of the poor. While a hundred thousand persons died of famine in Ethiopia from 1973 to 1974, Emperior Haile Selassie had some $16 billion to his credit in foreign banks. The secrecy of the Swiss banking system is a plaything of corruption at the world level.

The Swiss are proud to be thought of as a peace-loving people. But are they aware that they draw substantial benefits from the flow of ill-gotten funds to their bank accounts? Should not persons of good will expose rather than participate in and profit from this evil? If Swiss bank employees would take action to reverse this situation, they would help in reducing corruption all over the world.

Another example of the type of contestation needed is the analysis and exposure of the policies of big industrial companies, especially the MNCs. How do they get their raw materials? What is their profit margin? What is their impact on elites and governments of poor countries? Are they guilty of tax evasion? What are their labor practices?

Contestation has to take place at all levels—in corporations, universities, research institutes, newspapers and other mass media, legislatures, the armed forces, and at the United Nations.

The transformation of at least a section of the local elites of Third World countries is essential for the contestation of injustice globally. They hold a key role in the linking of peoples of good will in the rich and poor countries.

The world situation is similar to that of a village when thieves attack one household. The whole village is mobilized to defend the victims and capture the thieves. When a country is attacked by an enemy, the whole population is mobilized to ward off the invaders. Today we have a situation of worldwide robbery. Humanity can be truly human only by taking part in the struggle to eliminate exploitation of person by person, and country by country, through a system of global domination.

Political Action

Contestation of capitalism, both internal and external, will best be carried out with the support of the power and machinery of the state. Changes such as land reform and income redistribution brought about by law are likely to be more readily accepted. Some will always argue: Why should we make sacrifices when others are not? If changes are imposed on a nation as a whole, they are more likely to be accepted as just. But of course resistance can be expected from those with vested interests in exploitation.

The contestation of capitalism can be undertaken politically through influence on political parties or by persuading or creating a particular political party to adopt such a program. Within a democratic society that party may work to bring about changes through legislative processes. Where a democratic framework does not exist, such a party would have to plan on gaining power by whatever feasible means it may have. In any case, it must be recognized that the last bastion of capitalism will not be overcome unless the armed forces are on the side of change and will not impose military dictatorship to thwart democratically spearheaded social change.

Just as forms of domination have been embodied in the political, social, economic, and cultural structures of countries and of the world, so also the liberation of a people must have societal structuring. Thus, from a critique of the laws of a country, a revolutionary movement has to move on to a building of alternative types of laws, relationships, and structures. Ownership laws must be changed in the capitalist countries if all humankind's right to life is to be guaranteed. Similarly the prevailing international law—both public and private—must be contested and altered if there is to be a global respect for human rights.

The ordinary citizen will have to take a much greater interest in politics in order to bring about such changes within countries and on the world level. This means banishing the idea that politics is "dirty" or the task only of politicians and political scientists. Everyone is involved in politics; everyone is affected by political decisions. One of the reasons why the passivity of the masses continues is promotion of the idea that politics is a field restricted to a few.

Mass action can be developed through social awareness. Such action can take different forms in different countries. It is naturally more difficult under dictatorial regimes and where a people has never really exercised the power of choosing its own form of government or its own rulers. Mass political action can occur within the framework of law or may involve the breaking of unjust laws. Legal action may pressure parliamentary systems and government structures. Extralegal action may be necessary in the contestation of laws and structures. A workers' strike, if carried out against an unjust law, can be one such action. The strike can be a powerful weapon for bringing society to an awareness of its social responsibilities. Boycotts organized against the sale of certain commodities can also have an educational value in making a people aware of an issue. Setting up alternative international marketing arrangements is a means of bypassing the MNCs, helping disadvantaged producers,

getting better products for consumers, and developing global education.

Contestation in Socialist Countries

The historical experience of socialism proves that the setting up of
a socialist regime does not by itself bring about the full realization
of all human aspirations, or the end of all forms of exploitation.
The excesses of Stalin included a cruel suppression of all opposition
to his views, as revealed by his successor Nikita Khrushchev in his
speech to the Twentieth Party Congress in 1956. Mao Tse-tung tried
to eradicate the evils of bureaucratic elitism in the People's Republic
of China through the "Great Proletarian Cultural Revolution"
started in 1967. But it became an oppressive movement. The present
rulers of China have denounced the "Gang of Four" for the mis-
deeds of the period from 1967 to 1976. In Eastern Europe there
were massive uprisings in Hungary (1956) and Czechoslovakia
(1968).

The Polish workers' Solidarity movement is an example of how
workers can organize themselves for nonviolent action even in a
socialist state. They developed the weapon of the strike and na-
tionwide work stoppages as an affirmation of the peoples' will.
Their membership is so widespread, with over ten million workers,
that even the Communist Party had to move with caution. Their
demands include a more people-oriented economic planning, more
freedom of association, publication, communication, and religious
worship. Even the Soviet Union considered it unadvisable to interfere militarily in Poland, unlike its response in Czechslovakia in
1968.

Grassroots Movements

These events indicate that grassroots movements have a worldwide role and impact today. We are going through a process of
reeducation at a global level. Some of the methods of nonviolent
resistance to injustice developed and popularized by Mahatma Gandhi, and after him by Martin Luther King, Jr., have been lessons for
the whole of humanity.

Voluntary action groups everywhere need to develop an understanding and experience of different methods of nonviolence, as their situation and culture may indicate. In general the goal is to influence public opinion, amplify popular consciousness and power, and thereby put pressure on public authorities. Building up bargaining or counteracting power is a short-term goal toward more radical changes in society. Methods such as mass petitions, marches, protest meetings, fasts, prayer meetings, legal action in courts, and strikes are becoming increasingly widespread all over the world, especially where governments turn to repression as a means to maintain power. All these mean that more and more groups are becoming aware that the major public voice cannot be left to bureaucrats, diplomats, politicians, or the police and military. Unfortunately, where such nonviolent means are unsuccessful, more radical groups must resort to terrorism, guerrilla warfare, and armed revolt.

Forming Alliances to Contest Social Injustce

The impact of the contestation of social injustice, nationally and internationally, depends very much on the linkage of groups dedicated to this cause. The enemies of the people are linked nationally and internationally. Unless alliances are formed nationally and transnationally, the forces of liberation will stay weak. A linkup can help bring about a concomitant cultural revolution in persons' thoughts, attitudes, and behavior. The universalizing of alliances can manifest the worldwide extent of the will for liberation today. It can help remove prejudices and give weight to the values of togetherness and sharing.

The universalizing of action for justice must relate to persons of all age groups and families. The young, the middle-aged, and the old can cooperate in this. A noticeable phenomenon today is that both men and women are becoming radicalized as they grow older.

Women's powers of persuasion must be recognized for their potential in bringing about a cultural revolution. In the fight against consumerism, women have an important role. If their values change, the demand for nonessential consumer goods and for ostentation will be greatly reduced. Women of all age groups are already participating in liberative struggles in fields such as politics, trade unions, the media, and education. They bring immense moral and physical strength to campaigns against injustice.

The young are especially aware of and concerned with social justice, both nationally and internationally. In almost every country of the world there are young radical opponents of injustice. They are more sensitive to global issues and to the rights of the oppressed in other countries. The present generation of youth has been brought up with less chauvinistic attitudes, especially in countries open to economic cooperation with other countries, as in Western Europe. They are also more open to the future. They realize more intuitively that the structures of the past century are inadequate to meet the problems of the present world and especially the future world, which will be theirs to construct.

One characteristic of the modern age is that contestation is likely to be a regular feature in the lives of many throughout all the different stages in their lives. The true revolution is a long-term people's revolution.

Radical contestation of injustice has also to be universalized geographically. The building of a new world order involves all countries. The Third World cannot liberate itself without reference to the First and Second Worlds. The United States cannot humanize itself without relating to the human rights of the peoples that it exploits. The socialist countries cannot maintain their socialist ideals without participating in the struggle of oppressed peoples against capitalism, feudalism, and the expansionism of socialist powers. We have a situation, therefore, in which the struggle against the unjust world system has to take place everywhere simultaneously. The strategies and the short-term goals in different areas are bound to be different. The peoples of Papua New Guinea may have to contest Australian exploitation and their own apathy. On the other hand, radical contestants in the United States may have to fight the exploitation of Australia by U.S. companies. The more enlightened socialists in Czechoslovakia have to contest the trend toward consumerism within their country and the military domination within the East European bloc.

Chapter 6

Religion:
Foundational Inspiration
and Sociocultural Conditioning

RELIGION AND SOCIETY

Religion is a world-pervasive force that motivates human beings in their personal and social lives. Different religions seek answers to the meaning of life at its deepest level: Why do we live, suffer, have moments of enjoyment, and die? What was before this life, and what comes after? Is there a Supreme Being who governs the universe and human destiny? How can persons find meaning, joy, and peace within themselves and in relation to others? Are there any transcendent values?

The great religious traditions of the world give different answers to these fundamental questions. But they all participate in the search, recognizing human life to be on the way to some better state. Even Marxism has aspects of religion about it, giving an explanation of human life and the universe based on a faith in dialectical and historical materialism.

Faith, within the theistic religions, is the response of believers to what they regard as the revelation of God to humankind concerning the ultimate meaning of human life. Faith, for the Christian, is a personal acceptance of God's revelation in Jesus Christ concerning the meaning of human existence, both individual and collective. It is the acknowledgement of God as a loving Father/Mother revealed in Jesus Christ, through the outpouring of the divine Spirit to all humankind. It means facing life with the conviction that happiness consists in unselfishness, in self-sacrifice of oneself for others, that the real joy of life is realized through a process of death-resurrection: death to selfishness, life in selflessness.

Each religious tradition also bears a particular relationship to the society in which it takes root and lives; Hinduism in India, Islam in the Middle East, Christianity in the West. The religious intuition influences social forces. On the other hand, social powers tend to condition religions, making their teachings and practices consonant with the needs, values, and positions of those in power. Religion organized as a social group needs the support of the powers that be for continued peaceful existence and external growth.

Social powers can find in religion a valuable justification of their own position. Social power depends very much on physical and economic strength for its maintenance. It finds that religion can offer a meta-social legitimation of its power and a "spiritual" motivation for eliciting the obedience of subjects.

Religion correspondingly offers to the oppressed and underprivileged a compensation of rewards in the future life. Its teaching, spirituality, and ritual can help condition the oppressed to accept their lot in life without questioning the powerful or the social system. Religion may offer to dominant groups a sense of mission for helping the downtrodden to save themselves. This mission can satisfy those among the affluent who busy themselves "doing good" without fundamentally questioning the power relationships in society. This can cause an alienation of both the oppressed and oppressors, making the former submissive and the latter benevolent and complacent. Religion can thus be the opium of the affluent as well as of the masses.

Hence in a religious tradition or organization we must distinguish two elements: the core of its foundational message and its socio-cultural conditioning. The former is a basic intuition of life and should have a permanent value; if so, it should be a criterion for evaluating the organizational and external aspects of the religion. On the other hand, religion as a sociocultural phenomenon may relate more to de facto human groupings than to the content and quality of its faith. Faith is a response to the core message; it need not necessarily accept the whole of the sociocultural conditioning of a religious tradition.

Evaluation of Religion as a Social Force

We can apply here the criteria elaborated in chapter 5 concerning goals and means. Religious organizations too have their goals and means—verbally expressed goals and actually intended goals.

Religions claim to teach their adherents the way to salvation. This journey and the meta-natural means it may involve cannot be assessed by the evaluational criteria of the social sciences. On the other hand, religions use human organizations; they teach about interpersonal and social relationships; they have forms of worship and community organization; they run institutions and services; and they form a religious community within a wider social community. These can be seen as intermediate goals or means.

Hence we can evaluate the actually intended goals of the activities of religious groups. These may be the establishment of a fellowship or group, the forming of a believing community, the organization of churches into parishes and dioceses. These intermediate goals would relate to the final expressed goal of salvation, but they would also be within a given socio-cultural setting and conditioned by it. It is this latter aspect that we can evaluate with the criteria of the social sciences.

We can discern the de facto goals of building a religious community and the means used to relate to the actual powers present in a society. Here we can also bring in the criteria of social justice. How far do the activities of religious groups help or hinder the realization of social justice within a given community? Do they help to reduce or increase income, wealth, and power imbalances in society? Do they make opportunities and facilities available to everyone? Are human relationships improved and human rights and freedom more respected, or less so, because of the impact of a religion in its teaching and practice? These are the questions to be asked when we wish to evaluate the relevance of a religion as a sociological phenomenon. This analysis must be distinguished from the implications of the basic message of the faith, for this may not be actually lived out in practice.

Religion and the World Order

We can evaluate the social impact of a religion in different dimensions. There are the personal aspects, the relationship to the small group or the nation-state. There is also the impact on the wider reality of the human race, the world, and the universe.

We can and must ask, therefore: How have the religions, as organized bodies, related to the establishment of the world system? What have they contributed to this world system by their doctrines, worship, missionary endeavors, lifestyles, discipline, relationships to other religions, other ideologies, social movements, different cultures, races, and countries? We must also distinguish here between the expressed goals and the actually intended ones; we must try to see what the means used have actually resulted in.

This reflection has to be made in the context of the present world crisis and the tragic conditions produced by the barbaric relationships among the peoples of the world. The question is relevant because we are reaping the consequences of a long-term evolution. We are not questioning the personal motivation of men and women of religion, which, we presume, has generally been praiseworthy; but we must study the impact of their well-intentioned actions.

A reflection on the world's major religious traditions and the world order will help elaborate a thinking and practice that can aid the religions in responding to human aspirations for peace, justice, and happiness today. How can the different religious traditions meet these issues? Can they converge in their basic messages and even public expressions in order to serve humanity? These are challenges that the world situation poses to religions, especially in Asia, the source of the great religious traditions, the home of the world's proletariat, and the chief arena of the world's conflicts.

Christianity: Foundational Inspiration and
Sociocultural Conditioning

In Christianity we can distinguish the core message of faith and its sociocultural conditioning. Theology, too, is an admixture of the two. We must try to discern what is of permanent value in the Christian faith and what is purely human, temporal conditioning caused by the environment in which Christianity lives. The former can be accepted and the later rejected if not beneficial to human society.

There are some who propose that the whole of the Christian phenomenon is divine and binding on all believers. Others reject the whole of Christianity because, as a sociological phenomenon, it is seen almost entirely on the side of the exploiting classes and nations. Marxism rejects all religions on this ground.

A third attitude is possible: the core message of Jesus Christ is one of integral liberation—of the person, of society, and of the world in truth, authenticity, social justice, and peace. This is the main thrust of Scripture and the life of the early church. If we recapture these insights and try to live them in faith, then the basic intuition of Christ can have meaning for us today. While doing so, we must also try to rid Christianity of the narrowness and group selfishness that it has historically manifested in many areas of its life.

This is a challenge for Christianity today. How much and how soon can it return to the basic sources of the evangelical message and cease to be a sort of ideological superstructure of the domination of some groups by others? The world situation and the growth of human consciousness through the communications revolution is a challenge to Christian religious institutions to transform themselves into servants of a just world order. For this the Christian church will have to go through profound changes, for it is at present deeply compromised with the world establishment.

RELIGIONISM

We have earlier described racism, classism, and sexism as instances of extremism. Their extremist bias is shown in that one group thinks of itself as more important than and the norm for the others. Members of the other sex, other racial groupings, other classes are not respected as persons with their own identity, dignity, and equal rights. The others exist for and can be used and disposed of by the "superior" one.

We can see a similar phenomenon in religions. One religion deems itself superior to the others in such a way that the others do not have the same dignity and rights. Others are considered anticipations or partial reflections of itself, and less important. One religion tolerates or even promotes the proscription and persecution of others. Such a phenomenon can be called "religionism." All religions have shown an inclination to religionism.

Religionism can be particularly strong if a religion is tied to a dominant culture, ideology, or racial group. Dominance in the economic, political, military, and cultural spheres can be carried over to the religious sphere also. And a dominant secular power tends to want to make its religion dominant and to seek religious legitimation for its own dominance. In the Japanese empire the emperor was to be considered God, to whom all subjects owed obedience and worship.

Religionism seeks to express itself in the elaboration of the content of the beliefs of a religion. A religion tends to elaborate an explanation of salvation—a soteriology—in which it has a major, prior, or special role. It tends to interpret God as its special protector, in preference to other religions. It may believe that its adherents are the "chosen people," favored by God, unlike the rest of humanity. It would therefore be inclined to claim a special divine sanction for its teachings, decisions, and actions, which other religions do not enjoy. It may claim that it has a superior understanding of God and of the divine plan of salvation. It may consider its own sacred writings as more sacred, more authentically inspired, than any others. It will tend to look down on the spiritual leaders, traditions, worship, and values of other religions. When powerful it may be intolerant of the members of other religions. It would like to organize national life and the world system according to its perspectives.

A danger in religionism is that the dominant religion may find itself in a position in which it can hardly distinguish between characteristics derived from its foundational religiousness and the implications or consequences of its alliance with a dominant secular power. It may find it difficult to draw a line between the rights of the truth that it believes and the arrogance of the power that it exercises over others. It may tend to make the truth subordinate to authority, and the search for truth a function of obedience to religious power, exercised even in alliance with secular power. This is exactly the opposite of the present-day spirit of tolerance, dialogue, and ecumenism among religions.

Religionism has the effect of fostering the prejudices from which it is itself born. It tends to engender and intensify blindness in a dominant religion—a blindness that obscures the values in others and exaggerates its own good qualities. It tends to depreciate and despise what it cannot comprehend in other religions. Like the dominant male in sexism, it cannot understand why the other should not be subordinate to it.

Religionism is the result of a lack of respect for the followers of another religious faith. But, then, it is also a lack of respect for God. Religionism tends to make God to the image of the salient features of the dominant religion. It is a form of idolatry, for it ends up worshiping the image of its own power rather than a God who cares for all creation. It is also blasphemous, for it claims a proximity to God that it has no justification in denying to others. Like a dominant class, a dominant religion tends to think of its role as more important than that of other religions.

For a religion to cure itself of religionism it will have to undergo a deep purification. It will have to take more seriously the virtues of humility and service to others. It will have to understand that its own ennoblement is in respecting the rights of others, being prepared to learn from others, and sharing its perceptions and values with others. It will have to reexamine and purify its own creedal content tainted with religionism, learn a new language of respect and dialogue, and above all not try to make God its own monopoly.

Chapter 7

The Christian Churches
and the World System

If it is true that the present world system is largely the result of white, Western, capitalist expansionism linked to male domination and a pillage of nature, we must ask how the Christian churches related and reacted to this process during the five centuries of its evolution.

Many Christians have been concerned with the injustices of the emerging world system and were deeply interested in science and the humanistic trends in Europe. But the Christian churches as a whole have not been open enough to the world of science to inspire it, and tended to benefit from European expansionism without being critical of its deep inhumanity.

From Spain to Eastern Europe the centuries prior to Western expansion were those of warfare between Western Christians and Muslims. European religious, military, and economic interests were closely linked. This was true, too, in the religious wars between Catholics and Protestants: *Cujus regio ejus religio*. Those were the days of the "Holy Wars" and the Inquisition. Religious orthodoxy was enforced by political or physical power when deemed necessary.

Why should we remind ourselves of all this now, when colonial peoples have been given their independence and the churches have gone through the updating of Vatican II and the general assemblies of the World Council of Churches? Because, although national situations may have changed, the world system has not. Nor has the

Christian church as yet rid itself of the orientation it had during the millennia when it was identified with male domination and Western Europe. Christianity is only now beginning the process of purifying itself from being the religion of the Holy Roman Empire, Western culture, and Euro-American capitalism.

CHRISTIANITY AND THE WEST

With the conversion of Christianity to the religion of the Roman empire and later of the West in general, the gospel of Jesus Christ became deeply impregnated with the values, aspirations, and interests of Europeans. There was an unholy amalgam of the evangelical message with the secular interests of those peoples and powers. The geographical expansion of Christianity was linked to the military success of the Western powers, and vice versa. The understanding of the church, its mission, and its role in society was accommodated to fit that relationship.

Though the Protestant Reformation divided the church, it did not basically alter the attitude of Christians in their relationship to West European dominance over other countries. On the contrary, the Reformation eased the way for colonialist and capitalist expansion according to European interests and cultures. In such a situation, it is understandable, though regrettable, that some of the basic teachings of Jesus Christ were forgotten, played down, or even distorted in the interests of the link between Christianity and the West.

Christianity and Colonialism

A clear example of theological and spiritual deviation from Jesus Christ was the church's unquestioned acceptance of the West European model of expansion for its own growth. And expansion became an ultimate value. The church was conceived of as the only means of salvation for the world.

The preaching of the gospel was undertaken for the expansion of the church and, in the case of Catholicism, the subordination of non-European peoples to the Roman pontiff in all matters of religion—and other matters as well: consider the division of South America between Spain and Portugal by papal decree. It was a church-centered theology and spirituality that fitted the needs of

European conquistadores and colonialists. Soldiers, merchants, and settlers found missionaries valuable allies in their colonial enterprise.

The spread of the church being the highest value, everything else could be justified by it. There followed the usurpation of entire continents, the elimination of centuries-old cultural traditions, and armed combat with other religions. The popes of the time legitimized and blessed the colonial enterprise:

> This was exactly what Martin V did by granting perpetual rights to the royal Crown over all the lands that should be discovered beyond Cape Bojador, in his Bull *Sane charissimus* of April 4, 1418. The grant was confirmed by several successive popes, particularly by Eugene IV in 1442 and by Nicholas V in 1452. The following is an extract from the Bull *Dum diversas*, in which this last pope addressed the king of Portugal: "In the name of our apostolic authority, we grant to you by these present letters the full and entire faculty of invading, conquering, expelling, and reigning over all the kingdoms, the duchies . . . of the Saracens, of pagans, and of all infidels, wherever they may be found; of reducing their inhabitants to perpetual slavery, of appropriating to yourself these kingdoms and all their possessions, for your own use and that of your successors."
>
> The number of pontifical Bulls [dealing with colonial expansion] (69 have been counted), generally obtained at the request of the Kings, shows the importance of the religious legitimation. In order thoroughly to establish the Portuguese power, the same Nicholas V, in the document already quoted, threatened with excommunication every person, and with interdict every nation, that did not respect the rights of the Portuguese [François Houtart, *Religion and Ideology in Sri Lanka* (Bangalore: TPI, 1974), pp. 116–17].

Christianity and Capitalism

With colonialism came capitalism in its commercial and industrial embodiments, and eventually the MNCs. Capitalism also fostered many antievangelical values and practices, such as the destruction of the economy of a colonized people, the creation of dependence, the exploitation of labor and resources, unfair terms of trade, and the plunder of natural resources (gold from Latin America, diamonds from South Africa, for example). Gold decorations in basilicas, cathedrals, and monasteries bear witness to the church's share of the spoils of imperialist capitalism.

Capitalism breeds an acquisitive society and, more recently, consumerism. The churches have not, in practice, clearly contested these values. On the contrary, the school system that the churches helped build in colonies often spread the competitive and individualistic values of capitalism. They provide docile and skilled personnel for capitalistic enterprises and for colonial administrations. But the schools also indirectly helped in the political emancipation of the colonies by training future leaders of independence movements.

The churches, even up to the present, have not squarely faced the question of population and land and the racism motivating the Euro-American world system. Their approaches to the problems of world population are based on the presupposition that the present system of nation-states should continue.

The churches are more aware now of injustice as it relates to social classes. However, they have not yet come to a meaningful participation in the struggles of the poor to transform their societies and world structures. Confrontation with socialist and Marxist ideologies has been a long record of distrust and opposition. The Christian churches have been extremely reluctant to appreciate the positive values of socialist revolutions in the U.S.S.R., China, and elsewhere. In general the churches have not been attuned to accept revolutionary change. They took nearly a hundred years to reconcile themselves to the French Revolution and the democratic trends in Western Europe. After over sixty years the churches outside Russia are still not reconciled with the Marxist revolution in the U.S.S.R. The Chinese revolution is only now beginning to be even heard as a voice that must be listened to and may have a message for Christianity. The churches' linkage, first to Western feudalism and monarchy and later to Western capitalism, has paralyzed them from responding with discernment to the revolutionary trends of other ages and other parts of the world.

The linkage of the Catholic and Protestant churches to Western culture was such that, prior to the independence of colonial peoples, these churches were among the principal agents of Western cultural penetration into Asia, Africa, and the Americas. This brought with it some positive values. But the churches failed to appreciate—and even tried to obliterate—the significance of the cultural values of the African, Asian, and Amerindian peoples. Due to the same attitude they were blind to the inadequacies of Western culture that presumed itself superior to all others.

In the religious expression of non-Western Christians in worship, art, architecture, and music, there has been some change, especially after independence of Asian and African countries. In the Americas, white Western culture has been imposed as the dominant way of life. In Africa and Asia the churches have been rather reluctant to accept indigenous cultures as having a religious value and as capable of replacing Western culture elements. There is a willingness to accept the externals of another culture, but a distrust of its inner core if it is closely linked to another religion.

An even greater reluctance has been shown to acceptance of the liberative dimensions of non-Western peoples and cultures, which have supported ferments of resistance and revolt against Western domination and religious imperialism. Dialogue between these cultures and Christianity has not been adequately engaged in at this deep level.

The churches have also generally helped buttress the male dominance that characterizes the present world system. Theologically the interpretation of the Scriptures has been such as to favor patriarchy. This has been so from the way the first chapters of Genesis have generally been interpreted and applied. The life of Jesus, the nature of his apostolic community, and the writings of St. Paul have been utilized to give a religious sanction to male power. The world Christian churches, especially the Catholic and the Orthodox, have been particularly marked by the idea of male superiority in matters ecclesiastical, if not religious and spiritual as well.

The movements for the liberation of women from such domination have originated mainly from secular inspiration. Much of the thrust has come from North America, though now it is spreading to Europe and other continents. In this, unfortunately, the churches have been more obstructive than promotive of liberation, even though women comprise the majority of the church-going population. The relationships and structures of male domination that prevailed in society in general were also maintained in the churches, with perhaps greater conviction due to their supposed religious legitimation.

A dominative relationship to nature and the earth is another dimension of the modern world system. In the progress of scientific investigation, scientists tended to study the universe, the planet earth, and human life with the instruments of quantitative measurement and inquiry. They neglected the psychic and numinous relationships in nature. They did not adequately appreciate the balance and interrelationships of the physical, biological, and psychological orders. They tended in this direction partly because they could not find meaningful motivation for their investigations from the Christian thinking of their day.

Theologians, on the other hand, tended to study the numinous without a clear relationship to the earth and earth processes. The sources to which they turned were divine revelation and ecclesiastical tradition. They distrusted the scientific studies that seemed to them either naturalistic or atheistic.

The chasm was deepened by the strong presence of commercial capitalistic motivation in economic and social life. Science, technology, and communications were utilized for power and profit in disregard for ethical values and the rights of peoples. Nature itself was subordinated to the exigencies of a rapacious capitalistic appetite for materialities.

All these elements have helped bring on the present world crisis. The churches are only now beginning to understand the catastrophic consequences of the sundering of science and economy from morality on the one hand, and of theology, church life, and Christian mission from the concerns of scientific investigation, human relationships, and the care of nature on the other hand. They present a challenge to theology at deeply personal and far-flung planetary levels.

We can see in all this the impact of religionism on Christianity. Whereas genuine religion is disinterested service to the other, religionism tends to consider one religion an end in itself and superior to all others. Christianity, due to its uncritical alliance with Western power, culture, economy, and racial interests, was disrespectful of other religions, cultures, and peoples.

Whereas secularism helped confirm scientists in their amoral and sometimes atheistic attitudes, religionism tended to make Christians think their theology was self-sufficient and had nothing to learn from science and the rest of the world. Religionism prevents a male-dominated Christianity from learning from female insights, experiences, and research.

Theological Deviations in Christianity

With Christianity the prisoner of Western capitalism, its understanding of the Scriptures, of Jesus Christ, and of the mission of the church was deeply vitiated. The priorities of the kingdom of God were neglected. Ecclesiology was attuned to triumphalism rather than to evangelical service. Theology became heavily defensive— either defending the church against science, democracy, socialism, and human liberty, or defending antagonistic Catholic and Protestant positions.

In the moral teaching of the churches, the emphasis was on individual morality rather than the social responsibilities of Christians. The rape of continents was overlooked, even justified. Imperialist wars were not condemned. Teachings on ownership were not voiced to safeguard the rights of colonized peoples. Though international economic relationships were then developing, moral theology ignored questions of pricing, wages, use of resources, and human exploitation. Strangely, these issues were much in the Christian conscience during the Middle Ages with reference to feudalism. And some of the fathers of the early church—to say nothing of the Old Testament prophets—had an acute sense of social justice.

The rights of the human person were neglected in favor of the authority of the church or the state. As if to counterbalance these negligences, there was an overwhelming concern about sex and personal morality. But preachers and spiritual writers turned a blind eye to the unjust interpersonal relationships springing up in the world around them.

The Fatherhood of God

The theological implications of the doctrine of the universal fatherhood of God were not developed or lived in practice. That

God is a loving father of all, is just, and cares for all with a loving providence is a central theme in the teaching of Jesus. If Christians had reflected more on the common, divine filiation of all humankind, they could not have been so at ease within the growing colonial and capitalist world order.

The Bible speaks clearly of God as creator. In the general catechesis and life of the church, there was a neglect of the consequences of the revelation concerning creation. Creation implies the unity of the human race, the entrusting of the resources of the universe to all peoples, and the love of the creator for all. Such themes militate against racism, sexism, classism, religionism, the rape of nature, and the grossly unfair distribution of the world's land and resources among the worldwide human family.

Social Service vs. Social Justice

The central message of Jesus Christ—that God is love, and that we must love God and one another even to the extent of self-sacrifice—was not applied to colonized and exploited peoples. Instead, the emphasis of the church was on making Christians, just as the emphasis of capitalism was on making profits.

Jesus was concerned for others. But his message was applied more in terms of social service than of social justice. The centuries of growth of the church in the Third World were periods of extraordinary generosity by persons inspired by the gospels. Christians from Western Europe and North America went out over the world, sacrificing themselves in the service of colonized peoples. We do not doubt their sincerity and spirit of self-sacrifice. Unhappily, their efforts fitted all too easily into the Euro-American dream of world supremacy.

In both the Protestant and Catholic churches, the more recent charismatic and pentecostal movements, which had their origins in the United States, tend to take theological and ideological stances that fit in conveniently with Western domination over the world. Their emphasis on peace, joy, and love neglects the need of conflict, holy discontent, and struggle precisely in order to introduce the fruits of the Holy Spirit in a highly exploitive world situation. It is to be hoped that the charismatic movement will develop beyond its present stage, but it is noteworthy that, in its spread over the world, it has as yet no message on, or program for, world justice.

"Where Your Heart Is . . ."

The Christian churches, in spite of the heroic efforts of individuals within them, have not yet come to grips with the fact that the world order is barbaric; that some are affluent at the expense of the penury of others; that the escalating production of armaments is a crime against humanity; that male dominance dehumanizes both women and men; that the wasting of nonrenewable resources is a grave crime against the human race.

The goals of the churches at the world level are still primarily based on ecclesiastical interests. There is more concern for building and safeguarding the institutions of the church than in presenting the gospel of Jesus Christ or serving humanity in its global search for survival.

The churches have little awareness of the strategies necessary for the service of humanity. They do not make serious use of their multinational presence to combat the structured evil of our times and build mentalities and structures of justice. Even much of the spending by church-oriented funding agencies is counterproductive in that they build up new ecclesiastical elites even in Third World countries. These elites help bolster social conservatism. Little is used directly for critical awareness, organization, and action among the oppressed masses in the poor countries, and still less for the conscientization of Euro-American Christians to their sinfulness and the need for urgent and adequate remedial action at the national and world levels.

BUILDING THE FUTURE

Ours is a period of rapid and profound change. The coming years will see the most unprecedented changes if the present trends of evolution and revolution continue. We shall see either the growing maturation of the human race in global fellowship or destruction on a scale hitherto unknown. The peoples of the world are groping toward a new age of greater justice, while the forces of injustice are also gathering strength.

The church harbors a germ of hope for humankind. This is due, first of all, to the universality and radicality of the gospel of Jesus Christ. The Scriptures can present a message that is capable of motivating believers to respond meaningfully to the challenge of persons and of the whole world system in crisis. In spite of its accommodation to the world powers, the Christian churches represent an enormous reservoir of good will that can be harnessed for justice and peace. Christians are at the centers of power and decision-making. They can influence the course of future human evolution. The task is an urgent one. Millions of lives depend on it. But it cannot be achieved without a deep transformation of all Christians, a process of death/resurrection: dying to an exploitive world in order to rise with the whole of humankind in justice, sharing, and personal fulfillment.

Chapter 8

Asia's Challenge to Christianity

Christianity, like the other major world religions, was born in Asia. The Christian Bible is an Asian sacred writing. Jesus, Mary, the Apostles, many of the early Christians were Asians. Orthodox Christianity has always had a home among Asian peoples.

Why is it, then, that Christianity did not spread further eastward in the early centuries after Christ? Other religions of Asia have had such a movement. Buddhism went eastward from India to Burma, Thailand, China, Korea, and Japan, and southward to Indonesia. Confucian influence spread eastward from China to Korea and Japan. Islam went both eastward and westward from the Middle East.

Christianity on the other hand found it difficult to move from the West to the heart of Asia. Only in the Philippines is the majority of the population Christian. Efforts for several centuries at setting up Christian churches in Asia were not significantly successful. Outside of the Philippines, only about 1 or 2 percent of Asians are Christians, though there are significant Christian minorities in Korea, Vietnam, Sri Lanka, and India.

Is this because Christianity was not converted to Asia in the same way as it was to Rome and Greece and European culture? Asian peoples readily honor Jesus Christ as a spiritual leader and accept the Bible as a worthy religious book. But they have been aloof to the Christianity that has been presented to them. Is it perhaps because Christianity has not been open to learn from Asian values? Buddhism and Islam spread in Asia because they became truly part of the way of life of the people.

Asian people deeply appreciate Jesus of Nazareth. They accept his simple, evangelical values. Naturally they do so from within the framework of their own traditions.

Christianity has borne witness to certain spiritual values, especially in its dedication to the poor and needy. Christians have been influential in enhancing human dignity and respect for the downtrodden in Asian countries. Christianity has counteracted forces of fatalism, which tended to blame physical and other evils on one's past life. It brought an element of rationality to the consideration of personal and social problems.

Social service of an individualized nature has been a distinct contribution of Christians in all the Asian countries and has helped to contest such social evils as caste and racism.

Christianity has made a special contribution to the development of modern education in Asia. Christian schools are important educational institutions in every major city of Asia. Christian villages have had the advantage of education at the elementary level. The schools helped to prepare the first generation of Asian middle-class leaders, who were able to take over administration of their countries after colonial rule. Christians took a lead in the education of girls, which was generally neglected in Asian societies.

The openness of modern Asia to science and technology has been helped by the Christian presence, as in China at the time of Matteo Ricci. In a sense, the spread of socialist ideas has been indirectly helped by a knowledge of Jesus Christ and the gospels, even if the institutional church was wary of socialism.

The organization of parishes, dioceses, schools, social services, and communications media has given Christians a sense of cohesiveness. They are much admired for their organizational ability. In the more recent trend toward "development" activities, Christians have been a medium of contact with the West and a base for the widespread organization of relief, aid, and development projects—for example, in Bangladesh, India, and Indonesia.

Catholics have given a special testimony to new forms of religious living through the witness of members of religious orders, especially women. The seventy thousand nuns in Asia have contributed immensely to the enhanced status of women, who have long been underprivileged in Asian countries.

Thus has the church borne witness to some spiritual and personal values. Where it has failed is particularly in the larger sociopolitical aspects of life and in respect for spiritual values and experiences.

THE WESTERN CHARACTER OF ASIAN CHRISTIANITY

In India there are Christians who trace their history back to apostolic times. The Orthodox churches have had a continuous presence in the Middle East and later in India. In modern times Catholic and Protestant Christianity came to Asia hand in hand with Western colonizers, both military and commercial. This has deeply hurt the Asian peoples and remains imprinted in their memories. Asian Catholicism, for instance, was connected with Portuguese and Spanish colonial expeditions and expansion. From India to China, and especially in the Philippines, the Spanish and Portuguese traders established trading ports, military forts, and mission stations. The French colonial empire in Indochina was another point of entry of Catholicism to Vietnam. As Portuguese and Spanish power waned in the seventeenth and eighteenth centuries, missionaries from Europe and later from North America helped consolidate the Catholic Church in those countries. The Philippines remained under Spanish control until 1898, and the Spanish did a thorough job of converting the Filipinos to their faith.

Christianity in Korea had a different history. Lay scholars from China first introduced Christianity into Korea. The earliest converts were upper-class intellectuals who were impressed by the work of Western Christian missionaries of the caliber of Matteo Ricci.

A related characteristic of Christian origins in Asia in modern times is the intolerant manner in which it was introduced. Christians came as superiors—militarily, politically, culturally, and even theologically—and went about trying to save souls in an iconoclastic manner. Present-day Europeans and Americans can hardly imagine the cultural and spiritual shock this gave to Asian peoples. The resentment in China at the request of foreign powers for special privileges and protection of missionaries and at missionaries depending on and siding with foreign invaders had been particularly strong. This was one of the causes of the opposition to foreign missionaries after the Chinese revolution.

In the Philippines strong-arm conversion tactics were used, and no effective religio-cultural tradition opposed Christianity there. But in the rest of Asia, the ancient philosophical and religious traditions of Yoga, Hinduism, Buddhism, Taoism, Confucianism, Shintoism, Zen, and Islam were too deeply rooted in society to be vanquished by foreign conquerors and missionaries.

Christians did not integrate themselves with the main sociocultural groups in the Asian countries. Sometimes missionaries tried to convert kings and courts, and thus influence a whole realm, as in China. At other times they went to small disadvantaged groups: to migrants and those who suffered psychological and physical disabilities (lepers, the aged, orphans, the handicapped). This was partly within the evangelical tradition, but it was partly an evasion of the more difficult task of relating to socially integrated groups and the mainstream of the population.

As a result, almost everywhere today Asian Christians are sociological as well as demographic minorities. In North India they are among the depressed castes or migrants from the south. In Burma they are Katchins, Karens, Shans, Chinese, Chins, and Anglo-Indians, but very few are Burmese. In Thailand they are mainly Vietnamese and Chinese. In Cambodia they are Vietnamese and Europeans. In Malaysia they are mainly Chinese, Indians, Ceylonese, and Europeans; hardly any are Malays. In Indonesia many of them are Chinese, especially in Java. This characteristic gives Asian Christians a complex of defensiveness and inferiority.

Converts to Christianity were kept apart in separate settlements or parishes. Their lives were so conditioned that they would have little social intercourse with the rest of the community, the "pagans." Theology, canon law, foreign customs, liturgical puritanism, the ban on mixed marriages, the Christian school systems, and even geographical segregation helped build and keep most Asian Christian churches as sacral ghettos.

In some Asian countries, the Catholic Church is still foreign in that the leadership, especially the clergy and religious, are foreign. In Japan, Hong Kong, Korea, Malaysia, Thailand, and Indonesia many of the clergy, including some of the hierarchy, are foreign. Although this witnesses to the international character of the church, it adds to the foreign image of the local church. The liturgy, ritual, architecture, dress of the clergy and religious, canon law, allegiance to Rome, and dependence on Western countries also make Catholics in Asia seem less at one with their fellow citizens, except in the Philippines.

Asian Christianity lacked flexibility, suppleness, and growth from the base or grassroots. Asia comprises three-fifths of the human race and is extremely diversified, but Christianity in Asia, except for recent marginal trends, resembles the uniform European Christianity of half a century ago, not merely in externals but in basic mentalities as well. Christians in general are ghettoized, and the institutions of the church—parishes, schools, seminaries, religious houses—tend to be ghettos within a ghetto.

An attitude of spiritual superiority does more harm to Christianity than do any externals of rite, architecture, dress, language, music, or even political options. This attitude of mind dies hard. It is strongly enshrined in church thinking. It helps confine Christians to a fringe existence and a fringe role in most of Asia.

Being a nonintegrated minority has an important impact on the mentality of Asian Christians, particularly in the countries where they are less than 5 percent of the population. Self-conscious and defensive, they are afraid to join the mainstream for fear of being submerged in the process. They tend to be self-centered, concerned with their own preservation and growth. In the smaller churches there is little opportunity of developing original thinking and ways of Christian living. In order to maintain their identity, they tend to preserve their Western forms and outlook.

THE CALL OF HUMAN LIFE

The most fundamental fact of Asia for Christianity and theology is human life itself—the struggle for life, which is the basic issue for the vast majority of Asia's massive and growing population. This is more basic than issues of religion, culture, or ideology. For Asians die early, unnecessarily. They wither away due to malnutrition. Children die very young. Millions are homeless, landless, jobless. This is the reality of Asia. And it is worsening, while the rich everywhere grow richer.

The question for Christianity is compounded by its relationship to the affluent world, which is also the world that has long exploited Asian peoples. The philosophy and policies of Western capitalism have not resolved the main questions of social justice or even of mass poverty. Asia has learned much from the West, but the Asian peoples are also suffering much due to the power and influence of Western countries and values.

China under its communist rulers has tried to provide the essentials for human living for over one-third of Asia, and has been fairly successful—more so than feudal or capitalistic regimes of the past. How can this not affect our Christian evaluation of non-Christian ideologies, class struggle in Asia, and mass movements among Asian peoples?

Hitherto Christianity in Asia has failed to respond to this challenge adequately and seriously in action or even in thought. The churches as a whole are concerned with the poor, the aged, and the sick; but they do not deal with the causes of poverty or infirmity in such a way as to remove injustice and bring about a greater sharing. Christianity at the world level does not take human life seriously, even though statements of the popes and the World Council of Churches urgently call for it.

As far as the churches and theology are concerned, much of what was said earlier on the world system and on Asia boils down to this issue. Without radical changes in the world political and economic system, in our cultural values and our attitude toward populations and living space, poverty and hunger in Asia will not be remedied. Therefore participation in such a mental, cultural, and social revolution is incumbent on the followers of Christ. No other issue can come before it. Its realization is basic to love, to justice, to human relations, and therefore to spirituality, and to the fulfillment of God's will. What a loss the whole of humanity suffers in so many human lives truncated, unfulfilled, unrealized! How much sorrow this causes to so many fathers and mothers, brothers and sisters, in Asian villages and towns! In what deep contrast all this is to the superficiality of the lifestyles, concerns, and amusements of local elites and of the people of affluent countries!

Christianity in the world as a whole cannot absolve itself of the white racism that pervades the world system as such. Christians may not be made conscious of this in their religious gatherings. But racism is deeply entrenched in the mosaic of international relationships and in national policies, such as those regulating immigration. They condition the right of life of other peoples, especially Asians. An Asian challenge to Christianity and its theology is to face this worldwide racism squarely, genuinely, determinedly, and practically.

Within Asian countries Christians must face the internal problems of racism, casteism, and religious rivalries. Closely connected is the call to identify with the struggle of the poor for a decent life and for human dignity. For Asian Christians this means that those who are poor do not remain passive or let themselves be coopted by an unjust system, and for those who are relatively affluent a call to discard their class privileges and join in the cause of the poor with a clear view of the struggle involved.

Correspondingly, Christian theology has to motivate and itself grow out from identification with the poor in their struggle for life and for justice. This should be the main thrust of theological search in relation to the Asian reality of the half of humanity living in conditions of crushing poverty and unbearable oppression—in a world of plenty. Reflection on the ideologies of capitalism and Marxism, the cultural values of consumerism, and care for nature should all be linked to this struggle for life itself.

In the procapitalist countries of Asia, the churches have adapted themselves to the class structures of their societies. The majority of Christians are poor, and often among the marginalized in society. The poor are encouraged to be docile and accept their lot. They generally combine Christian church membership with a continuance of earlier animistic practices and superstitions.

The Christian elite is generally part of the local elite in Asian countries. In colonial times they were close to the centers of power and cooperated with imperialism. Chiang Kai-shek in China, the Diems in Vietnam, and the Marcos family in the Philippines are modern examples of such collaboration. The MNCs also tend to favor Christians due to their westernized education and anti-Marxist upbringing. The Christian elite is, in most instances, cut off from the masses by their lifestyle, political options, and class interests—even if they worship in the same churches. They are attracted to the idea of migrating to Western countries and form a considerable portion of Asia's "braindrain."

Church leadership in the hierarchy, clergy, religious life, and lay movements is usually drawn from the Christian elite, or is incorporated into it. The prevailing theology, the focus of seminary formation, the lifestyle of priests and religious all help in this. Social action and pastoral and educational work tend to be oriented toward social service, but not to social justice through the radical transformation of mentalities and social relationships locally and internationally.

In more recent years some among Christian elites participate in movements for liberation and exploitation. Their numbers are growing, especially in the Philippines and Korea. Otherwise the Asian Christian elites resemble their national counterparts and generally serve the prevailing world system.

Asian poverty and struggle for life are a call to the Asian churches and to Christian theology to return to the foundational aspirations of Christianity in the Scriptures, the life of Jesus, and the early church, which were all deeply concerned with human life and justice. The Asian reality summons Christians to a deep conversion based on reassessment of their positions within the prevailing world system and conflicting ideologies and movements.

IN THE CONTEXT OF THE OTHER ASIAN RELIGIONS

The Asian context brings another basic challenge to Christianity and to theology through its religious traditions. Asian religions have been seeking through countless generations for the meaning of human life, for an understanding of our universe, and for communion with the divine. There have been varied traditions from the Middle East with the Jews and Zoroastrians, to the Far East with Zen and Shintoism. India has been the home of yoga, a spiritual discipline of Hinduism—a search for identification with the Absolute—and of Buddhism, seeking an understanding of self and purification from mundane attachment.

From India these traditions moved southward and eastward in a nonviolent, symbiotic manner. Buddhism spread to all the countries of Asia without the military and without imposing a sense of cultural superiority. Buddhists in Burma are of the Burmese culture, in Vietnam, Vietnamese, and in Japan, Japanese. There was a deep centennial dialogue and osmosis of religions without force, without antagonism. Even the spread of Islam has mostly been by quiet penetration, though in some instances rulers did establish Islam after coming to power.

The Confucian approach to life is one of great respect for human relationships and a respectful concern for nature. The Confucian mentality is more practical, this-worldly, and seeks harmony and balance in relationships. Taoism also stresses the importance of seeking harmony within the reality of antinomies and in the perspective of Tao, the ultimate, all-pervading principle of reality.

Shintoism was the Japanese expression of the experience of the all-pervading numinous reality manifesting itself throughout the entire natural world. Shinto has provided the Japanese people with an identity, a fundamental sense of unity, a theory of political rule, and even a sense of historical destiny. Zen, which arose within the context of Buddhism, entails a search for deeper meaning in meditation, the mind reflecting on itself and all reality, perceiving its unity and beauty.

Islam arose from a stream of religious tradition closely connected with Judaism and Christianity. Islam stresses the transcendence of Allah, the one supreme personal deity who has communicated with humanity through Muhammad his prophet. The revelation to Muhammad has been transmitted to succeeding generations through the Koran. Islam became the basis of a new social and political community with specific directions for its relationships as detailed in the Koran. Islam too has shown a capacity for multicultural religious communion, spread from the west of Africa to the east of the Indonesian islands, and north to China and Russia.

These different religious traditions have been integrated in Asian countries with a core of primitive animism that still persists as the inspiration of Asian religion and superstition. Thus Asian religiousness is not merely a philosophical discipline or a meditative asceticism. It consists in a webbing of traditions, beliefs, customs, fears, and hopes that have given Asian peoples inspiration, narratives for finding meaning in life, in relationships with the cosmos, with an afterlife, and with the Absolute. For each area and people the religions they have been born into are part of their whole life process linking them with their ancestors for innumerable ages, with the earth, and with the universe. The religions have given them courage to face the stark realities of life and molded their values and character. The religions also had their weaknesses and unworthy alliances with unjust social systems. They tended to legitimize exploitation, casteism, feudalism, absolutism, and sometimes obscurantism. Yet these have been the life forces of Asia's millions.

Christianity entered this Asian religious scene like a bull charging into a china shop. It came armed with the power of the Western nations and allied to their merchants. The best among the missionaries were more understanding and sympathetic to human suffering. But the Asian peoples still retain the memory of the barbarous manner in which European invaders dealt with their religions, religious institutions, and traditions—and that in the name of another religion! My present purpose, however, is to ask what lessons there are for Christianity and Christian theology from this sad historical encounter, and consequently what orientations seem indicated for the future.

Part of the explanation of the mistakes that Christians made is that they gave themselves an exaggerated self-importance that easily led to religious arrogance. They showed a lack of recognition and respect for other persons, other religions, other views on life. We have to ask how far alliance with and influence of the European way of life was responsible for this. Can the irrelevance of Christianity to the Asian mind be eliminated by merely external changes in language, art, architecture, and music? Should there not be a profounder opening to accept Asian philosophies as vehicles of Christian thought? And should not the content of Christian theology be purified, deepened, and broadened to be able to respond to the challenges of Asia? It is my conviction that a profound change in Christian theology is necessary if the message of Christ is to be meaningful for Asia and Asians. This will mean a reconversion of all Christians to the core of the gospel.

In the first place Christians need to learn to dialogue with other religions in a truly respectful manner. This requires an openness in relationships, without ulterior motives. We must be prepared to lay ourselves open to others, and to learn from others in genuine humility. It will also mean a readiness to accept the fact that we do not have a monopoly on God, that God cares for all persons and peoples. God does not leave any people without the means necessary for their spiritual growth and fulfillment.

This will have serious implications for theology on the nature of revelation and redemption. No fruitful dialogue with the Asian religions is possible if we begin with the view that Christian revelation is the unique, privileged, and ultimate revelation of God in such a manner that all others are secondary, less valid, and in a sense less true. This may be difficult for Christians to accept. But it is a lesson we have to learn. God has spoken to different peoples in different ways. We can say that the Hindu understanding of God is different from that of the Bible. Comparison in terms of "right" and "wrong" is no way to evaluate revelations.

A connected issue is that of the nature of salvation or redemption and the necessity of the Christian church or explicit faith in Jesus Christ for salvation. This is sometimes posed as the question of the salvific power of other religions. We need to recognize the goodness of God toward all human beings and that God will not leave anyone without the means of salvation and redemption. We have then to seek further as to what it is that we have to be redeemed from, and in what way the religions, including Christianity, can help in it. The very fact that Asia's half of humanity is not willing to enter the Christian church as it is must make us inquire further into our own understanding of God and theology.

The Christian theology of the believing community on Jesus as the Christ, and on the Holy Spirit, are further areas that need elaboration in this context. Have we not understood the church too mechanically and sociologically, as the community of all those who are baptized, whether they be converted to the gospel or not? What is the conversion that is required of the Christian? How is Jesus, the historical person, related to the cosmic Christ spoken of in parts of the New Testament? How do we reconcile all these with the universal indwelling of the Holy Spirit? How is the God worshiped in Hinduism related to the God of Christians and of Islam?

From the point of view of the growing oneness of the world as an interdependent whole, and in view of the better understanding among religions, can we not advance toward an ecumenism of all religions so that there would be one common core of spirituality for the global community? Can Christianity be so purified that its message would be in keeping with such a spiritual core of human understanding?

Another related requirement is the contribution of Christianity and other world religions to the integral liberation of Asian peoples.

The Asian religions, in spite of all their limitations and defects, have been sources of motivation and strength in the search of Asian communities for personal meaning and societal liberation. In the struggles against European colonialism, in the resistance to what is undesirable in Western culture, the Asian religions have been a support of the peoples. Hinduism in India, Islam in the Middle East, Buddhism in Sri Lanka have motivated the leaders and masses toward selfhood and independence. These struggles are not over. Feudalism and capitalism continue to dominate many parts of Asia. Can Christianity, renewed by the call for human life against poverty and death, and the other religions be linked in the liberation struggles of Asian peoples?

In the socialistic societies there is a need for further action toward the promotion of human rights, because the march toward full humanity is not terminated by the capture of power by a socialist party. Can religions cooperate with each other and the positive forces in the socialist societies for the service of the half of Asia that is under socialist regimes?

What will all this mean for Christian theology and church life?

ACHIEVEMENTS OF THE CHINESE REVOLUTION

Modern China is an example of a whole social order built up after a revolutionary struggle without reference to a God, a religion, a church, or missionaries. On the contrary, it asserts a positive disbelief in religion. China has been largely successful in resolving many problems that baffled humankind—especially in the capitalist world—problems of food, housing, energy, employment, inflation, self-reliance, mass participation, and discipline. In most areas of life, China has opted for a form of development that is not based on the West European technological model.

We cannot justify some of the stances China has taken in domestic and foreign policy. Nor can we look with approval on the tremendous psychological pressure put on the people by the regime, the exaggerations of personality cult, and the absence of certain forms of political freedom. But even with these limitations, the Chinese revolution is, by any human standards, the main achievement of any Asian country in this century, and perhaps of any people throughout the course of history. It represents the greatest transformation for the betterment of the largest number of human beings in the shortest period of time. It is extraordinary in the sheer magnitude of its undertaking, in the depth of its impact, in facing immense odds—including isolation by the rest of the world—in an enormous effort of self-reliance, innovation, and creativity.

The revolution of Mao Tse-tung has given an Asian face to communism. It has adapted Marxism to the rural masses and to the traditions and culture of an Asian people.

China constitutes the largest and deepest challenge to the Christian churches, for this fifth of humanity has its own answers to problems to which the churches claim to have the only response. China was one of the biggest mission fields of the churches for centuries prior to 1949. But the churches have always had a difficult time adapting themselves to the Chinese way of life. Today, foreign missionaries are almost totally banned from China, and there is little contact between the Christians in China and the churches abroad.

In this situation, the churches themselves have gone through a process of self-examination with reference to China. They realize now how distasteful their activities were to the Chinese people during the years of imperialist penetration into China—from 1840 to 1909. During this period, prejudicial trade treaties were forced on China by foreign powers—Britain, France, Germany, the United States, and czarist Russia. These treaties contained specific guarantees for the toleration of Christianity and promises of protection not only for missionaries, but also for their Chinese converts. The missionaries could travel and work in any region of China under the protection of foreign powers. For the Chinese people, therefore, Christianity was not only foreign but also a close ally of Western imperialism. This was seen as undesirable not only by Chinese nationalists but also by more sensitive persons such as Cardinal Constantini, Catholic apostolic delegate in China, and Teilhard de Chardin.

Further, activities of the churches, such as the creation of parishes, schools, hospitals, and universities, did not oppose the exploitation of China by foreigners; on the contrary, they were ancillary to such exploitation. Christian churches failed to oppose such evils through their moral teaching and action. Hence we should not be surprised that China, after the revolution, considered the churches, particularly foreign missionaries, as obstacles to their self-improvement.

The mission history of China shows how it is not enough for missionaries to be self-sacrificing; they must understand a people's struggles and share in them. Have the churches learned the lessons of the failure of that stage of the mission in China? Did not the churches continue to make the same blunders in Vietnam until 1975? Are they not doing so in Namibia, in the Philippines, in South Africa, and countries such as Paraguay and Uruguay, in spite of more conscious and committed minorities? Some small groups of Christians are now open to rethinking on China, but their reflection has not yet reached the stage of a renewed missiology and ecclesiology applicable to the whole world.

As mentioned earlier, the churches have been slow to understand revolutions. This is partly because they have not been sensitive to human suffering on a massive scale. Their concern has been too "other-worldly," too church-centered. The Chinese revolution can also help us understand better the uses of violence in certain circumstances. During the second half of the twentieth century, the Chinese people, in spite of the Cultural Revolution, has experienced relatively more peaceful conditions than the rest of Asia, Africa, or Latin America. We can hardly imagine the turmoil there would have been if Chiang Kai-shek had continued in power in mainland China with the support of the U.S.A.

After more than thirty years since the final victory of communism in China, we can say that China has shown the feasibility of another path to development that does not need the capitalistic motivation of the West or the Stalinist methods of technocratic control. It is now opening to the West somewhat, from a position of strength and self-confidence. Christian theology has to consider how far this achievement is in keeping with the Christian gospel, insofar as the Chinese form of economic organization is more communitarian and more egalitarian.

The new openness of Christian groups outside China to the Chinese revolution should be coupled with caution that it not be merely a consequence of European and U.S. opening to China. It should rather be inspired by a sincere acknowledgment of the values of the Chinese revolution and a desire to rethink one's own Christian theology. Western Christians should be open to dialogue with socialist developments everywhere—including Eastern Europe and the Soviet Union—in independence of the foreign policies of their countries.

The reorganization of the churches in China since 1949 raise theological issues that have a global relevance. The Protestant churches have regrouped themselves in China under the Three-Self Movement: self-government, self-support, and self-propagation. They are evolving their own Christian life, after the ravages of the Cultural Revolution of 1967 to 1976. They are taking their inspiration from the Scriptures and the life of the early church. They work within the framework of the Chinese revolution. They do not want outside interference in church affairs. They have reached a stage that they call postdenominational. They no longer belong to their former Protestant denominations as such; they do not want money or personnel from them. They are evolving a new form of Chinese Christianity. The Protestants have not had much difficulty in establishing autonomous local churches. Their postdenominationality can be a good lesson for churches elsewhere: the denominations are a consequence of European divisions and need not be exported to the rest of the world.

The Catholic Church in China is going through a more traumatic experience. Though there were missions in China since the seventeenth century, Chinese were not appointed bishops until 1926. Most bishops were non-Chinese. With the revolution most of them were imprisoned or expelled. The Vatican did not approve of the Chinese revolution. It maintained diplomatic relations with the government in Taiwan. Catholics were forbidden to cooperate with the communist regime. Chinese Catholics were torn between loyalty to the church and to their country. But they began to see that the new government was doing many things that were more in keeping with the gospel—for example, land reform, and an end to the opium trade and to prostitution.

When several dioceses were without bishops, the Chinese clergy appointed bishops on their own, or asked the Vatican to appoint those named by them. The Vatican did not accept this. Thus a schism took place. The Chinese Catholic Patriotic Association was set up in 1957 under the chairmanship of Archbishop Pi of Shenyang. Since that time it has continued to appoint its own bishops. I had occasion to meet Bishop Fu Tieshan of the Catholic diocese of Peking, Bishop Tu Shihua, bishop of the Catholic diocese of Hanyang, and Fr. Wang Zi-Cheng, vicar general of the Catholic diocese of Yao-Yang, at the Canada-China Consultation in Montreal, October 1981. They insist that it is within Catholic tradition that local churches nominate their own bishops and that the Vatican should recognize this legitimate autonomy of local churches. This is an important theological issue that can be of great significance to the whole Catholic Church.

Catholics of the Patriotic Association also support the Chinese revolution. They are its beneficiaries. They maintain that they are Catholics, and they welcome the friendliness of Catholics and other Christians in other countries. Their dilemma deserves sympathetic appreciation. It is also true that there are Chinese Catholics who remain loyal to the papacy and are suspicious of the Patriotic Association. This is an issue similar to what the church had to face when radical changes took place at the time of the French revolution.

Pope John Paul II has admitted that blunders have been committed over the years and centuries in the church's dealings with China. Is it not time that this issue be reviewed in a spirit of Christian understanding and reconciliation? Can it not be done with a less rigid understanding of papal authority—an understanding of it more as a presidency of love than a depository of all power in the church?

While these changes have been going on in the Chinese churches, the communist regime there has also been undergoing an evolution. The Cultural Revolution was quite intolerant of Christianity. This was part of its general approach. The new regime, since the death of Mao Tse-tung, is more permissive to religion. Chinese Marxism now seems to realize that religion is not necessarily an enemy of socialism, and also that a people's religion cannot be exterminated by repression. This may open new doors for ideological dialogue.

The Chinese experience is an important lesson for Christian mission theology. It can teach Christians the importance of respecting other peoples, their culture, their desire for self-government, their revolutionary struggles, and their yearning for life and justice. The churches have still to undertake a deep reexamination of their attitudes and theology to discern why they were so insensitive to China and the Chinese. Why did they not see the harm that European and American—and Japanese—armies and companies were doing in China?

All this can help Christians realize how far they were from being real witnesses to the gospel values in China prior to 1969, in spite of so much personal good will and dedication—and draw the necessary conclusions for the present and especially for the future of the church in a planetary age.

WOMANKIND IN ASIA

Asian and African peoples have been well acquainted with male domination, in spite of the importance of women in the extended family community. Contact with Western Christianity in some ways helped to strengthen male domination and in some other ways fostered the liberation of women by the spread of education and of a more scientific attitude toward life.

Although there is some similarity in the problems faced by women in Asia and by those in the Euro-American countries, from which the women's liberation movement emanated, there are also important differences. Asian religions have generally been insensitive to the rights of women. Power in the major religions has been with males. The discrimination against women that is prevalent in society has been buttressed by religious teachings, customs, and sanctions. Islam has been particularly inflexible in this regard.

On the other hand women and men join hands in continuing other kinds of discrimination—based on class, color, or caste. In Asia these divisions can be very pronounced, as caste is in India, race in Malaysia, and class in the Philippines. This situation is somewhat similar to what prevails elsewhere in the world. The women's movement and theology have to face this issue—in theory and in practice.

Because the problem of life itself is the primary issue for the majority of Asian families, it brings women and men together. It has a higher priority, particularly if malnutrition is a fact of life. This is one reason why the more distinctive campaigns of the women's movement in Europe and America have not found much resonance among Asian women.

Third World theology and women's theology face similar hindrances in the dominant male Western theology. Both movements find it difficult to reflect and work from within the accepted tradition and interpretation of the Scriptures. Both find that God has been appropriated by the powerful and made male and white. Both base themselves on their conviction of the truth of Christianity to invalidate a tradition of male domination.

A characteristic of Asian women's movements is that they do not find it meaningful to form separate movements of Christian women, especially when they are in a minority position. Hence their theology too has to include women of other faiths or ideologies.

The women's movement contributes to the conscientizing of Asian women, but it also has much to learn from them. The theology of women needs to be broadened and deepened to include the concerns of women in the Third World, who are perhaps over two-thirds of the world's women, and 80 to 90 percent of the world's oppressed women. Here too we need a perspective that respects each movement in its autonomy, is willing to learn from others, and endeavors to cooperate toward integral human liberation.

BEYOND VATICAN II

It is now two decades since the Second Vatican Council met, in 1962. It had noteworthy influences on the Asian churches. There is a greater openness of Christians to other religions, ideologies, and cultures. The bishops' conferences have been strengthened and linked together in the Federation of Asian Bishops Conferences (FABC). There has been an acceptance of Asian languages in the liturgy and in India the development of an Indian rite for the Eucharist. Catechetical renewal has helped to move the accent from the letter of the law to God as love. Inter-Christian ecumenism has advanced toward cooperation in Bible translation, in social action, and sometimes joint worship. The relations of hierarchy, clergy, and laity are less formal and more cooperative than earlier. As elsewhere, Catholic religious sisters have been among the most outgoing and forward-looking as a group. Youth, student, and worker movements have been more progressive, but the official churches have often not been able to inspire them or cope with their joltings.

The Second Vatican Council was, however, inadequate for the

Asian context, and therefore also for the world context. This was mainly because it was a Euro-American council. Most bishops of the Third World were not yet sure enough of themselves to have significant impact on the council. The council agenda was set by the European theological debates of the 1950s and early 1960s. It was mainly a council of bishops, and its deliberations generally centered on matters of interest to the bishops. Instead of monolithic papal supremacy over all Catholics, local bishops and episcopal conferences were to have some authority delegated to them. The synods of bishops, to meet occasionally, were to be consultative to the pope, who decides their agenda.

The concerns of Vatican II were mainly intraecclesiastical and interecclesiastical (ecumenical) vis-à-vis other Christian churches. It was only in passing that it dealt with other religions and ideologies. Its general direction was, however, a welcome break from earlier dogmatic and ecclesiocentric attitudes. It advanced thinking in the direction of a more human and world-centered theology. It fostered more freedom and respect for persons within the church and without.

Its inadequacy was due partly to its lack of an adequate social analysis of what was going on in the world at the time. It had no real sense of the struggles of the poor, the working class, of women, of oppressed racial groups. It did not deal seriously with racism and white supremacy, with sexism and male dominance, with classism and capitalist exploitation. It did not come to terms with the Russian revolution or even consider seriously the Chinese and Cuban revolutions and the Vietnamese struggle. There was no deep dialogue with other religions, cultures, and ideologies as offering alternative analyses and worldviews to the white, Western, capitalist, male mind-set that still dominated Catholicism. Some of the main theologians of the council—Congar, Rahner, Ratzinger, Küng— rendered valuable service as far as they went, but their experience was European and church-centered. The council had no clear vision of the type of world it envisioned as against the present exploitive world system with its assault on nature by the exhaustion of nonrenewable resources and environmental pollution. Hence it did not propose relevant practical goals in the real world and strategies for transforming mentalities and structures. Its relationship to the world order and human development remained within the framework of "aid" to the poor by the rich.

Thus while the church as a whole limped along renewing itself from within, the world became more and more entangled in crises: the Vietnam war, oil shortages and price escalations, recession, national security states, unemployment, the arms race, during the 1970s and into the 1980s. In the Catholic Church, support of struggles for human liberation came more from small peripheral groups, sometimes backed by more progressive bishops and religious houses or even whole congregations. It was thus that Christians participated in liberation struggles in Latin America, southern and Portuguese Africa, South Korea, the Philippines, and other local movements in Asia.

This situation brought about a questioning of personal views, lifestyles, and the very concept of mission by priests and religious women and men in Asia. Although the majority are still in their traditional apostolates and relationships, many have had second thoughts on the efficacy of their own work. Some have moved to ashrams for contemplation and interfaith dialogue. Others have gone to action groups and movements for social change, including struggles for justice. Still others have given up the priestly and religious life—over 10 percent of the priests in Sri Lanka from 1965 to 1980. More sensitive persons in lay movements too feel the inadequacy of traditional church activities and perspectives. Vocations to the priestly and religious life and membership of lay organizations of the traditional types have decreased. The average age of the present membership is increasing, with a consequent decline in vitality. The bishops in general have tried to maintain the generally rigid line of the past, especially in seminaries, the consequence being that the younger clergy is less enterprising and more content with the traditional ministries of the pastoral clergy. The religious congregations, especially of sisters, are more reflective and creative, having both the resources and the personnel for new directions.

Throughout the Church in Asia, however, there is a search for a meaningful interpretation of Christian life and witness. Both clergy and laity, women and men, want a religion that is deeper and more related to the hopes and aspirations of the people. They are, therefore, experiencing a crisis of conscience and confidence in the prevailing traditional orientations.

Protestant Christians in Asia have been more open to secular currents and to the breathings of the Spirit among them. The influence of the World Council of Churches general assemblies, as at

Uppsala and Nairobi, and specialized groups has been less spectacular than Vatican II but more consistent and continuous. World Council units, such as Dialogue with Other Faiths, Evangelism and Mission, the Program to Combat Racism, Community of Women and Men in the Church, and units on science and technology, health, lifestyles, the multinationals, and urban rural ministry have kept up a regular activity and orientation based on a consultation that is more open and permissive to the Spirit's blowing from the periphery or grassroots than the Catholic Church has been accustomed to. The Christian Conference of Asia (CCA) links these at the Asian level. The CCA has fostered dialogue with other religions and with communist China.

All the same, Protestantism also counts conservative evangelicals, who are far more rigid and conscious of their election by God than Catholics are likely to be. The very freedom of Protestantism permits more extreme positions, whereas Catholics tend to move more slowly, preferring to act together under the hierarchy, which has been hard pressed to keep opposed extremes in harmony.

The Orthodox churches in Asia are as yet less involved in the movements for human liberation: they are smaller in numbers and more related to their own church projects. Their theology, however, is more open to the Spirit of God present in the world. They adhere to a tradition that is freer from central control than is the Catholic tradition, and yet they are more interrelated than Protestant groups.

Christians in Asia face explosive issues from several directions: massive and ever expanding population; hunger; demand for life and freedom; pluralism of religions, cultures, and ideologies; racism, casteism, and classism; the neocolonial thrust into their countries; the despoiling of nature in the quest for profit at all costs. Christianity is thus challenged to rethink its fundamental approaches in order to respond to these fundamental issues. Asia poses them, but they are global in their significance.

Chapter 9

God, the New Jerusalem, and the Cosmos in Jesus Christ

Unification of the world into one planetary context can be a grace for Christianity, as well as for the other world religions. Awareness of a planetary context can help Christianity to return to the basic message of its Scriptures and try to live it in the real world today. The dangers humanity as a whole faces demand that we return to more fundamental values in our personal relationships with each other and in the interrelationships among nations.

A planetary dimension of theology would have to be evolved by meditation on the Scriptures and on the world reality of today. From these sources Christians have to decide on courses of action in keeping with the message of the Scriptures and the demands of local and global situations. This will confront us with the challenge to live according to the motivations of our faith. Our spiritual growth will be guided by fidelity to the call of God in our times. We shall know what the mission of the followers of Jesus should be in a planetary context both for personal self-realization and integral human liberation.

The Bible clearly teaches that God created the universe, the earth, and human life. God entrusted the earth to the human family. God cares for all human beings and draws them toward their fulfillment in relationships of love and justice. God has promised eternal life after death to all those who are righteous in their conduct here on earth.

God has sent Jesus the Christ to communicate this message of salvation to all humankind. Jesus in turn witnessed to the Father in his life, in his teachings, and above all in his death. He was killed because of his teachings and his life, which contradicted the established powers of the day.

Jesus confirmed that the Spirit of God will be with all persons on earth to the end of time, helping each one to discern right and wrong and opt for the good. Jesus founded a community of disciples to announce his message to all peoples and follow his teachings.

When we read the scriptures from the perspective that through them God speaks to the whole of humanity, we begin to realize the planetary import of the basic beliefs of Christianity.

GOD

Creation

God as revealed in the Old Testament is the Creator of the world and of the human race. God entrusted the earth to the human family. God cares for the whole of creation and "saw that it was good." From a reflection of the infinite care that was needed for the evolution of the multitude of relationships in the billions of beings in the universe, we can have an inkling of the power and concern of God for everyone and everything. Nature as a whole is self-governing, self-propagating, maintaining itself in a wonderful balance of beginnings and endings, of movement and relationships. As the psalmist says, the whole universe speaks of the Lord of creation. The earth is given to humanity for its sustenance; the human race in turn is to develop the earth, to bring out its potential through human activity.

The doctrine of creation can be the basis of a theology of planet earth itself and of human relationships to it. We have to respect its norms and inner dynamic if we wish to preserve and develop it. The earth will sustain human life if human beings do not destroy the earth. If we ruin the earth, human life is ruined. There is an intimate connection between the earth and our own fulfillment. We are from the earth, and we return to it. We live from the earth. From it we get our food, all the other material necessities of life, and the enriching experience of natural beauty. We must, therefore, care for the earth, respect and revere it. By a wonderful design of creative providence, the earth has the climate that can foster human life. We are warmed by the sun, and yet not too close to it. The moon is at an ideal distance from the earth to contribute beneficially to earth processes—for example, the ebb and flow of the world's tides.

This is one of the vital perceptions that the creation story and the meditation on God can contribute to a planetary theology. Its implications are widespread. It tells us that we have a connaturality to nature; we have to respect and revere it, discover its laws, learn more about it, and use it for our good—and not to harm it by our carelessness or greed. The UN Draft Charter for Nature indicates the type of reverence and care we must have for nature.

Because the earth is the home of all humankind, and because rivers, oceans, mountains, and the atmosphere do not necessarily adapt themselves to our national frontiers, we must have international cooperation for the care of nature, for harnessing it as well as for cherishing it. National selfishness can harm humanity—for example, if one nation manipulates nature in such a way that another nation suffers from it. And the earth is for all time; it is ours to bequeath to future generations. If we pollute the earth or consume its nonrenewable resources in such a way that future generations will be harmed, we are acting in an irresponsible and selfish manner. We are hurting the human family itself. We are not imaging God in our care of nature. The limits of nature set conditions for the viability of civilization. If we promote the spread of deserts or the death of rivers, lakes, and seas we are committing suicide, or genocide, or both.

We should not be so terrified of nature as to deify it, or refrain from studying, exploring, and using it. But to want to dominate it without respect for its own laws, needs, rhythms, and limits is clear proof of a lack of love and concern for nature. Is it not also clear proof of a lack of love of God—the author of nature?

Through the ages—millions of years—the providence of God fashioned the earth to its present state. Now, thanks to human intelligence and inventiveness, we can use it well or destroy it. Millions of acres of forest can be destroyed by fire in a few days. Whole seas can be polluted in a few years. Are these not issues that call for planetary concern, global conscientiousness, and action by humanity to preserve our irreplaceable heritage?

The monotheism of the Bible is a revelation with a universal dimension. There is only one God, and this God loves and cares for all persons and peoples. Whatever may be the beliefs of others, those who accept the biblical teaching have to hold that the one and only God cares for all humanity. No religions, cultures, ideologies, or philosophies can ultimately stand in the way of this unique God and every human person anywhere and at all times.

Exodus

The Latin American theologians of liberation interpret the exodus in relation to liberation from the evil of capitalism in their countries. We can take this perspective further and see in the exodus the archetype of divine concern in all instances of human oppression— personal and societal, national and international.

Creation is not a once-and-for-all static act. God accompanies the human race through its history. Through his revealed word and his involvement in human history he reveals the plan he has for humanity, and the ultimate consummation of all things in a new heaven and a new earth.

Exodus 1 describes the oppression of the Jewish people under the Egyptian pharaoh:

> Then there came to power in Egypt a new king who knew nothing of Joseph. ''Look,'' he said to his subjects, ''these people, the sons of Israel, have become so numerous and strong that they are a threat to us. We must be prudent and take steps against their increasing any further, or if war should break out, they might add to the number of our enemies. They might take arms against us and so escape out of the country.'' Accordingly they put slave drivers over the Israelites to wear them down under heavy loads. In this way they built the store-cities of Pithom and Rameses for Pharaoh. . . . The Egyptians forced the sons of Israel into slavery, and made their lives unbearable with hard labor [Exod. 1:8–14].

The pharaoh ordered the Hebrew midwives to kill all newborn boys. When this was not done, he ''then gave his subjects this command: 'Throw all the boys born to the Hebrews into the river, but let all the girls live' '' (Exod. 1:22).

God is not indifferent to the groans of the Hebrews. He cares for them. He wishes them to have life and freedom. He sees their help-lessness and calls forth a leader to take them away from slavery to a land where freedom and abundance are promised:

> And now the cry of the sons of Israel has come to me, and I have witnessed the way in which the Egyptians oppress them, so come, I send you [Moses] to Pharaoh to bring the sons of Israel, my people, out of Egypt [Exod. 3:9–10].

God does not save his people without their participation. He calls Moses to be their leader. God's plan has to do with the material reality of his people's life, its suffering and liberation. It is thor-oughly this-worldly. It has to do with the masses, their economic and social relationships and their rulers.

When Moses hears God's call he is worried. He feels he is incapa-ble of leading his people. "I am a nobody. How can I go to the king and bring the Israelites out of Egypt?" Moses was fearful of his incompetence, his weakness. For God calls leaders to a task seem-ingly beyond them: to contest rulers, oppressors, the mighty. This was the attitude of other prophets too. They felt their incompe-tence, but they also felt impelled by the Spirit speaking to them. Even Jesus felt this when he prayed in the garden of Gethsemane.

> Moses said to God, "Who am I to go to Pharaoh and bring the sons of Israel out of Egypt?" "I shall be with you," was the answer [Exod. 3:11–12].

God is present to the leader; God is with him. There is an intimate union with God in the liberative task. Mission to the people is linked to communion with God. This is sanctity: to be with God, the God of the Bible, the God deeply concerned about his people and their struggles. He is the strength of those who struggle.

In the New Testament Jesus gives the same promise to his disci-ples: "I shall be with you . . . to the ends of the earth."

What a different spirituality this is from the traditional spiritual-ity that tends to cast the dedicated follower of God as a recluse, or one concerned only with social service, shying away from socio-political struggles. Traditional spirituality betrayed not only the people, but also the God of the Bible "who hears the cry of the oppressed" and calls believers to struggle against the pharaohs of this world.

We see this human frailty of Moses strengthened in dialogue with God. This is prayer; it is contemplation. Prayer has to do with the fact of oppressed peoples and our personal responsibility for liberation. If we genuinely meet God in prayer, will he not speak to us about the oppression of so many today? If prayer does not motivate us to serve the masses, must it not be an indication that there is something essentially lacking in our prayer?

Moses is still worried; he asks in whose name he is to speak to his people and to the pharaoh?

> And God said to Moses, "I Am who I Am. This," he added, "is what you must say to the sons of Israel: 'I Am has sent me to you' " [Exod. 3:14].

We too must go in the name of God—in the name of the God who calls us to justice, to freedom, to march together to the promised land.

God warns Moses that the pharaoh will not give in easily: "For myself, knowing that the king of Egypt will not let you go unless he is forced by a mighty hand, I shall show my power and strike Egypt with all the wonders I am going to work there. After this he will let you go" (Exod. 3:20). God sees that the suffering of the Hebrews will not be alleviated without some form of physical intervention on their behalf. He sees a hard and long struggle. He knows of the unbending desire of oppressors to keep slaves captive. The benefits of slavery are too attractive to the Egyptians for them to agree to respect the human dignity of their slaves.

God is not a tame, spineless God; he acts. He is not neutral. He clearly takes sides with the oppressed. His is an option involving a challenge to the political power of the day. The exodus is revolutionary in its political implications.

The Egyptians have been so dehumanized by having slaves that they do not want to give up their wickedness. The good news of the liberation of the Hebrew slaves is bad news for them. It means an end to cheap labor. Their lifestyle will have to change. Oppressors are always reluctant to liberate their slaves or even improve their lot. Pressure must be brought to bear on them for the sake of the oppressed.

Even the oppressed do not always respond gladly to the call for liberation:

> To Moses they said, ''Were there no graves in Egypt that you must lead us out to die in the wilderness? . . . Leave us alone, we said, we would rather work for the Egyptians! Better to work for the Egyptians than die in the wilderness! [Exod. 14:11–12].

The oppressed sometimes want quick and easy results. They are dispirited by failure. Their oppression, internalized over a long period of time—like the four hundred years of the Jews in Egypt—breeds a mentality of dependence. They tend to distrust leaders who emerge from among themselves.

Action for liberation must be undertaken as a long-term process. We should not be disappointed with the slowness of the process. Both the oppressor and the oppressed may be obstacles to radical changes. The situation may be worse today in some respects due to the seductive power of the mass media and the repressive measures at the disposal of the powerful. The armies and defense forces of modern pharaohs hold their peoples in check. They allow oppression to continue for decades and generations.

Exodus gives a long description of the way God dealt with the recalcitrant pharaoh. He sent ten plagues, one after the other, with increasing intensity: water turned to blood, hordes of frogs, mosquitoes, flies, animal diseases, boils, hailstorms, locusts . . . death of the eldest sons in the Egyptian families.

After each plague the pharaoh first relented but later hardened his heart. He tried to win over the Israelites with partial solutions and palliatives—anything but an end to slavery and permission to leave Egypt. He permits the Israelites to leave only when the situation of his own people becomes unbearable.

In today's world we can see humanity's part in warnings and punishment of God vis-à-vis the injustice of our age: world wars, pollution, inflation, unemployment, high suicide rates, the disruption of family life, nuclear threats, and the like. Yet how little we learn.

Even after the Israelites are allowed to leave, the pharaoh changed his mind after three days and gave chase. Thus he and his troops perished in the tragedy of the Red Sea.

Those who struggle for liberation have to be prepared for resistance by oppressors. All too easily can the gains of justice be withdrawn. Victories of liberation can be reversed by countermeasures. The quest for the promised land required clear options, determination, and ever watchful defense of freedom.

The liberation of the exodus was a mass movement. It entailed a whole people. The journey to the promised land did not take place by individuals acting in private. God's concern was not merely with the individual salvation of souls; it was with the people as a whole, in their common destiny as a people. Hence the importance of people's movements, of the mobilization of the masses, today.

The festival of the unleavened bread is a memorial of and thanksgiving for the success of the exodus liberation struggle. Later on, in the New Testament, the Eucharist is seen as a memorial of and thanksgiving for the human liberation that Jesus struggled for and initiated in his life, passion, and death.

The liberation of the Hebrews required a radical rupture of relationships with their oppressors. It was a revolutionary change. They rejected the structures of oppression and walked out into the desert. It was not a "natural" development, but a liberative struggle. Centuries of suffering had taught them that hope for deliverance could not be placed in slave masters.

When the Egyptian king and army were engulfed by the Red Sea and the Israelites were thus liberated, they sang out in joy. Moses led in the celebration with his song of praise (Exod. 15:1–18).

Moses sees in this liberative action the glory of God: "Yahweh I sing: he has covered himself in glory." Miriam, Aaron's sister, sang and danced along with all the other women.

The historic liberation signaled festivity in Israel's history. It was its "independence day" celebration. The paschal feast reminded the people annually of the great mass movement, liberation struggle, and march into the unknown. Do our church festivities today celebrate struggle and victory, or do they help to further consolidate the oppression of the masses?

The Liberator-God

The liberation from bondage in Egypt is the foundational event in the history of the Jews in the Old Testament. It is referred to in the first commandment: "I am Yahweh your God who brought you out of the land of Egypt. . . . You shall have no gods except me." Human liberation is part of God's revelation. God did not reveal simply a kingdom beyond this life, outside human history and this world. He is concerned with persons and peoples in a this-worldly way. In the Old Testament he teaches his people the meaning of life, suffering, justice, struggle, victory. He wants the loyalty of his people. They must have confidence in him. They are not to have strange gods, false idols. To do so is to be a harlot, an adulteress, for the people is the bride of God. He will be with his people, he will tell them what to say, he will lead them and provide for them. This is the substance of its faith and the basis of its hope. God is holy because he is just, because he is a liberator.

The Israelites left Egypt and marched out into the unknown. They did not know what the future had in store for them. All they had was a faith in the promises of God, of giving them a land flowing with milk and honey, and a holy city—a Jeru-salem. It grounded the hope of the people.

A vision of hope is extremely important for a people's conscientization to and mobilization for liberation. Unfortunately Christians often fail to recognize this. One of the strengths of Marxism is the messianic vision that it proposes in the form of a classless society. But the Bible has a much brighter vision of humanity's destiny.

A NEW HEAVEN AND A NEW EARTH

Isaiah 65 fleshes out the promise of the new kingdom in greater detail:

> For now I create new heavens and a new earth, and the past will not be remembered, and will come no more to men's minds. Be glad and rejoice for ever and ever for what I am creating, because I now create Jerusalem "Joy" and her people "Gladness." I shall rejoice over Jerusalem and exult in my people. No more will the sound of weeping or the sound of

cries be heard in her; in her, no more will be found the infant living a few days only, or the old man not living to the end of his days. To die at the age of a hundred will be dying young; not to live to be a hundred will be the sign of a curse. They will build houses and inhabit them, plant vineyards and eat their fruit. They will not build for others to live in, or plant so that others can eat. For my people shall live as long as trees, and my chosen ones wear out what their hands have made. They will not toil in vain or beget children to their own ruin, for they will be a race blessed by Yahweh, and their children with them. Long before they call I shall answer; before they stop speaking I shall have heard. The wolf and the young lamb will feed together, the lion eat straw like the ox, and dust will be the serpent's food. They will do no hurt, no harm on all my holy mountain, says Yahweh [Isa. 65:17–25].

"I create new heavens and a new earth. . . . Be glad and rejoice" (65:17). God's plan is not for suffering but for happiness. He does not want the death of infants, but that all persons enjoy the fulness of life. God promises to lead his people to a new Jerusalem, the Holy City, where "he will wipe away all tears from their eyes" (Rev. 21:4).

Inhabitants of the new Jerusalem will live in the houses they build, and eat the fruit of the vineyards they plant. They will not build houses only for others to live in, or plant only for others to eat. They will long enjoy the produce of their hands. They will not toil in vain (cf. 65:21–23).

This touches on the concept of exploitation, which Pope John Paul II refers to in his encyclical *Redemptor Hominis*.

Inhabitants of the new city will enjoy the fruit of their labor. They will not be exploited. They will not help build luxurious apartments while they themselves live in slums and shanties. They will not work merely to enrich others.

It is this concept that Karl Marx developed in the concept of "surplus value" and exploitation. Christians had quite forgotten the God of the Bible in the nineteenth century when capitalism was building its wealth on the misery of the working classes and the exploited foreign colonies. There is a close connection between the Marxist analysis and vision and the biblical message in the Old Testament.

The promise is that of a long, meaningful life. The newborn are not to die young. Nor are they to live in vain. They are not to be frustrated in their growth due to a lack of means. They are not meant to be victims of crime, drugs, delinquency, broken homes, prostitution, hunger.

"The wolf and the young lamb will feed together. . . . They will do no hurt, no harm on all my holy mountain" (65:25). There will be no exploitation. The wolf will not take food away from the lamb or eat the lamb. These are images of sharing; there will be peace, not plunder. Is this not the idea of the new society that transcends differences of color, class, or sex? This is the classless society, one in which state power is not abused. How far it is from the powerlessness of the exploited and the power of the rich! Do not the wolves eat up the fat of the land as well as the flesh of the lambs? What of the mounting cost of living and inflation that eats up the low incomes and savings, if any, of the poor? How different is the provision for old age and sickness for the multinational investor or executive and for the roofless shantydwellers!

Mother Zion

In Isaiah 66 we have the same concept of the holy city but in terms of the loving mother Zion who cares for her child:

> Rejoice, Jerusalem,
> be glad for her, all you who love her!
> Rejoice, rejoice for her,
> all you who mourned her!

> That you may be suckled, filled,
> from her consoling breast
> that you may savor with delight
> her glorious breasts.

> For thus says Yahweh:
> Now toward her I send flowing
> peace, like a river,
> and like a stream in spate
> the glory of the nations.

> At her breast will her nurslings be carried
> and fondled in her lap.
> Like a son comforted by his mother
> will I comfort you.
> (And by Jerusalem you will be comforted.)
>
> At the sight your heart will rejoice,
> and your bones flourish like the grass.
> To his servants Yahweh will reveal his hand,
> but to his enemies his fury [Isa. 66:7–14].

The child "may be suckled, filled, from her consoling breast"—that is, children are to be well fed, cared for, comforted, consoled. Zion is a mother to all. The earth is to be truly a home for humanity: caring, providing, consoling, comforting, that the needs of all may be provided. "Toward her I send flowing peace, like a river." God is a God of plenty and of just distribution, of rejoicing and celebration. She is the God who punishes the unjust, the enemy of her beloved people. We also have here a representation of God as Mother, and this is a necessary corrective to thinking of God only as Father.

The concept of God as revealed in the Old Testament, especially in the foundational event of the exodus, is clearly relevant to our times. Those who believe in the God of the Bible are called to recognize the present-day forms of mass human bondage and work toward a new exodus of the whole of humanity to a better future of more humane relationships.

Universality of Jesus' Teaching

The basic teaching of Jesus concerning God as love and the inherent dignity of every human person forms the inspiration for a universalist approach that can have a great importance for us today in our search for global order. Jesus came at a time when Jewish particularism was considered a virtue. He contradicted its narrowness in religion, in social relationships, in its attitudes toward minorities. He opposed its elitisms: of class, profession, race, sex, and even virtue. If he sided with anyone, it was with the poor, the oppressed, the marginalized, the lowly. Children were for him an example of a single-minded, universal, uncorrupted openness to everyone. We cannot say that Jesus elaborated a detailed, universalist perspective, but he proposed elements essential for it.

"Love your enemies" is one basic approach of his universality. This goes far beyond any form of narrowness, or even the strict demands of justice. This is to be the type of sharing that is to characterize the new society to which humanity is called. Jesus' appreciation of the peoples of other racial groupings and religions is quite explicit in many of his statements—for example, on the centurion in Matthew 8:10–11, "I tell you solemnly, nowhere in Israel have I found faith like this. And I tell you that many will come from east and west to take their places with Abraham and Isaac and Jacob at the feast in the kingdom of heaven . . . (parallel, Luke 13: 28–29). His parable of the banquet highlights the apparent paradox of invited guests' refusals and of strangers being called in from the byways.

In Jesus' teachings there is the widest possible universality based on a love that is self-sacrificial, nonexclusive, and disinterested. His words of institution at the Last Supper confirm its centrality in his own life: "This is my body which will be given for you" (Luke 22:19).

God Is Love

A central theme of the teaching of Jesus is the revelation of God as "Abba," Father. He had a loving trust in the Father. He reveals clearly that God is love. God loves us, understands us, fulfills us. In return we must love God and all human beings in God. This is the substance of his message—his summing up of the law and the prophets. If anything is to give specificity to the followers of Jesus it has to be the living out of this understanding of the divine nature and of human fulfillment in response to the love of God, in the context of our interpersonal and societal relationships.

With this central theme Jesus introduced a new understanding of the human person and of social institutions. Every human being was important and had to be cared for. This was the criterion for admission "take for your heritage the kingdom prepared for you . . . for I was hungry and you gave me food" (Matt. 25:34–35). Jesus preached a new view of life that was to be the fulfillment of the revelations in the Jewish religion. Against the abuses and shortcomings of the religions of his day, he witnessed to God as love. Where there is genuine love, there is God; and where there is no real love, God is not present.

The love of God for us is such that anything done unselfishly for someone else counts as being done for God in Christ: "In so far as you did this to one of the least of these brothers of mine, you did it to me" (Matt. 25:40). God's love is universal; it does not discriminate between Jews and Samaritans, fishermen and publicans.

The message of Christ has love as its principal virtue, motivation, and constituent. This love has to be active, effective, creative. Love bridges gaps, seeks to unite, to build solidarity and communion. Love shares, is self-sacrificial and other-centered. In this sense love is radical; it does not compromise with injustice, corruption, waste, and unconcern for others. It is most energetic when a loved one is in danger—as a mother when her child is endangered.

Jesus proclaimed the good news that God is the Father of all— "Our Father." All human beings are brothers and sisters. God is present to all, he speaks to all. The Spirit resides within us. Human beings are very precious in God's eyes: "Think of the ravens. They do not sow or reap; they have no storehouses and no barns; yet God feeds them. And how much more are you worth than the birds!" (Luke 12:24).

There is no fundamental need for masters other than the spirit within each one of us (Matt. 23:8–12). Jesus bestowed a basic dignity and auto-sufficiency on each person in the context of the fatherhood of God and the inner voice of the Spirit. He thus deemphasized human authority of all types. He helped liberate persons from fear of soothsayers, sorcerers, and others who preyed on human ignorance and misery.

The spirit of God whom Jesus promised will guide those who accept him. "When the spirit of truth comes, he will lead you to the complete truth" (John 16:13).

The Trinity

Through the teaching of Jesus we have come to know of the Father and the Holy Spirit. In Christian theology the supreme example of persons is the Trinity. Three persons, yet one God; three who are completely equal to one another, three who know and love one another eternally and everlastingly. They lack nothing. Yet their interrelationship is dynamic, communicative, and creative. The created universe comes into existence as a flowering of their inter-personal relationships. The Trinity is personal; the Trinity is social. In the Trinity everything is in common. Jesus bears witness to such a God.

The teaching of Jesus concerning himself, the Father, and the Spirit is also the revelation of our own personal fulfillment in a concern for others. Humankind is enveloped in the relationships among the divine persons. Human persons too can be, as it were, divinized by keeping his new commandment of love; for thereby we abide in him and in the Father with the grace of the Counselor, the Spirit. We touch here the mystique of Jesus' inner life and his call to personal and societal liberation. It is in working for others that we truly realize ourselves and become one with God.

The trinitarian God as revealed in the New Testament is for every-one, and in everyone, in all times and places, persons, and things. No religion or culture can monopolize or coopt this all-loving God.

Personal Liberation

The God revealed in Jesus Christ is also the source of personal liberation and fulfillment for everyone. This is prior to and tran-scendent of all institutional religious affiliations and ritual. He teaches a way of disinterested liberation and fulfillment in service to others. His way does not follow the path of violence. We cannot, all the same, rule out recourse to violence in the discipleship of Jesus. What he insists upon, however, is self-donation for the sake of others. He offers himself and his life as the example and invites others to follow him. In Jesus we can more clearly identify personal and societal selfishness and sinfulness and transcend them in loving service to others.

Personal liberation has to be liberation from selfishness—the desire for self-promotion strongly rebuked in the apostles, who were concerned about their places in the messianic kingdom. It includes liberation from materialism, which places its trust in wealth and not in God's providence. Rejecting the ruling ethic of the time, Jesus proposed the Beatitudes. True human happiness is in loving service and in struggling to bring about a just society even at the cost of personal suffering.

He preached a message of interiority, sincerity, authenticity, and honesty—values that the modern world is beginning to recognize better in the young. He detested all forms of hypocrisy and duplicity.

He motivated Zaccheus to part with a large portion of his wealth. He called the apostles to leave all their possessions and follow him. Their formation was a process of liberation from their own selfishness, narrowness of perspectives, and Jewish chauvinism. He revealed to them the real meaning of life. He entrusted a mission to them. He gave them a sense of purpose, a new hierarchy of values, an understanding of a deep relationship with God, the courage to be their better selves.

Jesus explained to the Samaritan woman that the worship of God was to be "liberated" from fixed places:

> Believe me, woman, the hour is coming when you will worship the Father neither on this mountain nor in Jerusalem . . . But the hour will come—in fact it is here already—when true worshipers will worship the Father in spirit and truth: that is the kind of worship the Father wants. God is spirit, and those who worship must worship in spirit and truth [John 4:21–24].

Jesus strengthened his followers to face civil and religious authorities with an inner courage and trust in the Father: "But when they hand you over, do not worry about how to speak or what to say; what you are to say will be given to you when the time comes; because it is not you who will be speaking; the Spirit of your Father will be speaking in you" (Matt. 10:19–20). Personal liberation leads to a courageous commitment to social justice.

St. Paul explains in the Epistle to the Galatians how Christ has freed them from their earlier bondage to ignorance and fear:

> When Christ freed us, he meant us to remain free. Stand firm, therefore, and do not submit again to the yoke of slavery . . . You were called, as you know, to liberty; but be careful, or this liberty will provide an opening for self-

indulgence. Serve one another, rather, in works of love, since the whole of the Law is summarized in a single command: Love your neighbor as yourself [Gal. 5:1, 13–14].

The Kingdom

Jesus lived in a situation similar to ours in many respects. Persons were not respected for what they were, but according to their social status. Exploitation was rampant. The poor, the weak, the ignorant, women, children, publicans, and "sinners" were all exploited in different ways by the rich and powerful, by local elites and foreign rulers. Religion too played a role in exploitation. Sicknesses were considered a consequence of one's sins or those of previous genera-tions. Public sinners were ostracized and had to undertake a long period of penance before they were restored to social communion. Jesus cured the paralytic man, lowered to him through the roof of the house, to make the point that he could also forgive sins. The scribes thought this was blasphemy: "only God can forgive sins." They dominated the weak through the alleged connection between sickness and sin. Jesus liberated the paralytic of both sin and sick-ness (Mark 2:1–12).

Within a context of such deep-seated exploitation Jesus presented a radical new teaching, backed up by the witness of his life. He announced it as the "kingdom of God." In today's terminology we may say that he was speaking of a new person and a new society, of new personal and societal values. This was his good news, his gos-pel. He dethroned the prevailing values of money, power, prestige, and group selfishness. Instead he proposed sharing, service, selfless love of the human person, and a universal human solidarity. Natu-rally this was not well received by the sociopolitico-religious estab-lishment of the day.

Jesus emphasized the kingdom or rule of God over us rather than rule by an earthly power or organization. The kingdom of God is primarily within us. He did not stress the power of religious author-ity or of a church. His evangelization pursued the values of the kingdom rather than of an institution or power of a temporal na-ture. It was a movement rather than an organization. He spoke frequently of the kingdom and very seldom of the church. To be precise, Jesus speaks only twice of the church in the four gospels:

"on this rock I will build my Church" (Matt. 16:18) and "if he refuses to listen to these, report it to the community" (i.e., the church; Matt. 18:17). The bulk of his teaching is on the kingdom of God: seeking first the kingdom of God (Matt. 6:33); the rich enter the kingdom of God only with difficulty (Matt. 19:24); harlots enter the kingdom of God (Matt. 21:31); preaching the kingdom of God (Matt. 14); better to enter the kingdom of God with one eye (Mark 9:47); the poor are happy, for theirs is the kingdom of God (Luke 6:20); the kingdom of God is among you (Luke 17:21); the kingdom is near (Luke 21:31).

Jesus speaks also of his kingdom, the kingdom of heaven, the kingdom of the Father. "Your kingdom come, your will be done" (Matt. 6:10). Reward is in the kingdom of heaven: "Happy those who are persecuted in the cause of right: theirs is the kingdom of heaven" (Matt. 5:10). "It is not those who say to me, 'Lord, Lord,' who will enter the kingdom of heaven, but the person who does the will of my Father in heaven" (Matt. 7:21).

Jesus preached such a kingdom at the time of the Roman empire, when the Jews were being cruelly exploited by the Romans. The values he proposed implied a fundamental critique of Roman power and domination. The idea that "the kingdom of God is among you" implied an inner personal liberation from total allegiance to any temporal power. His preaching relativized the authority of both civil and religious leaders. God alone is Absolute.

The community he gathered around him was to live the values of divine dominion. This is a very fruitful perspective at the present time when humanity is looking beyond the narrow confines of particular churches and religions to more universal values on which global understanding can be based. The doctrine of the kingdom of God is also a criterion for evaluating particular historical churches.

His kingdom means that the plan of God for humankind is already being fulfilled. It represents a reversal of the usual condition of society. The poor become rich (Luke 6:20), the first are last (Mark 10:31), the littlest are the greatest (Matt. 18:4), the hungry are filled, the sick are healed, the humble inherit the earth, prisoners are freed, the lowly are exalted, the oppressed are liberated, and the dead live. Those who lose their lives find them (Matt. 23; Luke 14).

The kingdom of God is among us as a transforming power that is communicative and expansive. It grows like the mustard seed, the

leaven that transforms the whole mass of dough. It is power of the
spirit that can be released in human relationships. It can transform
entire peoples. It is the stuff out of which battles for liberation are
fought and won. It is the force of truth that sets the imprisoned free.

These are the strange promises of Jesus to be realized in this life
by individuals and by the human family over the ages. We can discern the outlines of the kingdom by faith, and contribute toward it
by struggling in hope. Love is its fulfillment, joy its fruit. To live the
values of this spiritual mastery over our lives is to realize a new
power, a joy that surpasses all other joys. It is a pure, selfless, active, creative, and liberating joy. It is the joy of the wedding feast to
which liberated humankind is invited. It is for us to respond will-
ingly by a conversion of heart, to live in solidarity, friendship, and
effective sharing in love. Then heaven begins for us here on earth.
Death will be the final confirmation of the continuance of a liberated life in the never-ending kingdom with the Father.

Sin is turning away from God, who is love. Sin is lovelessness.
Love is sharing; sin is selfishness. Sin is untruthfulness, insincerity,
a turning away from God who is the truth. Sin, lovelessness, selfishness, untruth, and injustice are overcome in the kingdom of God,
and love, mercy, truth, and justice prevail. Mercy and forgiveness
are essential conditions of the reign of God over us. It can even be
said that Jesus conditions God's mercy upon our forgiveness of
others: "forgive us our debts, as we have forgiven those who are in
debt to us" (Matt. 6:12).

A shift of accent from a church-centered theology to a kingdom-
centered theology will inspire Christians to be more concerned with
their neighbor and human society than with their own personal
interests.

Those who accept discipleship of Jesus must endeavor to rediscover the dynamism of his teaching. Rigidity in worship practices,
preoccupation with dogmatic formulas, and the institutionalism of
churches dull its thrust and render it innocuous.

Jesus transcended racist, classist, and religious bigotry by freely
associating with sinners, including women of bad repute, tax collectors, Zealots, and Samaritans. He contravened prevailing religious
customs and laws about food, fasts, table companionship, and the
like.

He was truly a liberator of the human person and of oppressed groups in society. At the beginning of his public ministry he defined his mission in the words of Isaiah. "He has anointed me. He has sent me to bring the good news to the poor, to proclaim liberty to captives, and to the blind new sight, to set the downtrodden free" (Luke 4:18). He contested the alienations of the day to which the poor and others were subjected. He introduced into religion an element of contestation with the evils of institutionalism.

Jesus and the Rich and Privileged

Jesus loved all human beings. But his love for them did not lead him to justify their personal or social sinfulness. His attitude toward riches and the rich is clear from several examples. He dined with Zaccheus, the senior tax collector. As a result of the visit Zaccheus said to him: "Look, sir, I am going to give half my property to the poor, and if I have cheated anybody I will pay him back four times the amount" (Luke 19:8). Earlier the crowd had murmured "he has gone to stay at a sinner's house."

Jesus knew how difficult it was to convert the rich to share their wealth. It is the central theme of the parable of Dives, the rich man, and the beggar Lazarus. After Dives died, he was in torment in Hades. He wanted Father Abraham to send Lazarus to his father's house, "since I have five brothers, to give them warning so that they do not come to this place of torment too." But Abraham replied that Moses and the prophets had not been able to convince the rich to live as true believers. "If they will not listen to Moses or to the prophets, they will not be convinced even if someone should rise from the dead" (Luke 16:31).

The incident of the rich young man who came to ask Jesus what he should do to inherit eternal life shows once again the centrality of sharing in Jesus' teaching. The young man said that he observed the Commandments; what else was required of him?

> Jesus said, "If you wish to be perfect, go and sell what you own and give the money to the poor, and you will have treasure in heaven; then come, follow me." But when the young man heard these words, he went away sad, for he was a man of great wealth [Matt. 19:20–22].

Jesus was not neutral in his attitude toward the rich and the poor. He called for a clear option in favor of poverty and the poor. Though he was gentle in his ways, he did not mince his words when he had to speak to the rich.

"Yes, I tell you again, it is easier for a camel to pass through the eye of a needle than for a rich man to enter the kingdom of heaven" (Matt. 19:24). It is perfectly clear that Jesus did not understand belonging to the kingdom in terms of external, nominal affiliation, or of attending to or watching temple ritual. He demands a total conversion of heart and life. "You cannot be the slave both of God and of money" (Luke 16:13).

Jesus dined with a Pharisee, but this did not stop him from castigating the social injustices and hypocrisy of the Pharisees:

> Alas for you Pharisees! You who pay your tithe of mint and rue and all sorts of garden herbs and overlook justice and the love of God! . . . Alas for you, because you are like the unmarked tombs that men walk on without knowing it! [Luke 11:42, 44].

A lawyer then said that when Jesus spoke as he just did, he insulted lawyers as well. And Jesus replied:

> Alas for you lawyers also, because you load on men burdens that are unendurable, burdens that you yourselves do not move a finger to lift. . . . Alas for you lawyers who have taken away the key of knowledge! You have not gone in [the kingdom; cf. Matt. 23:13] yourselves, and have prevented others going in who wanted to [Luke 11:46, 52].

These are clear stands taken by Jesus against the elitism of the privileged classes of his day.

The criterion of the final judgment brings all these points into clearer relief. In the ultimate reckoning, God is not pictured as asking us about our external sacramental life or even our particular religious beliefs. The unique criterion of judgment is that of loving service to the neighbor in need:

> Come, you whom my Father has blessed, take for your heri-
> tage the kingdom prepared for you since the foundation of the
> world. For I was hungry and you gave me food; . . . I was a
> stranger and you made me welcome; . . . in prison and you
> came to see me [Matt. 25:34–36].

It is important to keep in mind that this is the criterion for judging
every human being who has ever lived or will ever live on this earth.
It also founds an ecumenism as wide as the whole of human history
and as deep as the innermost depths of our individual personalities.
It is clear too that this criterion—service to others—is applicable to
every man, woman, and child. This is the one indispensable
sacrament—the sacrament of fellowship, of solidarity with the
neighbor in need.

The full theological implications of this teaching of Jesus still
remain to be elaborated in different directions, such as international
relationships, political commitment, and the meaning of Christian
community, sacraments, worship. In a world of immense poverty
side by side with unparalleled affluence, this criterion must be a
shattering challenge to a believer's conscience and way of life. True
love of God and neighbor cannot agree to a compromise with poverty in a world of plenty, of vast empty continents and the com-
pulsory sterilization of the poor in overpopulated countries, of the
enormous waste on armaments when the majority of humankind
needs food to combat malnutrition and starvation.

Jesus offers a profound challenge to the social conscience of those
who wish to follow him. In him there is no separation of the divine
from the human, of the supernatural from the natural, of the verti-
cal from the horizontal, of the spiritual from the socioeconomic.
Those who ask for bread should not be given a stone. Bread for
oneself is a material concern, but bread for another is a spiritual
concern.

The social teaching of Jesus has a great relevance for today when
whole societies have been built on individualism, elitism, consumerism, and the exploitation of the weak by the strong. We are
highly civilized barbarians, for we condemn millions to death by
starvation while others feast themselves to an early death. We are

technologically evolved, but spiritually retarded in living up to the message of the world religions. If only Christians would live out the basic message of Jesus, there would be so much more sharing in the world, and the whole of our socioeconomic life would change. Society would be more egalitarian. Those who have two coats would give one to the person who has none. The land resources of the earth would be more equitably distributed. The world, as Mahatma Gandhi said, has enough for everyone's need, though not for everyone's greed.

Jesus and the World System of His Day

Jesus was born as a colonial subject of a world empire. Very early in life he was a political exile, a refugee in Egypt, until Herod died and the Holy Family, making a political judgment, could return to their native land. Later on he was killed as an enemy of Caesar, a danger to the empire. Thus his life has much relevance to us when we consider the role of Christianity with reference to the world system today and the future of humanity.

The Roman empire was then at the height of its power. The emperor Augustus had given it a sense of unity and administrative cohesion. But its decline had already begun to set in. The Roman empire was built on discipline and military valor; good morals and filial piety were in high honor among writers of the time. But the decline of the empire was due to the ills of that same society. Booty from conquered territories had a corrupting influence on the nobility and the military.

Roman society was basically unequal and exploitative. Slaves formed about a third of the population. With the success of the empire, the upper classes gave themselves to lazy, luxurious living and moral debauchery. Family life broke down and divorce was widespread. Slaves were not regarded as "persons" with legal and human rights; they were "things" that belonged to their masters. Slaves had to labor hard and long while their masters and mistresses amused themselves. Discontent was rampant. It gave rise to several revolts of urban and agricultural slaves.

The Romans despised the peoples they conquered, though they

ruled them with a mixture of tact and firmness. They extorted heavy taxes from the colonies. They ruled them with the help of local collaborators, such as the traditional elites among a subjugated people.

Though the Roman soldiers were the ultimate defenders of the imperial rule, the Romans made use of traditional authority patterns for governing the Jews. Jewish society too was very unequal and hierarchical. The high priests represented religious as well as political and social authority. Jewish religious leaders lorded it over the ignorant poor.

Neither the Roman nor the Jewish concept of human freedom was applied to all persons. The human being was not respected as having intrinsic dignity, value, and rights. Power was used in the defense of the privileged classes. The majority of the Jewish people lived in fear both of nature and of social authority.

The Jews were unhappy with their exploited situation under the Romans. They had a proud feeling of racial superiority as the chosen people of God. Hence there were revolutionary currents among them. The Pharisees were more intransigent in their opposition to the Romans than were the Sadducees, who favored peaceful collaboration. The Zealots were a group that fomented armed rebellion to overthrow the Roman yoke.

We have to understand Jesus and his message against this background. Today we take the universal heritage of human rights almost for granted, even though dictatorships dominate the majority of the world's peoples. But at that time to propose a doctrine of the human dignity of every person was truly radical and revolutionary.

Jesus stressed the personal worth of all human beings regardless of their social condition or status. He helped persons understand that their worth did not depend on the prevailing social values of power, wealth, social position, physical strength, intellectual acumen, legal eminence, or even religion. Merely external laws had no moral binding force before God if they were unjust. This is the foundation of universal human responsibility and freedom. Historically it has been the ultimate stand of champions of freedom and justice over the centuries. Jesus laid down the principle of the rights of every human person as a child of God and a bearer of free will. He challenged persons not to fear even death, but to stand firm for truth, honesty, and justice.

Jesus lived his message of universal fellowship. He moved about with all. He offered all his love and friendship. Only the arrogant, the hypocritical, and the hard-hearted merited his reproaches. He was close to the socially rejected and marginalized. It is perhaps difficult for us today to understand this—we who live in a "democratic" age. How few of the elite of our society, even religious leaders, would feel at ease in the company of slum dwellers, migrant farm workers, or frustrated rebellious youth—not to mention prostitutes? Jesus was a threat to the social power elite because he practiced what he preached.

His interpersonal relationships carried a deep social significance. He was breaking through the taboos of his environment. Here was an eminently holy teacher making common cause with the down-and-out rabble. This was unthinkable in the Roman way of life, or even for the Jewish establishment. The way he lived was a challenge to others; his friendships were a threat to those who despised the ignorant masses.

In every instance of a clash of values he favored the dignity and freedom of the human person. He opposed the domination
- of the rigid law over genuine love;
- of the learned lawyer over the ignorant layperson;
- of the hypocritical Pharisee over the humble publican;
- of the shrewd priests over the simple faithful;
- of the guilty accusers over the adulterous woman;
- of the vendors in the temple over the worshipers outside;
- of the sumptuously well-fed Dives over the beggar Lazarus;
- of the exploiting rich over the miserable poor;
- of the supercilious Jew over the disdained Gentile;
- of the letter that kills over the spirit that vivifies;
- of superstition over true religion of the spirit;
- of formalism over sincerity;
- of unjust power over weakness;
- of hate over love.

Jesus is essentially a religious and spiritual leader. Hence his teaching has a much wider significance than that of a political strategy for a particular place or time. His message is universal; his life is an example for all time. He dealt with the most fundamental concerns of human beings. He was not trying to substitute another political regime for the Roman rule over the Jews. But he did open deeper channels to the human quest for righteousness in the political field too. As a Jewish religious leader he could not refrain from relating to his people's political issues. They were basic to its contemporary situation and expectations. Suffering under the yoke of alien oppression the Jews awaited a Messiah who, they thought, would be their political liberator. Politics and religion were so closely connected in the ancient world, including his own country, that Jesus could not have been without a political message and option. The high priests were not only religious leaders but also shared in the civil powers of the ruling class.

However, the liberation that he proposed in the political field also was at a deeper level. He taught that all power was to be put to service of others, especially the needy. He attacked the ways in which authority was being exercised by the civic and religious rulers of the day—who lorded it over their subjects. His community and his kingdom were to be different. "Anyone who wants to become great among you must be your servant, and anyone who wants to be first among you must be slave to all" (Mark 10:43). He was laying the foundations of a new humanity to be governed by an authority that is an expression of love and service, and not of brute force and exploitation. He washed the feet of his disciples, and he wanted them to do likewise. "If I, then, the Lord and Master, have washed your feet, you should wash each another's feet" (John 13:14). Power and authority has to be genuine service, honest and uncorrupt, not self-seeking and not wanting to perpetuate itself.

In all this Jesus contested the political structures and rulers of his day. He saw that Roman rule was maintained with the cooperation of the corrupt, hypocritical Jewish religious and social leaders. He recognized the responsibility of the collaborating local elite in the continued exploitation of the masses. Hence he castigated the Jewish oppressors even more than the Romans. He wanted the Jews to understand that the guilt of tyranny disfigured and burdened them too. So long as they did not give up false values of material wealth, sanctimonious prestige, power hunger, and narrow racialism they could not achieve lasting liberation even if they overcame the Romans. On the other hand if they continued merely in the adventurist Zealot way, he was afraid that Jerusalem would be destroyed by the Romans, as actually happened in A.D. 70.

For the political success of the total revolution that he preached, there had to be a profound change in values in the political field too among the Jews themselves. They must love their enemies (Luke 5:44). This was much more than any spiritual leader had ever asked of them. It meant an inner triumph over jealousy, selfishness, and revenge. It was the condition for a lasting triumph in which one oppressor would not simply replace another. It would also be the definitive victory over domination—for no one can really dominate those who are interiorly liberated.

Jesus and Imperialism

It is often argued that Jesus did not oppose the Roman empire and hence he did not condemn imperialism. The text "render to Caesar what belongs to Caesar, and to God what belongs to God" is usually quoted in this connection. This text has been subject to much controversy over the centuries. Temporal rulers have often used it to claim the loyalty of their subjects. Others have argued that loyalty to God sets limits to civil authority.

The Pharisees and the Herodians, who held opposite views, conspired to trap Jesus in some public statement. He dealt with them in a way that confounded both the Herodians who wanted taxes paid subserviently and the Zealots who were for armed rebellion against Rome. Jesus did not make a categorical statement in favor of the payment of taxes; the Zealots and even the Pharisees would have denounced him as a traitor to the Jewish cause. What Jesus did was to expose the hypocrisy of his questioners. He more or less told them, "you yourselves accept and use the coins with which the Roman tax is paid; this means you acknowledge Caesar's sovereignty. Sort it out among yourselves. But remember there are also the claims of God." They were dumbfounded because they were exposed as hypocrites before the crowd. He had also shown them to be the real exploiters of the poor. This reply is similar to Jesus' masterly response to the accusers of the woman taken in adultery. "The one who is without sin, let him throw the first stone."

It is, however, significant that one of the chief accusations against Jesus at his trial before Pilate was: "We found this man inciting our people to revolt, opposing payment of the tribute to Caesar, and claiming to be Christ, a king" (Luke 23:2). When Pilate sought to release him the Jews cried out, "If you set him free you are no friend of Caesar's; anyone who makes himself king is defying

Caesar'' (John 19:12). The chief priests shouted for his crucifixion saying ''We have no king but Caesar'' (John 19:15).

Jesus said, ''my kingdom is not of this world''—that is, he does not subscribe to the values of power, money, and prestige as do earthly kings. There is a contradiction in values between his kingdom and the Roman empire. If he did not think they were contradictory, he could have explained it to Pilate, the chief priests and the people. Why was he silent against the charges? Jesus, who could give such devastating answers to his critics, would not have wanted to die under false accusation, if he was in favor of Roman imperialism. He had only to say so and the Roman governor and soldiers would have protected him.

The role of the Roman governor Pontius Pilate in the trial and crucifixion of Jesus was a clear indication that the Roman authorities feared Jesus because of his teaching and his popularity. Pontius Pilate participated in the torture of Jesus (Matt. 27:1–31, Mark 15:16–20).

Roman soldiers went to apprehend Jesus in the garden of Gethsemane (John 18:3); Roman soldiers tortured him inside the palace of the governor; they led him to Calvary; '' they crucified him and divided his garments.'' They put up the inscription ''King of the Jews,'' implying sedition; they reported his death to Pilate and guarded the tomb (Matt. 27:27–38; John 19:12–24; Mark 15:16–39, 44–45). Pilate allowed his soldiers to participate in the arrest, trial, torture, and execution of Jesus. Philo of Alexandria, the Jewish philosopher, and Josephus speak of Pilate as brutal, corrupt, and harsh in the suppression of Jewish nationalists and insurgents.

Jesus was not an armed rebel like the Zealots (some of whom were among his disciples); nor was he a conformist pro-Roman like the Herodians, or a hypocrite like the Pharisees who were in theory opposed to the Roman taxes but in practice paid them. He criticized the Zealots for their narrow nationalism, racialism, and Jewish sense of superiority in matters of religion.

Though Jesus was not a violent insurgent, he was killed on the charge of subverting the people and inciting them not to pay taxes to the Romans. Pilate authorized his crucifixion. Jesus did not deny these charges, and consequently had to face death.

Jesus may not have condemned the Roman empire directly but his entire teaching and way of life were opposed to the values of the empire, especially in its corrupt stage. The Roman empire was based on military conquest, and no one will doubt that the use of armed power for building empires is contrary to the teaching of Jesus. The Roman empire was built on and for greed, and this is opposed to Jesus' teaching on unselfish sharing. The Roman empire used power to dominate and exploit other peoples, and this was condemned by Jesus in his teaching on power as service. Roman society was one in which slaves were ill treated as mere "things" and not persons; Jesus taught that all human beings are children of God and lovingly cared for by the Father. The Roman way of life at the time was one of an aristocracy given to extortion, moral debauchery, and the assuaging of the masses with bread and circuses.

There was an inherent incompatibility between the values of Jesus and those of the decadent Roman empire. This was seen more clearly in later years when his followers spread to Rome and other parts of the empire. They refused to accept Caesar as God. They were persecuted. They had to go underground. They were tried and put to death. Over three centuries, martyrs numbered in the thousands.

What Jesus taught concerning love, justice, and freedom became in the course of the centuries the rallying point of revolutionary struggles for these values. The political traditions of Western countries bear its mark, derived from Christian thought via St. Augustine, through the Middle Ages, to modern times. Marxism too is profoundly influenced by the Judeo-Christian tradition of struggle for a just society.

At the present time the teaching of Jesus concerning power as service can be an inspiration for an emphasis on a pattern of socio-economic development in favor of the masses rather than of privileged elites. It can also be the motivation for questioning a militarism that relies more on the power of armed forces than on the consent of the people.

Christianity, along with the other world religions, can be a profound, motivating force for a permanent revolution in history. Mass secular revolutionary forces have a powerful impact on a people, especially when led by charismatic self-sacrificing leaders. But once the major battles are won and revolutionaries are installed in political power, the vision tends to fade and human selfishness asserts itself. The dedicated radicals of yesterday are soon replaced by power-seekers, bureaucrats, and others who seek the fruits of revolution without paying their price. Revolution tends to breed its own power elite that gradually alienates itself from the masses.

Jesus and Women

Jesus lived in a society that was oppressive of women. It is said that the devout Jewish man used to thank God for not having been born a woman. We may not be able to find in the life and teaching of Jesus all the elements required for shaping a theological foundation for the women's movements today. We see, however, from his life that he was against the exploitation of women.

He was a liberated person in his relationships with women. His parables reveal an understanding of feminine psychology—for example, the poor widow's mite, the woman with the lost coin, the joys of childbirth. We see him relaxed in the house of Mary and Martha, sharing in their joys and sorrows as one of them. He teaches them the deeper meaning of life. He was friendly and affectionate to Mary Magdalene. He was understanding to the sinful woman who spent money on oil to anoint his feet; he appreciated the meaningfulness of the gesture, the repentance and affection it implied. He chose married persons as his disciples and apostles. He healed the mother-in-law of Simon Peter in whose house he stayed. When she was cured she ministered to them with characteristic feminine solicitude.

Women cared for him. They were part of his group of followers. They went with him to Calvary. They believed in him beyond death and were the first to find the empty tomb and proclaim the resurrection. Mary, his mother, must have given him a love both tender and strong. Mary was with him throughout his life. She followed him to the foot of the cross—a source of strength and sorrow to him. In his dying moments he shows his solicitude for her, entrusting her to John, his beloved disciple.

Jesus' human concern for women in difficult circumstances is seen in his attitude toward prostitutes. They are mentioned in the gospels as being among his followers. That Jesus appealed to them can indicate many things to us. He was open to them; he probably listened to their life stories. They must have felt free to speak to him. They must have had confidence in him.

It was not an honorable thing for a religious leader to be found in the company of prostitutes, and that at a time when men and women did not mix so freely in society. Jesus was accused of being a person of unsound mind and ill-repute because of the company he kept, or because of those who followed him. But he was prepared to face the difficulties of being an innovator, of being unconventional. He risked public ridicule by being friendly to persons hypocritically rejected by the "respectable" society of the day.

He probably understood the plight of the prostitutes, why they were reduced to a condition of selling their bodies, why they accepted a role that men privately desired and publicly scorned. He may have seen the causes in the social conditions of the time—that these women could not earn a living otherwise. He was much more critical of those who prostituted their minds for power and wealth and were unrepentant.

Even if there were no women among the twelve apostles, there were many among his disciples. At his passion the women who had come with him from Galilee followed behind him. They saw the tomb and how his body was buried. Then they went home to prepare spices and perfumes. On the first day of the week, at dawn, they went to the tomb. They found the stone rolled back from the entrance. On their return, they told all these things to the eleven and the others.

Womanhood had a central role in the most significant events in the life of Jesus: his conception, gestation, birth and childhood; his public ministry; his death on the cross. His dead body was cared for by women, and the risen Jesus appeared first to women. Is it not strange, then, that some churches should consider women unfit to preside over the celebration of the sacramental presence of the body of Jesus in the Eucharist? Some of his apostles—Simon Peter, for instance—would not be admitted to a seminary today for training for the priesthood: he was married. Cultural conditioning has here been allowed to have a greater impact on church discipline than even the example of Jesus. The churches would be helped in their self-purification from sexism if they adhered more loyally to the example set by Jesus.

Jesus and Religion

Jesus distinguished clearly between real spirituality and the mere externals of religion or religiosity.

The traditional Jewish religion of the day had become very much a matter of religious formalism. Emphasis was on external rituals. Religious authorities dominated the lives of believers by imposing onerous obligations on them. The letter of the law was considered more important than its spirit. In the main spheres of life—in work, food, social relationships, family life, private prayer, public religious observances—a plethora of minute details had to be scrupulously adhered to. The religious and sociopolitical authorities controlled the ideas and actions of the people by dominating its mentality and customs. Religion was a factor of social domination; it implanted in the mind of the people the sense of obligation to observe all the customs and rituals. The authority of God and of the law was invoked for this.

Jesus made a powerful critique of the Jewish religion of the day. He came into the world to liberate human beings, and this included liberation from religious structures that embodied sin. Judaism at the time was an alienation, a corruption of what religion should be. It had built up a system of taboos, inhibitions, formalisms, and rites that were walls of separation between person and person, and between the people and God.

Jesus was severe in his criticism of the prevailing religion:

> Alas for you, scribes and Pharisees, you hypocrites! You who travel over sea and land to make a single proselyte, and when you have him you make him twice as fit for hell as you are. Alas for you, blind guides! You who say, "If a man swears by the Temple, it has no force; but if a man swears by the gold of the Temple, he is bound." Fools and blind! For which is of greater worth, the gold or the Temple that makes the gold sacred? [Matt. 23:13–15].
>
> Oh, you Pharisees! You clean the outside of cup and plate, while inside yourselves you are filled with extortion and wickedness. Fools! Did not he who made the outside make the inside too? [Luke 11:39–40].

Jesus exposed and corrected the ostentation that surrounded religious practices of the day:

> Be careful not to parade your good deeds before men to attract their notice. . . . When you give alms, do not have it

> trumpeted before you. . . . When you give alms, your left
> hand must not know what your right hand is doing [Matt.
> 6:1-3].
>
> When you fast do not put on a gloomy look. . . . When you
> fast, put oil on your head and wash your face, so that no one
> will know you are fasting except your Father who sees all that
> is done in secret [Matt. 6:16-18].

Jesus invited his followers to great spiritual heights. Sanctity is unselfish love:

> You have learned how it was said: You must love your
> neighbor and hate your enemy. But I say this to you: love your
> enemies and pray for those who persecute you; in this way you
> will be sons of your Father in heaven, for he causes his sun to
> rise on bad men as well as good, and his rain to fall on honest
> and dishonest men alike. . . . You must therefore be perfect
> just as your heavenly Father is perfect [Matt. 5:43-48].

Jesus teaches that the essence of religion is in a deep inner relationship to the Father and one's conscience. It does not consist in
mere externals such as almsgiving, fasting, praying. True holiness is
in the interiority of our actions: rend your hearts, not your garments
(cf. Joel 2:13). The essential value of worship is in your inner participation in the spirit of self-sacrifice that love implies: the offering
at the altar should be accompanied by purity of heart and genuine
love of others. In this Jesus was reemphasizing the basic message of
the Old Testament, especially of the prophets. Being deeply spiritual
implies authentic human experience and witness.

In this context we can understand better his attitude toward the
religious institutions of his day. He was not a priest of the Jewish
religion. If we regard him as a priest—and high priest—it is not in
terms of a cultic or administrative priesthood, even of a Christian
denomination. He is a priest in a more fundamental sense; he medi-
ates between God and humankind at a deeper level of being and
with a more universal significance. His priesthood is one in which
sacrifice is to consist not so much in externals as in love and service,
in which prayer is not merely with the lips but in the heart, and in
which ritual is for human beings and not human beings for ritual.

He did not seek privileges for himself. He did not want to stand apart from others with symbols of distinction—not even sacred symbols. The lesson he teaches us is that it is more important for the teacher and leader to be identified with the people than to be separated, distinguished, and elitist.

He was a priest who did not belong to a priestly caste. He did not distinguish himself from others in anything except his loving service and self-sacrifice. As the master he washed the feet of his disciples and invited them to follow him.

He wanted to liberate men and women from the dominance of cult, from the tendency to make of religion a sacred ghetto outside the so-called profane world. He placed the sacred within the depths of the secular, the profane, the human. He was a lay teacher of religion, a rabbi. He encountered God in the context of ordinary life—as a carpenter's son, in the streets, in homes, in boats, on the wayside, by the lake, on the mountain, in the desert. The cultic aspect of religion was to be brought into alignment with justice, mercy, and love. Religion was to be of spirit and truth: religious ceremonial was to be patterned on the most elemental features of earthly life—sharing bread and wine, anointing with oil, laying on of hands.

Jesus began a movement of fellowship and community; he did not found a canonical or administrative organization. But there has always been a tendency for organized religion to become more a structure and less a community, more a legalistic inertia and less a moral force for renewal. He advocated sincerity, truth, justice, sharing, and selfless love. These are permanent values in all religious experience and expression. They inspire the liberation that Jesus came to bring to religion.

Jesus was opposed to the religionism of the Jews. They were proud of being called the chosen people and proud of their religion as a legal system whose external performance was thought to be salvific. But all religionism is incompatible with Jesus' view of life, virtue, and true religion. Insofar as Christianity is religionist, it militates against Jesus' respect for and God's love of all human beings.

Christianity needs to be at once more deeply human and more intensely God-centered: more human, in understanding the human predicament of persons and the contradictions within our exploitative societies; and more God-centered in understanding that the depths of spiritual experience are in a relationship to the divine, beyond everything that mere external religious organizations can interpret or mediate, much less control. Contact with the other religions can help Christianity rediscover this dimension of an integral liberative thrust within its own inspirations. In certain countries small groups of Christians are becoming more and more aware of this deeper meaning of Christian religious and spiritual experience.

THE COSMIC CHRIST AND UNIVERSAL FULFILLMENT

The human life of Jesus of Nazareth is a supreme example for us of personal commitment to human liberation; the revelation of Jesus as the cosmic Christ gives us further insights into the evolution of the entire universe and of human history. The historical life of Jesus helps us especially in our understanding of the micro-level of our personal own lives; consideration of the cosmic Christ brings a deeper revelation of the wider macro-significance of our own lives within the whole of reality. Jesus teaches that human beings acquire a radically new relationship in doing the will of God. "Who is my mother? Who are my brothers? . . . Anyone who does the will of my Father in heaven is my brother and sister and mother" (Matt. 12:48–50).

Jesus himself tells us in the gospels that his is not the last word in revelation. The Father will send the Spirit who will be given to all humankind. The Spirit will reveal many more wonderful things and achieve more than what Jesus himself achieved. "I will not leave you orphans," he promised.

The Gospel of St. John begins with a universalist vision of the whole of reality and the place of Christ in it.

> In the beginning was the Word:
> the Word was with God
> and the Word was God.
> He was with God in the beginning.
> Through him all things came to be,
> Not one thing has its being but through him.

All that came to be had life in him
and that life was the light of men, . . .
The Word was made flesh,
he lived among us [John 1:1–14].

Christ is related to God from eternity and to the whole universe in
its return to the Creator in a fulfilled manner. Jesus the Christ,
through the mysteries of his incarnation, death, resurrection, and
second coming, links the divine and the human. In him God, nature, history, and all human beings of all time are mysteriously
intertwined in a manner that we cannot fully fathom. We can only
contemplate it and try to have it reflected better in our own lives.

St. Paul gives us a deeper intuition into the role of Jesus as the
cosmic Christ. According to Paul, Jesus Christ holds all things
together. He is the deeper being of all things animate and inani-
mate.

He is the image of the unseen God
and the first-born of all creation,
for in him were created
all things in heaven and on earth:
everything visible and everything invisible,
Thrones, Dominations, Sovereignties, Powers—
all things were created through him and for him.
Before anything was created, he existed,
and he holds all things in unity.
Now the Church is his body,
he is its head.

As he is the Beginning,
he was first to be born from the dead,
so that he should be first in every way;
because God wanted all perfection
to be found in him
and all things to be reconciled through him and for him,
everything in heaven and everything on earth,
when he made peace
by his death on the cross [Col. 1:15–20].

In the fullness of God dwelling in Christ, all things are reconciled; there can be no discrimination based on color, religion, economic status, education, ethnic background or sex:

> In that image there is no room for distinction between Greek and Jew, between the circumcised or the uncircumcised, or between barbarian and Scythian, slave and free man. There is only Christ: he is everything and he is in everything [Col. 3:11].

Christ is also the principle of a universal human solidarity. Paul attributes a wide cosmic role to Christ, englobing in his being everything that was, is, and ever will be, uniting in him the Creator and the created, "in whom all the jewels of wisdom and knowledge are hidden" (Col. 2:3).

It is important for us that we understand the nature of all being that is thus revealed. This is the deepest level of Christian ontology, a grasping of the nature of being or reality. Christ the Lord implies a much wider dimension of being than does Jesus of Nazareth, though Jesus is the Christ. It is not my intention to try to work out the exactness of the relationship between Jesus of Nazareth and Christ the Lord, but rather to point out the different dimensions of their riches. Unfortunately Christian reflection has largely neglected the cosmic implications of the lordship of Christ, or has been satisfied with affirming it in terms of the divinity of Jesus. The historical conflicts concerning the personality of Jesus have to some extent clouded the magnificent vision of the understanding of all reality as in Christ or "christic."

A Fundamental Theological Inadequacy

One of the reasons for this neglect of the ontological universality of the christic has been the penchant of Western theology to maintain the difference between the Creator and the created, the infinite and the finite. The Western mind has emphasized this difference partly because its logic is based on the principle of contradiction: what is, is not what it is not. On the contrary, oriental logic is more analogical, more synthetic. It seeks unity of being more than divergences; it sees continuity as more basic than discontinuity. The

West has been preoccupied with avoiding pantheism and has thus drawn a categorical dividing line between God and nature. Oriental thought sees one as emanating from the other, one suffused by the other, even though dependent and transitory. These rather subtle differences of approach have had profound implications in the interpretation of theology and spirituality.

Another influence on Christian theology has been its attachment to Aristotelian philosophy. In the Aristotelian tradition, God was at best a being of himself—an *ens a se*—the uncreated cause. This cause was distinct from the *ens ab alio,* dependent being. Such a view helped in the scientific, rational analysis of the world, of matter, and of human nature. It was a valuable point of departure for the study of nature as a separate being, having its own "autonomy." Western science and rationality of analysis benefited immensely from this approach. However, the Western tradition and Christian theology tended to neglect the intimate link between matter and spirit, universe and God, the natural and the numinous, between Jesus and the cosmic universality of Christ. The baptizing of Aristotle by Thomas Aquinas did not help much in elucidating the underpinning of all being; rather it tended to sharpen differences.

The Protestant Reformation and the Catholic Counter-Reformation further saw to it that Christian theology concentrated on intraecclesiastical debates, if not diatribes. For many centuries, while the modern world was being constituted largely by Western rationality, the churches concentrated their attention on issues such as the real presence of Jesus in the Eucharist, the relationship of Scripture and tradition, papal infallibility, auricular confession, apostolic succession, Latin and the vernacular in the liturgy, celibacy of the clergy, divorce, indulgences, and the like. The tragedy was not merely that the churches were divided and stayed divided, but also that they were blinded to the larger dimensions of Christian revelation itself. The cosmic ontology of the Scriptures was bypassed in favor of narrow, exclusivist "Christian" theologies.

A return to the cosmic dimension of Christ can be an important contribution for rendering Christians more docile to the Spirit of God and more open to genuine dialogue with persons of other religious traditions and ideologies.

Due to the neglect of the universal and cosmic Christ, Christians claimed a monopoly of Christ. They did not differentiate between the founding of the church by Jesus of Nazareth and the much wider influence of the cosmic Christ. The church was founded at a particular time, in a particular place, but the work of Christ is universal—being the alpha and the omega of all things. Christians tended to monopolize not only Jesus and Christ but also God. They understood the church as the unique medium of salvation—and here the church was understood narrowly as the historical institutional church, whether Roman Catholic, Orthodox, or Protestant.

Today there is a general malaise in Western theology. The limitations of earlier approaches are seen. The theology of Christendom has led to a dead end. Theology at peace with individualistic capitalism has been incapable of inspiring Christians to a responsible attitude toward a more just social order. A church-centered theology is inadequate for Christians to relate meaningfully to the planetary reality of our times.

Theology in Western countries is being challenged from two principal directions. On the one hand it has to respond to the personalist revolution of women and men affirming their own personal dignity and individual responsibility. This is leading to a deep questioning of the legalistic mentality still lingering within many traditional and authoritative church circles, including religious congregations.

On the other hand the churches have to respond to the social revolution of our times, which today has a global dimension. The countries of Asia, Africa, and to a certain extent Latin America want not merely to achieve political independence. They wish to undo the whole world order set up as a result of Western expansionism and colonialism. They demand a new relationship among peoples with reference to imports and exports. A further evolution to be expected is the call for a restructuring of the world power system, the restricting of national sovereignties, as well as the redistribution of the earth's resources and land surface among the peoples of the earth in a more equitable manner.

Western theology is still very far from dealing satisfactorily with these two basic issues facing humanity today: the personalist and social revolutions.

The Christic Dimension

Meditation on the cosmic dimension of Christ can lead us to a reevaluation of some of the basic injustices of what has passed for

Christian thought. Creation has to be rethought in terms of the christic presence in all created reality. Our attitude to the universe will be deeply influenced by such a consideration. Respect for nature and the prevention of its pollution, exhaustion, and destruction would acquire a christic dimension.

The incarnation and redemption would have to be thought out not only in terms of the life and times of Jesus of Nazareth but also in terms of their associated universal significance as engaging the cosmic dimension of Christ. Human history would then be reevaluated as the privileged area of the christic return of conscious and intelligent humanity to the Creator. Revelation would have to be understood as a continuing process, begun with creation itself and never ending. The message of God to humankind would have to be humbly discerned in nature, in history, and within our own selves—in addition to the written Scriptures and Christian tradition. The other religions, ideologies, and movements of humanity will also have to be discerned as part of this christic manifestation. A spirituality for a planetary age will then be a consequence of meditation on the world, on the agony of human beings in it, and on the designs of a divine providence for all creation.

The Scriptures too contain an eschatological vision of the ultimate stage of human evolution—the final realization of the kingdom of God:

> Then I saw a new heaven and a new earth; the first heaven and the first earth had disappeared now, and there was no longer any sea. I saw the holy city, and the new Jerusalem, coming down from God out of heaven, as beautiful as a bride all dressed for her husband. Then I heard a loud voice call from the throne, "You see this city? Here God lives among men. He will make his home among them; they shall be his people, and he will be their God; his name is God-with-them. He will wipe away all tears from their eyes; there will be no more death, and no more mourning or sadness. The world of the past has gone" [Rev. 21:1–8].

This apocalyptic vision of the new Jerusalem is an inspiration for believers to hope in the final achievement of a universal happiness. It is also a promise and a teaching that salvation is communitarian.

The kingdom of God is a common state of beatitude shared by all. Some place it outside the universe and its history. Others see it as causally linked to the evolution of the universe and of humanity.

Reflection on the cosmic dimension of Christ can be a source of theology and spirituality for a New International Economic Order. It can point to the struggle that the peoples of the world have to undergo for there to be an effective restructuring of the world order based on justice and fellowship. At the global level the exploited peoples of Asia, Africa, and Latin America are in the process of trying to work out their own economic and political liberation. Christians of the so-called Third World can contribute much at this stage of world history by relating the intuitions and inspiration of Jesus Christ to their own aspirations and struggles.

Unfortunately the economic and power gaps among the world's peoples are widening. The countries whose wealth is growing rapidly—at the expense of others—are mainly ones whose people claim to be followers of Christ. The universal church has still very far to go before it even articulates a theology adequate to meet the challenge of a total restructuring of the world in the direction of the kingdom of God. Strangely it is mainly in the socialist countries—which do not officially accept the sovereignty of God—that principles of sharing are better realized. Communism proposes universal principles for the realization of international social justice through world socialism. Other ideologies and social systems have not yet even elaborated a plan for the ending of exploitation of person by person and of nation by nation.

The love and service of Christ is, in a sense, something more than the love of the historical Jesus of Nazareth, for the christic dimension implies a universality. The spirituality of the Christian must therefore include a love of the whole of humanity in its return to the Creator; it also requires a love and service of the universe, and of our planet earth. Christian spirituality has to be open to the good in all others whatever be their religion or ideology, for Christ is all in all. Christians have to be both radical and conservative—radical in order to participate in the revolutionary changes that reshape our societies for the better and conservative in order to preserve what is valuable in all ages and cultures. They are called on to conserve the radicality of the revelation in Jesus Christ.

This is an important challenge to all believers in Christ, especially those in the Western countries and the local elites of poor nations. A rethinking of Christian theology is essential today for both the personal fulfillment of each unique human person and the global survival and evolution of the human race and of the universe.

Chapter 10

The Churches Called
to Radical Conversion

From a consideration of the core of Christian revelation, of the search of human beings for meaning in life, and of nature under attack by human exploitation we see that the principal mission of Christians and the churches as communities of believers is to foster the conditions for the self-realization and fulfillment of each and every person and for the full flowering of nature. This has to be undertaken in concert with all other persons of good will, whatever be their faith or ideology.

THE PLANETARY CONCEPT OF MISSION

The traditional concept of mission and evangelism gave priority to presenting the Word of God in an asocial, individualistic, nonhistorical manner. The objective was to establish a group of believers as a local church or denomination in a given area. What was most important was the quantitative growth of the church and the acceptance of the core of dogma, the moral code, and the worship forms of the missionizing church.

Each church set up its own institutions: parishes, schools, hospitals, social service centers, development projects. All these, however, had little to do with a transformation of social relationships in the national community. Each church tended to think of its own self-promotion as the only goal of its activities.

193

The motivating vision was that Christianity was the best, if not the unique, essential channel of salvation. Because so many non-Western peoples had no opportunity of knowing Jesus Christ and his teaching, Christians had to undertake the arduous task of planting the church everywhere on earth, so that more and more persons would have access to eternal salvation.

This perspective in fact generated much generosity and evangelical activity. It resulted in the birth of thousands of local churches in Africa, Asia, and Latin America. However, the entire undertaking was vitiated in its alliance with an exploitative world politico-economic system, and Western ideological, cultural, ecclesiastical, and sexist domination.

A renewed, planetary concept of mission and evangelism has to give priority to the fostering of relationships of solidarity among persons and peoples based on the biblical values of the rule of righteousness, the kingdom of God. The churches must be directly and primarily concerned with just relationships among peoples and in regard to nature, so that human life may be happy and fulfilling for all, within the limits of our human capabilities and the resources of nature.

A new ecclesiology or self-understanding of the churches is implied by such an orientation. They are to be part of the movement of humanity to go forward collectively toward the kingdom of God in the course of the evolution of human history over time and space. The understanding of God's word has to be within this context. Worship should relate to this collective effort, should motivate, purify, and celebrate it.

Proclamation and Witness

The proclamation that Jesus desires is an invitation to genuine discipleship—that is, to love one another as he loves us. It is a call to self-sacrificial love of one's neighbor. Proclamation by evangelism and building the Christian community by evangelization must be primarily an effort to foster love and sharing among persons and nations. The evangelizer who proclaims the Word and makes known the name of Jesus as savior, but does nothing about a tragic social situation is like the priest and the Levite in Jesus' parable of the Good Samaritan (Luke 10:30–37). Evangelical witness must integrate word and deed. If there is any doubt about which is prior, Jesus himself made clear that it is not the one who says "Lord, Lord" who is saved, but the one who does the will of the Father.

Difficulties arise when witness to evangelical love goes against the interests of one's own nation. Some church groups see evangelism as a way to promote their own national priorities, or to prove the superiority of their way of life. Church groups sometimes rush aid to poor countries in order to show how defective their governments are, but do nothing about similar issues when caused by their own government. The different attitudes of such groups concerning present-day problems in Afghanistan, Poland, Somalia, Uganda, Vietnam, El Salvador, South Africa, Guatemala, Haiti, Chile, and elsewhere make it clear that Christians do use the gospel for their own denominational or national advantage. Procapitalistic groups may lament the sufferings of refugees in Afghanistan, but turn a blind eye to the problems in El Salvador. Some Christians stress the repression in Haiti and South Africa, but gloss over similar or worse evils in Kampuchea or Somalia.

The gospel is a call to our collective conversion to the values of the kingdom of God. Conversion is especially difficult when we ourselves are oppressors or beneficiaries of oppression. It is a betrayal of the gospel when evangelistic groups accept invitations by repressive foreign regimes and carry out high-powered evangelical campaigns there, preach peace and resignation, but say hardly a word about the yoke of oppression forced on the masses by the same rulers. This is the proclamation of a disincarnate and caricatured Christ. It is bad witness as well as bad evangelism. It is a mockery of God and his kingdom.

Whatever the social order in a given locality, Christians are called to relevant and consistent proclamation and witness. The only real option is between genuine Christian witness and conformism—whatever be the social system: capitalist, socialist, or other. Conformists tend to accept the prevailing social order, for what they seek is their own advantage and survival. On the other hand those who stand for the values of righteousness are never fully coopted by any prevailing system.

The cross is encountered mainly in witnessing within one's own situation and suffering the consequences of Christian obedience and discipleship. That is how Jesus suffered under the prevailing powers of his day. And the early Christians were martyred by imperial Rome. This is also why there are many genuine martyrs for the faith in many places today—in the First, Second, and Third Worlds. Jesus promised to be with his disciples until the end of the world— for there will always be need of his sustenance.

Secular Reality and the Kingdom of God

Secular reality is the whole world. It is the place and time in which the kingdom of God has to come into being. In that sense the whole of secular reality is the focus of Christian mission.

The world, or secular reality, is also a subject of Christian mission, and not merely its term or object. The world can bear a message from God to Christians also, as well as to the churches individually and collectively. God is present in all reality by the power and love of creation. The Spirit of God is in the world. "God so loved the world that he sent his only Son" to give his life for the world. God cares for the world more than he does for churches. Churches began only about 1950 years ago, whereas humans have been on earth for hundreds of thousands of years. Christian church membership has never constituted the majority of the world population. God's revelation and grace operate in very large measure beyond the confines of institutional church membership. This is no less true in the modern world of secularization, when so many baptized Christians are "unchurched" persons.

Historically too the churches have been often evangelized by secular society. It was persons who were not close to the churches who helped open the churches to such values as modern science, democracy, socialism, women's liberation, the emancipation of workers, youth, and the peoples of the Third World. Secular forces helped free the churches from intolerant attitudes toward the freedom to read, write, publish, speak, to have control over one's own body, marry, respect other religions, and respect intellectual freedom including biblical research.

God of History

The God of creation is also the God of history, drawing humanity and the earth toward its fulfillment in the ultimate kingdom. He showed by his concern for the oppressed people of Israel in Egypt how he cared for them and their liberation. A church that does not pay serious attention to society to discern the signs of needed liberative action is a church that does not listen to God speaking to it in the medium of human events. Such a church worships a God made to suit its own needs, rather than the God of the Bible who marches at the head of the crusade for human liberation. The dechristianization of the European working classes in the nineteenth century is easily understandable: the churches were linked to the capitalist class and did not seriously listen to the groaning of the workers under the cruel yoke of oppression. It was in such a situation that Karl Marx and Frederick Engels wrote the *Communist Manifesto* of 1848.

All of us have a tendency to make God suit our own needs and justify our privileges. Then we become idolatrous, worshiping our own creations rather than the liberating God. But inasmuch as the God of history sides with the poor, it can be said that the poor, the marginalized, and the oppressed are a *locus theologicus,* a source of revelation, to us of God. They make known the exigencies of the kingdom of God. So too does nature when it groans under the weight of its exploitation and misuse.

Vision and Goals

Because God cares for persons individually, in and through society and history, the mission of the churches has to be discerned in relation to a vision of personal fulfillment and integral societal development. Each person's search for meaning in life can give an idea of what can contribute to the true happiness of individuals. Christian revelation sees personal fulfillment in giving oneself for others in as unselfish a manner as possible, without, of course, neglecting one's duty to oneself.

Our collective, overall goal must be integral human liberation. This demands an acceptance of persons and groupings and nations by one another and the dismantling of socioeconomic structures based on the exploitation of one group or nation by another. This is an ideal, a utopia, an almost unrealistic dream. Yet the better urges of the human spirit and the promises of God in the Scriptures are of such a nature.

The churches should try to identify the feasible goals toward which they could contribute at different levels: personal and social; local, national, and international. Society will always give evidence of issues that may require priority attention. Long-term goals can be worked out from an evaluation of the broader issues that the world as a whole has to face. We have identified some of them in chapter 4. They include an end to the arms race and the despoiling of nature, the adoption of a simpler lifestyle by the affluent, the redistribution of resources and land among peoples, a world authority, and the subordination of the use of technology to human needs and rights.

RADICAL CONVERSION

In discussions on Christian concern for social issues an argument that is often put forward is that Christians and churches should be concerned with personal, spiritual issues and not be involved with public affairs, which are really political and should be left to other agencies and to persons in public life.

We must retort that the New Testament makes it perfectly clear that there can be no true love of God that is not also love of neighbor. "Anyone who says 'I love God,' and hates his brother, is a liar, since a man who does not love the brother that he can see cannot love God, whom he has never seen. So this is the commandment that he has given us, that anyone who loves God must also love his brother" (1 John 4:20–21). In the world of today, love of neighbor cannot, for example, be indifferent to the fact that millions of human beings suffer from malnutrition. And food necessarily involves employment, which in turn will involve local, national, and international policies and decision-making.

The true contemplative is called to a radical love of neighbor, and the revolutionary is a type of contemplative who has opted for an active struggle to realize the vision seen in the meditation of God, humanity, and the universe today. The central act of conversion required in human lives and societies is to accept and respect each person and group for their own intrinsic worth, dignity, and rights.

We become our better selves when we are truly other-centered and not self-seeking. This is what underlies the yearning of the human heart for a nobler existence. This is what makes human life more respectful of others, more responsible, more bearable, meaningful, happy, beautiful, and fulfilling. It is also a difficult and permanent struggle that has to be waged throughout life, because selfishness is so ingrained in us and in social structures.

Personal and Societal Conversion

Throughout our reflection on the planetary tasks facing mankind today, we have to keep in mind the twofold perspective of the internal and the external, the personal and the societal. Transformation of both are essential for genuine conversion. They are inseparable in real life. The truth of change in one can be verified by its impact on the other.

A social structure is a more or less permanent solidification of relationships. Relationships, in turn, embody values, attitudes, and mentalities. Real changes in social structures must therefore be based on and lead to changes in mentalities of the persons in a society. Similarly, a conversion of minds must lead to transformations in social relationships and structures. The external is a manifestation of the internal, and the internal mind of persons is formed in relationship to society. Genuine conversion has to be both internal and external, personal and societal, contemplative and active, self-fulfilling and other-centered.

This is at the core of the teachings of the world religions, the substance of their ancient wisdom. Jesus teaches it and exemplifies it in his life. It is the "passover" from death to life, the dying unto self to which Jesus bears witness. All the major living faiths have a similar call to self-transcendence, to living for others, beyond selfishness, in harmonious relationships with others and therefore with oneself and the divine. All the major religions teach that unselfish service to others is the secret of human happiness. The best in the ideologies of democracy, socialism, and humanism have the same core message.

The Christian churches should therefore consider such a twofold conversion essential to their mission. For the followers of Jesus, some form of participation in the struggles for human liberation from oppression of all types should be the norm, the minimum required of discipleship. Some are called to go further and, like the master, offer their life for others. "A man can have no greater love than to lay down his life for his friends," as Jesus said (John 15:13).

The believer has to participate in struggle for liberation in a spirit of love for all, without bitterness and hatred. This is a service that religion can render to revolutionary struggles for human liberation. For revolution, too, needs to be humanized by deeper values of such a nature. Revolution in turn can help purify institutionalized religions and teach them some aspects of their deeper call to conversion.

A New Type of Person

Churches and all groups concerned with the future of humanity must try to bring into being a new type of person, whose loyalty to humankind and to our planetary home is primary. Such a person would not neglect her or his own home, locality, or country, but rather so care for each as not to hurt others and the earth.

Given today's consumeristic waste and ruin, such persons would try to simplify their wants. They would not find joy in acquiring as much as possible, but in sharing with others and in demanding little for themselves. Service to others would not be only a duty but also the source of profound inner joy and societal harmony. Instead of profit maximization for self or a small group, service to all would be a powerful motivation for creativity and a fair distribution of natural resources and of the fruit of human labor.

Respect for nature will enable such persons to rediscover the original and organic beauty in the ordinary things of life—bodies of water, trees, fresh air, the sunset, the moon, birds, fish, flowers, music—and in the creative arts. This is a quality of life that urban technological culture tends to neglect. It needs to be rediscovered for the human person to find fulfillment in a way that excludes greed, acquisitiveness, destruction, and waste.

This is an eminently spiritual vocation that is consonant with the best inspirations of all the world's major living faiths. It is a call to a radical conversion because it entails transcending our narrow selfishness and loyalties to smaller groups that we have tended to absolutize. In accepting the other as other we have to learn to respect other races, the other sex, other religions and cultures, and not be a party to the exploitation of one by another.

The present world crisis summons us to growth in awareness of and sensitivity to others. This is a never-ending process. It is the path to other-centeredness and holiness. Those who follow it will naturally also bring an influence to bear on family and social life, on national and global relationships.

They will think of family life in relation to the good and the rights of other families. Though claiming a legitimate freedom for themselves, they will exercise that freedom with a sense of responsibility to others. In employment they will seek to make public and economic life serve the common good.

Motivation for this new type of person will be drawn from the theology we discussed earlier, in which God is seen as caring for all, Jesus is a brother to all, the Spirit is present universally, the earth is our common mother, and society and history are where we can meet God in service to others. It is also a guarantee of personal fulfillment and happiness in living not for the possession of things but in service to others.

Respect for Religions and Cultures

If mission means the building of the kingdom of God on earth, then dialogue with other religions is not an option but a necessity. Dialogue can be genuine and respectful of others as they are, because its goal is not an increase in numbers for the church as an institution. This is not a denial of mission, but a widening and deepening of the concept of mission.

Other religions can help us understand other peoples, their inner yearnings, and the universe as a whole in ways that are at least complementary to and sometimes corrective of Western approaches. For such a cross-fertilization of traditions, Christianity has to dialogue with the mainstream of the vital Asian, African, and Amerindian religions and cultures.

The more or less general acceptance among Christians today that God's grace is offered to all human beings and that visible membership in a visible church is not essential for salvation helps interreligious dialogue to be more disinterested and more in the service of integral human liberation. On the other hand the mass media today communicate knowledge of Jesus Christ to many more persons than direct missionary activity could hope to achieve.

Collaboration among the major religions can be a very valuable and powerful contribution to integral human liberation—both personal and societal, national and international. Religions can help purify each other of their narrowness and their compromises with injustice. They can also bring out together the core of their message, where they are in general agreement that genuine service to others is the way to personal fulfillment and to justice and harmony in society.

Increased contacts of different cultures too present challenges and opportunities for a renewal of the Christian churches. It is now generally acknowledged, at least in theory, that the churches should be open to the different cultures in the world. The postindependence revival of African and Asian cultures further necessitates this. Beyond adaptation to the externals of culture—such as dress, art, architecture, and modes of communication—acceptance has to be at the level of values, ethics, ways of life, and philosophies. Religions, including Christianity, can help in the purification of the isolationist aspects of the local cultures of all countries by introducing the perspective of genuine liberation. Casteism, tribalism, and feudalistic relationships need to be contested to safeguard human rights.

We have to learn to respect the positive values in other cultures. In traditional African and Asian societies there has always been a respect for the values of community and family life, for nature, and for personal search for communion with the divine, the Absolute. A certain simplicity of relationships and respect for elders still pervades these societies.

Western culture has positive values in its democratic and scientific traditions. Western humanism, influenced by Christianity, has been the source of many improvements in society. Socialism too is basically of Western origin in its modern organized form.

In the coming decades culture contacts will increase. A global type of lifestyle may emerge to some extent, at least at a certain level of living. On the other hand racial, religious, and cultural identities may seek to reaffirm themselves, in reaction to the global unifying process.

One challenge to the religions is that of sharing in the communication of the positive values of different cultures to enrich humanity and of helping in the contestation of the less human, more domesticative aspects of all cultures. A revolution in thinking implies a change in cultural values. Cultures have to be evaluated in the way *all* persons and nature are treated by them.

The rule of righteousness is a criterion for the desirability of cultural traditions. But all cultures have to learn to respect others as equal in rights and dignity. This can be particularly difficult for those who have been accustomed to cultural domination within a given country or internationally. This is precisely where conversion to accept other cultures is most necessary. Cultural liberation is an essential process for our being able to genuinely accept all human beings as equals, as brothers and sisters, in one multicultured human race.

Systemic Conversion

The churches must learn in the coming years to understand better the existing world system and plan together for its transformation to bring it into better alignment with the rule of righteousness that should prevail. Our mission is not only individual conversion, but also systemic transformation or conversion. In the global community the impact on the nation-states and groups is a very important aspect of conversion. Churches should join together, along with other groups, to make nations and groups, including corporations, converge toward building a more human world. This is an aspect of Christian service in which the churches will learn how to die to themselves so that the common human cause may prosper.

When the Christian churches thus subordinate their narrow concerns, such as self-propagation, to the urgent tasks of human survival and justice, they will be really bearing witness to the gospel of Jesus Christ. This is the paradox of the cross that is life-giving: "Anyone who loses his life for my sake will find it," said Jesus (Matt. 10:39).

Within the churches there is still a serious difference of opinion between some who emphasize the proclamation of the name of Jesus as savior and others who stress the concern for social issues. The two groups tend to be wary of each other. The first tends to think that the other neglects the proclamation of the Word; the second tends to think that the first is not really present where the gospel has to be lived in deed. These two need not be contrary to each other. Proclamation of the gospel means to fulfill the mandate of Jesus to "go, therefore, and make disciples of all the nations; baptize them in the name of the Father and of the Son and of the Holy Spirit, and teach them to observe all the commands I gave you. And know that I am with you always; yes, to the end of time" (Matt. 28:19–20). This text includes both aspects. Baptism must be preceded by evangelization, which includes acceptance of the commandment of love; otherwise it is mere ritual.

Baptism is not merely of individual persons, but of "all the nations." How is a nation to be baptized? The conversion of the nations is a primary task of the church as such. Because this task is to go on to the end of time, it may be presumed that at no intermediate period will it be completed. This may imply that never will the whole world be baptized; the church will always have the task of announcing the Word and witnessing in deed, for the kingdom is always coming, and never fully realized.

Planetary vs. National Interests

The churches as institutions with a pervasive presence can be powerful agencies for helping persons to transcend their narrow loyalties to color, class, religion, culture, and family where the common good of humanity requires it. The churches have in the past legitimized more limited loyalties that seemed important at the time. Throughout the later Middle Ages the Catholic Church encouraged the crusades against the Muslims. There was thus a buildup of hatred that went on for centuries—on both sides, in the name of God and Allah. Thereafter the wars of religion between Catholics and Protestants ravaged Europe for more than sixty years. The colonial campaigns of European powers had the blessings of the churches. During the two World Wars of the twentieth century the churches supported the combatants on both sides. In the cold war since 1945 the churches have generally placed their moral weight on the side of anticommunism.

A conversion that the churches should endeavor to achieve in this generation is a change in the mentalities of whole nations in favor of placing the good of humanity ahead of their own national interests. Eventually world political structures would help in this. But religious groups can help bring about a prior transformation of the public mind in their nations. The churches can and must now undo the damage of past legitimations by educating their followers to refuse to tolerate national policies that are damaging to other nations or to nature.

STRATEGIES

From an analysis of the world situation we can know not only what our vision and short-term goals should be, but we can also discern strategies at the national and global levels for trying to achieve those goals. There is likely to be disagreement on them, especially because it is at the point of choosing strategies that the real choice of goals becomes clear. Chapter 5 treats of the type of goals and strategies world society needs today to satisfy the human needs for survival and justice. The churches must opt for suitable strategies in given situations for the integral liberation of all persons—oppressed and oppressors. Strategies for the maintenance of peace may be easier to arrive at than those for promoting justice.

Strategies for implementing the mission of the churches must take into account the obstacles to the realization of goals and the resources the churches have for it. We know, for example, that hunger and malnutrition are widespread today—affecting over five hundred million human beings daily. The churches should utilize their resources to discover the causes of this situation—and they could benefit from studies that have already been done. Agencies such as the FAO and UNCTAD may be able to supply reliable data and recommendations. Then the churches should motivate their constituencies to give attention to the causes and to suitable remedies. This should be a priority in their activities—because of the gravity of the situation.

Terms of trade have worsened for poor countries over the past three decades. The U.S. government policy on food sales, given under PL 480 agreements, amounts to a selling of excess food in a nondomestic market to keep domestic food prices high and build up future markets for the U.S.A. and funds for use in poor countries. The churches should deal with an issue such as this with all the skills and dedication they can muster. Fortunately the churches are becoming aware of their responsibilities vis-à-vis nuclear weapons, which represent the threat of potential genocide. However, they have not yet given sufficient attention to the world food business, which has been effectively genocidal for several decades.

Strategies of the churches will have to be many-sided, according to the causes and the urgency of the problems. Food for the world's sixteen million refugees requires immediate and direct action. Other problems call for developmental action for food production in the future.

There are many other problem areas, as mentioned earlier: peace, the arms race, drugs, housing, population, land, basic human rights. Each Christian community and church—and, where possible, churches joined together—should plan policies and programs on these issues at diverse levels, from local to global. The internationality of the churches can help forge global linkages.

The ecumenical movement for church unity would gain much by such collaboration, and the coming together of the churches would quicken hope for global justice. There could be very effective ecumenical cooperation at different levels of action for global justice: research, documentation, education, creation of world public opinion, mobilization of the oppressed and needy, pressure on governments and power elites, and in a special way theological reflection and the motivation of believers. Most of this could be done along with persons of other persuasions. Ecumenism would become truly universal, relating to the total *oikoumene,* the world that God so loves.

Such action will not be without its dilemmas, ambiguities, and conflicts. There is no agreement today among Christians as to what should be done so that everyone may have daily food. There is room for us to grow in knowing each other better, educating, and even challenging each other to greater fidelity to our call. And we have to expect misunderstandings and even suffering at the hands of the powerful, or rejection by those in need of liberation, be they oppressed or oppressors. I shall discuss some aspects of specific strategies and priorities as pointers to further reflection.

CONVERSION TO LIBERATION

Conversion to liberation is a human process, aided and guided by the Spirit. It need not and does not always take place in a logical manner. However, some of its stages and processes can be set down in a sort of logical order. They parallel the stages of the development of a strategy for liberation.

Consciousness or awareness of domination and its deeper causes is essential for a meaningful and organized combat against sexism, classism, racism, and other forms of domination. This is necessary both for oppressors and oppressed. Awareness is more than mere information. It implies an evaluation of a situation in terms of good and bad, desirable and undesirable, in relation to rights and duties and the goals and vision for just social relationships.

With such a judgment the motivation for change can be born and nurtured. Motivation is related to what we call the heart or the will; it is not merely an intellectual exercise. The whole person has to be involved and engaged in it.

Liberation must be desired as a value for which one is prepared to pay a price. The kingdom of God is a pearl of great price as Jesus says. The oppressed must motivate themselves to struggle fearlessly against domination and pay the price for it. The long march through the desert may be a necessary part of the process of struggle for liberation. Oppressors too need self-purification in order to reverse their attitude toward exploitation of others, to rid themselves of long ingrained prejudices, and work with others toward the goal of a just community. When they take such a stand they may be alienated from their own class, religion, or culture.

The dominated can contribute much to the conscientization of oppressors, some of whom are persons of good will who simply never saw things any other way. They are trapped by the presumptions and prejudices of their environment. On the other hand dominators who have acquired a liberated consciousness can help in awareness-building among both oppressors and oppressed. Converted elites have had a radicalizing role in mass movements. They can be powerful agents for cooperation and change.

Group formation is an irreplaceable step in the process of liberation. Trade unions, political parties, and action groups are examples. The women's movement has shown the importance of group formation. The Christian base communities, especially as evolving in Latin America, are a type of such group formation with social and Christian consciousness. Prayer and meditation can strengthen the consciousness, motivation, and solidarity of the group.

Friendships, alliances, and networks can grow from the functioning of groups. Sharing of the gains and losses of commitment generates mutual understanding, respect, and togetherness. In a situation of global exploitation, networking for liberation is an essential stage of the convergence of groups for effective action. There can be linkages across national frontiers and among those who have opted for justice across the barriers of discrimination.

A wide mobilization of the oppressed is essential for a successful struggle for liberation. It has to go counter to the divisions among the dominated, which are a major obstacle to liberation. Oppressors are clever at fostering and maintaining such divisions; their power depends on it, for the oppressed are the majority, and if they come together they will win.

Conversion to liberation entails an option for action, to change mentalities and social structures. It is a positive choice that is not generally considered to be a feature of the Christian life, or of baptism, though it should be. It is an option that is made once and for all, but has to be renewed from time to time, especially in a group context. This option is also a decision to obviate the obstacles to genuine liberation: internal and external obstacles.

Mental or psychological obstacles are generally the harder part of this conversion process. For it requires a break with the past, our accustomed subserviences, self-legitimations, fears, and convictions of goodness and holiness. It demands a rupture with our own sinfulness with which we had earlier come to terms. Overcoming our inner obstacles requires that we know the strengths of our weaknesses and the weaknesses of our strengths.

External obstacles include public criticism, ridicule, ostracism, repression, religious taboos—all forms of power used by the dominant to maintain their privileges. In racial and classist liberation struggles in many parts of the Third World, imprisonment, torture, and murder are not uncommon.

The option to struggle is sustained by the struggle itself. We have to strengthen ourselves against giving up, becoming frustrated, turning back to the easier path of subservience or seduction. Such perseverance is not easy. In the case of a people opting for the hard way of self-reliance rather than dependence, it calls for a determination to accept present sacrifices for long-term national objectives.

Awareness of domination and injustice may arouse a certain anger or moral indignation. Such anger can have a positive role in channeling discontent to action. It should, however, not entail a hatred of persons, for this is both unchristian and not self-liberating.

FORMS OF STRUGGLE

As discussed in chapter 5, struggle is necessary for human liberation. There is conflict in the world today for the lands and lives of entire peoples. The churches have to participate in it. Their first and normal approach has to be the development of nonviolent forms of struggle. This is necessary simply to prevent a further escalation of violence. For it is the nonchallenge of the uncommitted that permits exploitative situations to continue.

The churches have hitherto formed members for a type of Christian living in which struggle for the rule of righteousness was not considered essential. It is only in recent years that Christian groups have been evolving nonviolent methods for contesting social evils. The churches will now have to think more seriously and concretely of training programs for relating to and motivating members toward forms of struggle: the creation of public opinion, formation of popular organizations and movements, collective bargaining, lobbying, demonstrations, picketing, fasts, strikes, boycotts, the forming of alliances with the oppressed. The churches in the past have not found it incompatible to have military chaplains. It is time now to furnish chaplains for peace movements.

Action in the cultural sphere can be a very specific contribution by Christians. The educational services of Christian institutions need to be converted to the promotion of peace with justice, rather than continue providing trained, docile personnel for exploitative systems.

A more difficult issue arises when peaceful means fail to overcome exploitation, and when there is armed conflict for liberation as against colonialism or in Nicaragua against the 45-year misrule of the Somoza family. It is easy to say that Christians must always use nonviolent methods, but this offers no solution to the problems caused by the violence of oppressors. We cannot condemn Christians for participating in local armed conflicts for liberation, particularly if we do not oppose the existence of armed forces for the defense of privilege and domination.

The Christian churches as such do not, and cannot, claim to be guides in military strategy—or for that matter in political strategy. The churches can, however, motivate Christians to lines of action and coordination that can lead to the victory of righteous causes. This is of great significance in the countries of Latin America, which are largely Christian.

Issues concerning participation in armed conflict for liberation cannot be decided merely at the theoretical level. It is only in concrete situations that persons and groups must decide on the course of action that seems best for the furtherance of the rule of righteousness, the kingdom of God. Every means of peaceful struggle must be tried before resorting to violence. In today's world if peaceful struggle is well organized and on a massive scale, the armed forces cannot control a people. On the other hand unless the armed forces and state power are in the hands of persons dedicated to righteousness, nonviolent pressures will not lead to effective and lasting change in social structures. The lessons of Allende's Chile and the success of the procapitalist armed forces in overthrowing a democratically inclined, elected, socialist regime cannot be overlooked in discussions of contemporary strategies for liberation.

The strange thing is that churches—like civil governments—ultimately find little difficulty in recognizing the legitimacy of the legal controllers of violence. Most modern states, including the U.S.A., were born of violent revolution. Questions arise when illegal violence challenges the injustice of those who exercise a monopoly over legal violence through the mechanism of state power!

These are real issues in our real world. The churches need to deliberate on them more articulately, to elaborate Christian thinking and spur Christian action for liberation.

CHRISTIANS AND MARXISTS

Christianity and Marxism necessarily encounter each other in today's world. About a third of the human race is under Marxist rule, and about a third is Christian. Both of them have a worldview that embraces the whole of life. Marxism incorporates a philosophy, an interpretation of history, a vision of a classless society, a strategy for revolution, and practical policies for the reorganization of society.

During the century from 1850 to 1950, the two were quite antagonistic to each other. Marxists were excommunicated by Christian church hierarchies, and Christians were persecuted by Marxist rulers. Then there was a period of coexistence, as Marxism had spread to many countries and Christian groups began to reconsider their position, especially in Europe. By the 1970s there were Christians fighting side by side with Marxists for national liberation in Vietnam. The Cuban revolution and the Christian churches were coming to terms. In Latin America Christians were evolving a theology of liberation in which Marxist social analysis was incorporated as an aid to Christian reflection.

With growing détente between East and West, there was a greater atmosphere of freedom to evaluate capitalism and socialism in practice. In Eastern Europe some Christians were demanding a greater liberalization of communism. In Western Europe and North America the critique of capitalism grew stronger, especially as the world economic crisis intensified.

Conflict has given way to coexistence, and coexistence has led to forms of cooperation, with both Christianity and Marxism influencing each other. In Western Europe Marxists evolved a theory of Euro-communism to harmonize Marxism and the values of Western democracy and affirm their independence from Soviet control.

In the African liberation movements in Angola, Mozambique, and Zimbabwe, Marxists and Christians fought together. And they were successful in military combat against European imperialism. An even more noteworthy example is Nicaragua where prominent Christians and Catholic priests were among the national leaders of the people's revolution, along with the Marxist Sandinistas against the repressive dictator Somoza.

In the coming decades the relationships between Marxism and the world religions will be a key factor in the evolution of social and political life. Marxists are learning that religions, including Christianity, are not necessarily opposed to social change. They are beginning to see a liberative dimension in religion, as the experience of revolutionary praxis has unveiled. They are also more conscious that religions are part of the tradition, culture, and way of life of most peoples, especially in the Third World. Although Marxists oppose the domesticating aspects of religion, they are learning that religions can motivate peoples to accept the values of socialism and even struggle for them when necessary. Both the Soviet Union and China have learned that religion cannot be eliminated by persecution. They are now more tolerant, though, as Marxists, they may still expect that religion will eventually disappear as socialism advances.

Christians too have been changing. In Eastern Europe they are evolving their own modus vivendi within socialism. They are becoming more disenchanted with capitalism, especially because of the way capitalist rulers oppress the poor, many of whom are Christians, in Latin America, South Africa, the Philippines, and South Korea.

Marxists can teach Christians some aspects of the social significance of the gospel. Christians must be humble enough to accept this. They can also help Christians evaluate their methods, for the Marxist impact has been through methods that have emphasized the formation of persons and action programs in real situations. Today, when there is an increasing alienation of youth, workers, and intellectuals from the traditional institutional aspects of the church, dialogue with Marxists can be a great help to the church in discerning areas of relevant action, analyzing them, and choosing action strategies, while maintaining its critical judgment on them.

Christians on the other hand can bear witness to the human values of freedom and justice to Marxists, especially where Marxists are in power and tend to be authoritarian. Religions can help to humanize revolutionary processes, provided the religions remain faithful to their calling to bear witness to genuine integral human liberation.

Marxists too need to understand the challenge of the global reality and their own limitations. Marxism is not merely a philosophical theory, nor is there only one Marxist country as in the period from 1917 to 1945. It is a worldwide political and social reality. Divisions among Marxists are facts of world political life. In some ways their internal divisions and quarrels weaken the poor peoples and countries vis-à-vis the oppressive forces of capitalism. Further, historical Marxism has not yet demonstrated a capacity to incorporate the values of democratic political processes within the framework of a viable socialism. Evidently this is not easy, as Allende's Chile learned to its own cost, due to local resistance and foreign intervention.

CHRISTIANS AND SOCIALISTS

If Christians and socialists are to foster human liberation, jointly or separately, they must learn to respect each other critically and help in each other's self-purification and reeducation.

Socialists must see that Christianity and Christians are not necessarily allies of capitalism. Christians must understand that the socialist approach is necessary in the poor countries as a defense of the weak against capitalist exploitation. Socialism implies a state or public ownership of the means of production and distribution. Such communitarian organization is necessary because local, private enterprise cannot stand up to the giant MNCs.

It is important that the distinction be noted between socialism as a necessary means of ensuring human rights and socialism as linked to an atheistic ideology. There are forms of socialism that are not Marxist. Due to the opposition of church leadership to socialist measures, Christians who see socialists championing their cause are often alienated from the church in their sociopolitical options. It is also important to ask whether the opposition to socialism is not due to institutional and personal investments in property and buildings. For instance, the churches often equate Christian education with church ownership and management of institutions. Christians therefore tend to oppose the nationalization of schools on the basis of the rights of religion. They find it difficult to see that the state can ensure greater equality of opportunity through the provision of public education.

This is an area in which Christians must do much soul-searching, especially in the free enterprise countries of the world. If the affluent are prepared to adopt a simpler lifestyle for the sake of the common good, they will not be so opposed to egalitarian measures. Moreover, when churches are less taken up with institutions and property, they can be freer to exercise their prophetic role of criticism—even within socialist societies. This is a difficult issue, inasmuch as freedom is often the first victim of large-scale socialism. On the other hand, poor countries can hardly hope to resolve their problems without large-scale state intervention. Even economic giants such as France have recently opted for nationaliza-

tion of certain industries to defend their national interests against
the MNCs.

REEVALUATION OF MINISTRIES AND SERVICES

The oppressed can help the churches to reevaluate their own
ministries and services. The educational work of the churches must
be critiqued by asking how far they help in the liberation from oppression. In general, church educational systems tend to perpetuate
the prevailing values and power relationships in a society, unless
they generate a critical awareness. A keener awareness of the present
world system can help churches everywhere to analyze their involvement in schools, colleges, and universities in terms of the curriculum
taught, admission qualifications, values incorporated in the educational process, and the future social commitment of their graduates.
Reevaluation in terms of these criteria can show how far an educational system helps maintain the competitive, capitalistic values in
Western society, or helps reproduce a conformist mentality in socialistic countries.

The same applies to health services and other social service activities. Do they really help liberate the oppressed, or are they only
palliatives, when more radical solutions could reduce or even eliminate such ills as malnutrition, tuberculosis, or infant mortality? For
health itself is to a large extent a function of justice—within the
limits of human frailty and mortality. The poor are often sickly
because they are poor.

Self-review in light of the option for the liberation of the poor can
also be a help to institutions such as religious congregations vis-à-vis
their own orientations, spirituality, and activities. Most Catholic
and Protestant foreign missionary societies and agencies were inspired by what is now an outmoded theology of mission. They went
out to other countries to propagate a faith and church heavily
Western-oriented. Their motivation had little to do with the
kingdom of God or rule of righteousness as we consider them today.
In spite of extraordinary sacrifices and good will, they were largely
insensitive to the injustices imposed on the oppressed. Even in the
abolition of slavery they did not play a major role.

Lay movements in the churches and the more recent charismatic
movement should also be evaluated by the criterion of the option

for the liberation of the oppressed. The St. Vincent de Paul societies have done much work for the relief of poverty for more than three centuries, but they did not oppose the pauperization of peoples by colonialism. Likewise agencies such as the Red Cross did not contest the human causes of the misery of the weak, though they did extraordinary relief work at times of emergencies and disasters.

The crisis of vocations to religious congregations in many parts of the world and the lessening of enthusiasm for older forms of lay apostolate may be due to an awareness among the younger generation today that these forms of Christian mission are less meaningful: they do not go to the root causes of the problems they set out to tackle. Pope Pius XI lamented in the 1930s that the neglect of concern for the rights of the working classes in Europe was a cause of their dechristianization. And it is the consequences of this dechristianization that are afflicting the West European churches today.

On the other hand where the churches have been with the oppressed, the poor have rallied round the church. The history of Catholic Ireland demonstrates this. In recent decades, however, Ireland has advanced economically, and the church too has prospered financially. Those who have been marginalized in this process—the unemployed, aged, handicapped, single women, prostitutes, fishermen, landless farm laborers, urban poor—feel alienated from the church. They expected a greater solidarity from the traditional leadership of the church. Catholic Poland too is an example of a people loyal to a church that has stood by them for centuries of foreign invasion and oppression.

With the reduction in the proportion of church members in the First World and an increase of Christians especially in Africa and Latin America, the balance of numbers in the churches is moving in the direction of the Third World. This is particularly true of the Catholic Church, inasmuch as the Latin American peoples are in great majority Catholic. Over half the membership of the Catholic Church lives outside Europe and North America.

Thus it is that the majority of the world's oppressors call themselves Christian, and the majority of baptized Christians are oppressed peoples. This is a travesty of the values of the kingdom of justice that the churches are supposed to symbolize and help realize. All the same, the churches can serve as channels for a communication of the sufferings and demands of the oppressed to their oppressors. Traditionally the opposite was what took place. Church activities help to domesticate the poor and weak and legitimize their subordination to the powerful. Conversion of the church today will consist in the reversing of this process for the sake of justice. In many areas the churches are the most powerful voice for the voiceless and hence their strongest hope for peaceful solutions. This is particularly true of Latin America.

The irony of the overall situation is worsened when we consider the domination of women. The majority of church members and active exponents are women. Yet the churches are among the strongest and most entrenched bastions of male domination, and some may well be the last to abandon it—if they ever will.

There is at present a revolutionary upsurge in the countries of the Third World, seeking liberation especially from capitalist oppression. To participate in this revolution of our times the churches must courageously articulate an adequate teaching on social justice, as did the prophets of old for their day. We must stand unhesitatingly for the liberation of the oppressed, for the removal of the onus of debt from the poor, for the provision of land to the landless, work to the unemployed, homes for the shelterless, food for the hungry, freedom for political captives, and justice for all. These are among the basic goals of the modern revolution of the oppressed, and they are also central demands of the gospel message. The Christian churches must interpret this revolution to the rest of the world.

If the churches participate in revolutionary processes at the time they are taking shape, they can also be creatively present in the shaping of the new societies that will emerge from the present turmoil.

We have had too much of a stagnant theology, of rigidly fixed relationships, and hence we are ill-prepared to understand revolutionary times. We need a new theology that seeks to understand the world in its dynamic evolutionary processes and in light of the demands of the Scriptures. Such a theology can evolve only in honest dialogue with the more forward looking forces—youth, workers, urban and rural poor, intellectuals, political leaders.

With or without or even in spite of the affluent, the poor of the world will affirm themselves and their God-given right to life and liberty. Whether theology will be able to relate to them will depend on the willingness of Christians to dialogue in life with the revolutionary movements of our times. They are part of God's providence for our age.

CHRISTIAN MISSION TO THE FIRST WORLD

Planetary perspectives demand a change in the concept of mission and a reordering of our priorities in mission. Belief that the West had been converted to Christianity and the rest of the world needed conversion triggered the extraordinary missionary effort of the past few centuries. But even to this day the concept of mission implies going out to areas that are not considered part of the Western world.

Although not wishing to dilute enthusiasm for missionary witness in foreign lands, but keeping in mind too the Chinese example of self-reliant churches, it seems time for the Christian churches to put major emphasis on mission to Europe and North America. This may be called mission, or reevangelization, or mission in reverse. Whatever be the term used, what is meant is that a much more serious effort must be made by the Christian churches to orient the First World toward a respect for human dignity and a concern for nature—in other words, toward the values of the kingdom of God.

Christian mission to Europe and North America is a matter of urgent necessity because it is these countries that do the most harm to humanity and nature as a whole; exercise more power for good or evil; call themselves Christian and hence are more damaging to the witness of the gospel; and are more dehumanized, more alienated from the values of the kingdom, and more difficult to convert. Such a mission is less romantic, less satisfying to our sense of paternalism, and yet more necessary for the self-purification of the churches because they benefit from the exploitative social system of the First World.

That the Western nations exercise immense power in the world hardly needs proof. If their economic and technological power were used for better purposes, many of the unfulfilled basic needs of humankind could be realized—in a short time. Just as the world community was able to eliminate small pox from the face of the earth by joint action, much more could be achieved if the Western powers were prepared to subordinate their selfishness to the global common good. The money spent on armaments, liquor, advertisements, or cosmetics would be enough to rid the world of hunger and malnutrition. The resources and technology available for planned human development are such today that, were it not for the obstacles set up by the powerful nations, the world could satisfy the basic needs of its entire present population and plan ahead for the future. Is it not, then, a primary Christian responsibility to strain every nerve toward a healthy directioning of this immense, unprecedented potential?

That Western nations regard themselves as Christian lends a legitimation to governmental policies. Of greater importance, though, is the fact that the churches themselves tend to think that Christian evangelization in these countries has long since been achieved. This judgment derives from a sociological and ritualistic understanding of what it is to be a Christian. All those who are baptized are presumed to be Christians. Acceptance of the values of the gospel or of the person of Jesus Christ as a guide for one's life is not considered an essential qualification of a Christian. An executive of a multinational corporation that produces armaments or operates in such a way that food does not reach the starving may be considered a Christian. Even torturers of other human beings pass for Christian. Unfortunately church practices sometimes favor this false identification. A divorced person may not be allowed to receive communion, but an exploiter is not barred. Communists may be excommunicated, but not capitalist exploiters.

Mahatma Gandhi once said that he admired Jesus Christ but there were many Christians he could not admire. When we think of witness to the gospel in elaborating mission strategies, perhaps we do not give adequate weight to the scandal that the so-called Christian countries offer to the rest of the world. Is this one reason why Asian countries have been so reluctant to embrace Christianity? On the other hand where witness has been seen to be credible, Christianity gains more adherents, even without much evangelistic propaganda.

Christian churches do not reflect adequately on the seriousness of the damage done to Christianity by the way the Western powers act. The churches in the West do not like to be reminded of their alliance with colonialism. They prefer to regard it as something of the past. Someone in authority in Rome wrote to me that church officials think that raising issues of this nature is like blaming the Jews for crucifying Jesus. These are things of the past, he said. Not so; the present world order is a continuation and consolidation of the past.

The churches in Europe and North America control power in the churches worldwide. Most churches have their central agencies in Europe and North America: Rome, Geneva, Canterbury, New York—and we might add Moscow too. Those who exercise power over the churches are mainly Europeans and North Americans. The financial power bases of the churches too are in these countries, and it is difficult to dissociate finances and policy-making even in the churches, for they too have their human side.

First World churches will not change their policies unless Christians effectively make an option for a different type of person and world based on a rediscovery of Jesus Christ and his gospel. This is why reeeducation of European and North American Christians is vital for worldwide church renewal.

Today the peripheries are provoking change in the centers. Often missionaries returning from Latin America, Asia, and Africa are the ones who challenge the central churches, their agencies and institutions. This is somewhat similar to the impact of Paul and Barnabas at the Council of Jerusalem concerning the circumcision of Gentile converts (Acts 15). For such an impact to take place there must be dialogue between the peripheries and the central churches, and those at the centers should be prepared to be influenced by what they hear.

The churches at the centers of power can help effectively in the formation of linkages, alliances, and networks among the churches, especially at the level of leadership. This is a form of ecumenical cooperation that will be possible and effective only insofar as the churches at the power centers are willing to come together for joint service to humanity. So long as their priorities are their own advancement, such cooperation will not be wholehearted. This was seen in the experiment of Sodepax, which the World Council of Churches and the Vatican set up for cooperation in development and peace. After an experimental period of three years, the powers of this agency were so watered down that it became ineffective. The Vatican was not prepared to give Sodepax direct access to its rank and file on the peripheries.

If the gospel is a message of salvation, and if it is more difficult for the rich to be saved than for a camel to pass through the eye of a needle, are not those in the exploiting affluent societies the ones whose salvation is more in jeopardy? If so, should not those concerned with mission for the sake of salvation give a higher priority to the presentation of the integral gospel to the rich?

It might be argued that this is a difficult, useless, or thankless enterprise. But, then, should not the zealous disciple of Christ be more eager for the really tough assignments—eager to accept the most difficult missions, as some religious congregations have written into their constitutions?

What has been said about mission to Christians in Europe and North America is also valid in most respects for Christians among the local elites of Third World countries insofar as they are exploitive of the poor and linked to the unjust world system.

Similarly, socialists in Eastern Europe and elsewhere should see to it that socialism is not unjust and exploitive where it is in power. Today the Soviet presence in Afghanistan and its hegemony in Eastern Europe are a counterwitness to socialism. So too the China-Vietnam conflict and Vietnam after 1975.

On the other hand the poor in the rich countries and the racially exploited in the U.S.A. and Europe are in a position similar to that of the poor in the Third World. They have to struggle for their own liberation. They may be tempted to identify their interests in international relationships with those of their rich fellow citizens as against those of the poor countries. This may be the situation of women in rich countries: exploited domestically, but sharing in the world exploitative system. Such persons must opt for a total liberation from exploitation—including whatever form of exploitation of which they may be guilty.

REORGANIZATION OF CHURCHES

One of the lessons that the planetary age is teaching Christianity is the irrelevance of many of the organizational structures and other baggage that the churches have inherited from the past. Universality, grassroot presence, and international linkages have a tremendous value. In this the churches have a potential for global communication that very few other bodies can ever hope to have. The churches have also a power of motivation and a potential for community building to which the gospel message and Western organizational practicality have contributed.

However, moving into a new age of global interaction and of a mission in which the rule of righteousness is to be the ultimate guideline, the churches have to be made more aware of the unfortunate divisions that exist among them. There is first the threefold division into Catholic, Orthodox, and Protestant communions, with all manner of subdivisions, especially in Protestantism. This sundering cuts right across the globe and divides Christians everywhere. Each church has its own inherited prepossessions as to doctrine, clergy, laity, worship, evangelism, and so forth. These must all be reviewed, at their roots, for a more credible gospel witness and functional efficiency.

At the national level Christian communions must endeavor to close the gaps between them. One way would be for all the churches to relate more actively to the needs of the people and liberation from being oppressed or oppressor toward more just human relationships. In this the churches must learn to listen to the poor, the weak, the disadvantaged, the marginalized. In doing so they will be closer to their people, and they will hear better the demands of the gospel. They will then be motivated to relativize their doctrinal and disciplinary differences—that is, relate them to the more urgent needs of the people and the deeper message of the gospel. The poor can be a revelation to the church of what its mission and priorities should be today. The agenda of local secular agencies concerned with the rule of righteousness can help articulate these issues.

The churches should be able to dialogue together on their response to these demands. What resources do they have? What obstacles have to be faced? What steps can they take together and separately? These are normal stages in a planning process. The churches should be able to meet interdenominationally on such issues and in joint action move toward a postdenominational rapprochement. This will be an important stage of growth, though it will be difficult due to institutional and organizational issues. The divisions of past centuries are not so relevant for Christians today, especially in Asia, Africa, and Latin America, where they were exported from Europe and North America. Action together on more relevant issues is one way of building ecumenical unity among the churches.

THE LIBERATION OF WOMEN

Women are coming to an awareness of their rights to equality and dignity, which are essential for genuine human relationships of justice and love. They are organizing themselves in many parts of the world and beginning to make a collective impact. They are asking for a fundamental restructuring of mentalities, relationships, and structures of society. They want to be accepted as full and equal persons in their own right, not merely as an adjunct of a male world.

Both men and women must seek equality in service to each other and the community. Seeking equality in the capitalistic rat race or in hedonism is bound to harm both men and women—and future generations. We must, however, be careful that this argument is not used to deny women their just demands for equality and respect, or their right to pursue liberation.

The churches have been very sexist in their thought patterns and structures. They are therefore particularly called to a conversion from sexism to respect women and men as equals. The churches will find this difficult, due to the centuries-old incrustation of male superiority—with theological backing.

A totally unprejudiced reorientation of the content of theology will affect much of Christian thought—concerning God, revelation, human relationships, the study of Scripture. The churches must desist from transmitting a prefabricated theology: made by males only, or whites only, or the bourgeoisie only. Such a theology cannot but be sexist, racist, or classist.

The Scriptures have to be read by women in the light of their own perceptions. The Scriptures have to be read also by the poor and oppressed, as well as by persons of all religions and beliefs. In this way it will be seen that their basic teachings are universalistic.

There is a generally accepted opinion that the sources of Christian theology are revelation and tradition. Revelation is thought to have ended with the written Scriptures. Tradition is taken to be the theology that has prevailed in the churches. The problem with this is that the Scriptures were written by males in male-dominated societies, and the same is true of traditional theology. Can these be adequate sources for a theology of men *and women*?

Women have a specific contribution to make to Christian theology by rereading the Scriptures, reevaluating tradition, and articulating their own theological insights. In this their own life experience as dominated, as seeking liberation and fulfillment, bears a message from God for the churches and the whole of humanity. The contemporary lived experience of women is a source of theology, a mode of God's presence and word. No *consensus fidelium* can be had if their point of view is excluded. If the learning church, the *ecclesia discens*, is infallible, and women form more than half of it, then their contemporary views cannot be erroneous. They are a credible source of theology.

Women can make a very valuable contribution to the correcting of a theology that is male dominated. They must express their thinking as believers from within their own consciousness of their rights as free and responsible persons. For them to work within the old framework of tradition, or even Scripture only, would mean confinement within prejudiced limits. They should not be satisfied with a mere "promotion" of women when what is required is a radical liberation to be equals in church and civil society.

The structures of the churches need to be liberated from the constraints of male domination and monopoly. There is no theological, psychological, biological, or pastoral reason why women cannot exercise any function in any of the churches. There is nothing inherently masculine about the functions of priest, bishop, or pope. One can understand the limitation of these roles to males in a historical context that was male dominated. But that is no justification for continuing it, any more than there was for popes to be Italian.

On the contrary, if the church is a community in which love is the binding principle, it can be argued that women should be in positions of authority, for maternal love is the most gratuitous and generous.

Within the churches it is necessary that women form groups for ensuring that they be given their due place as equal partners. These groups must develop an awareness of the demands of justice and of Christian communion. They need to motivate each other to take the steps needed for transformation. This includes theological reflection among women's groups, an analysis of the way power is exercised in the churches, and a decision on strategies to bring about changes.

The church is a free community. Hence methods of bringing about change will have to be of a moral nature. Pressure will have to be brought on decision-makers in the churches so that women may have a just share as equals in all activities and responsibilities. This will mean more participation in church life. It will also bring with it changes in attitudes and administrative styles within the churches.

From our reflection on the common aspects of domination and liberation in sex, color, and class, we can see that the increased participation of women in decision-making in the churches can help bring the churches to the side of human liberation on the issues of color and class. This will require self-abnegation for those women who are in a privileged position and who share in the benefits of the oppression of color and class, though oppressed themselves as women.

Women must participate in the struggles to change the structures of society. But this cannot be realized so long as the women of an oppressing class prefer to be associated with the men of that class in their options and lifestyles. This is a most difficult passover or conversion to be worked out in one's life.

The most marginalized women are those of the Third World. They are two-thirds of womankind. Concern for women's rights must necessarily involve the struggle of these women for mere survival. The women of oppressed peoples have to realize that their struggle can be helped and purified by an alliance with the women of affluent countries.

The struggles for liberation within the churches would be strengthened by being integrated. The same applies to the struggles of women in all the churches. Unfortunately they do not have many opportunities for meeting. They have no churchwide base for operation, especially in the Catholic and Orthodox churches. Perhaps the religious congregations of women could take an initiative in this direction. The Catholic sisters in the United States, who are the best organized in this regard, may be able to take a lead in such an initiative.

The movements of Third World Christians should join with the women's movements in all the churches. They could then challenge the churches to rid themselves of the racist and sexist domination. And insofar as these groups truly represent the poor of the world, they could join in the movement to make the churches support liberation from class exploitation. There would thus be a planetary strategy for integral human liberation.

In any case, if the churches fail to recognize women's rights at this stage of human history, it is the churches that will suffer; women will forge ahead toward greater liberation without them. The same is true of oppressed racial groups and exploited classes. The upsurge of the poor, the despised, and the marginalized cannot be kept down forever. The ferment of revolutionary changes in today's world is thus a challenge and an opportunity for the renewal of theology and of the churches themselves. It is a call to them from the God of history.

Chapter 11

Catechetics for Integral Conversion

Individuals and groups concerned about personal fulfillment, human rights, and ecological problems have long recognized the need for a much broader awareness of and reflection on these issues. They recognize also the inadequacies of educational systems that are controlled by dominant business interests, political parties, or local elites.

Catechesis—the Christian instruction of those who belong to the churches—has this regard. This has been due to the type of theology that has prevailed almost universally in the churches. In the past decades there have been many attempts to heighten the consciousness of Christians to the social dimension of Christianity. The movement is fairly widespread now, even though in most countries it is still marginal to the mainstream of church life. The Latin American theology of liberation, black theology, women's theology, action groups for civil rights, the peace movement, and liberation movements in Africa and Asia have evolved methods of bringing about a new social consciousness among Christians. Paulo Freire's experience and writings on conscientization have had a worldwide impact. But a socially-attuned, planetary understanding of Jesus and the gospel is largely absent in the churches.

Why is it that the Christian catechesis is still silent in the field of human relationships concerning justice, freedom, and national and international sharing? It is because of the view that Christian life is

226

primarily a matter of individual sanctification and salvation. Catechesis dwells on the law of God and of the church and even presents God as love, but stops there; it avoids social analysis and its political implications. It often teaches that churches should be neutral in the field of politics. However, the reality is that politics influences human lives and decides whether persons will have food, houses, jobs, education, civil rights, freedom, water, energy, clothing. Their denial or unfair distribution goes counter to the values of the kingdom of God's righteousness.

Most catechists are not prepared to participate in the making of political decisions necessary for justice. Most teachers of religion have not been educated to analyze society: its social dynamics, power, political realities. They have been trained to teach individual relationships to God and the Christian community, but without an awareness of the demands of the kingdom of God and the structural nature of sin.

Catechesis has generally been limited to the instruction of children. It is often conducted by elderly persons and is directed toward the very young who have not yet joined the dynamic forces of society. Moreover, in the Catholic Church many catechists are religious and priests, and the lives of most nuns, priests, and brothers are as yet not geared to social change. Hence they are not capable of leading or participating in the orientation of catechesis toward social change.

Another limitation of catechetics is that it is carried out within the educational system of religious schools, or of the state, or in connection with such organizations as the Confraternity of Christian Doctrine, which form part of parochial and diocesan structures; and all these have tended toward social conservatism. Almost everywhere the educational system conditions children to social conservatism. Catechetics can hardly relate, therefore, to the currents that seek to bring about fundamental alterations in society. It is only indirectly and in the very long term that institutions such as educational systems or parishes relate to social change.

Textbooks used in catechetics focus chiefly on intrachurch affairs and on relating the Scriptures to private daily life. They should include discussion of world and cosmic principles, the nation-states, the struggle of peoples for human liberation, and other religions and their significance.

RETHINKING THE CONTENT OF CATECHESIS

Catechesis can and should relate to the present situation in the world. It can at least awaken Christians to present social trends and thus help render the churches and religion in general more relevant to de facto situations and less a force for unjustifiable conservatism.

Inclusion of social dynamics in catechesis will lead to a major change in the life of the church. It will not be the teacher of religion who decides what is to be studied, because the problems of society will determine the areas of interest. Catechesis will also involve believers in a certain measure of conflict in society, a certain polarization, forcing them to take stands on issues. Social justice is not possible without deep personal commitment, consequent upon study and reflection.

This will require a rethinking of the content of catechesis. In the new vision, much greater emphasis is placed on those elements in the faith that are of universal relevance to the human race. Churches would thus have to work out in greater detail the consequences for social justice of teachings on the creation of humankind, the universal fatherhood of God, and the oneness of the human race. Social and collective ownership of property, limits on national sovereignty, control over national property, concepts of race and culture, economic and social relationships, distribution of wealth within a country, oppression for reasons of color, caste, sex, or age, the care of nature—all these would be basically affected by a rethinking of Christian values in terms of social justice.

The concept of sin also needs rethinking. When a particular structure or environment impedes the realization of the fatherhood of God and justice among persons, it is sinful: it separates God from his people. The concepts of repentance, reparation, and forgiveness must also be enlarged. Repentance would be understood in its collective nature, and would have to include a collective effort at changing mentalities. It would also be intimately connected with collective compensation.

RETHINKING THE TEN COMMANDMENTS

Much of the teaching of Christianity is directly or indirectly related to moral life. For the most part, morality has been conceived of in individual and negative terms. It is important that we discover the deeper and wider significance of the commandments, which have to do with our relationships with God, our family, our neighbors, property, and nature. These must be understood from within the whole perspective of Christian revelation, especially in view of the unique commandment of love and the spirit of the Beatitudes.

The Beatitudes and the gospel teachings set the direction in which our lives can find fulfillment. It is in loving, selfless service, in the building of our inner strength and detachment from all transitory things, that we can find self-realization. Within such a perspective of inner liberation, we see how the Ten Commandments give guidelines for our social relationships.

The First Commandment reads, "I am Yahweh your God who brought you out of the land of Egypt. . . . You shall have no other gods except me." This reminds us of God's liberative commitment and demands from us an unreserved loyalty. It demands a dethroning of false gods of all kinds: money, power, status, racism, sexism.

The Second Commandment is that we are not to take the name of God in vain. Both these commandments affirm the supremacy of the Absolute, God. Hence, no one else can claim to be God, or absolute sovereign over our lives, or have complete authority or power. This calls for reflection on the limits of national rulers, and on the responsibility in conscience to obey God above all others. Hence the need to disobey demands for injustice. The Second Commandment calls for the exposure of all those who falsely claim that God is on their side.

The attitude toward the Sabbath was changed by Jesus himself. Christian churches have interpreted the Third Commandment too legalistically. Church attendance once a week was often regarded as the main Christian obligation and sign of religious affiliation. The real meaning of worship and community needs rethinking. It is taken up in chapter 12.

The Fourth Commandment has been an inspiration for the Christian teaching on the family, especially in raising children. It can be broadened to include the conversion of family members to respect and care for each other, to a greater sharing of the burdens of parenthood, to love of parents, and care for the aged. In contrast, it is a fact that the family tends to encourage consumerism, elitism, and racial, classist, and sexist prejudices. Family loyalties are often a means of enforcing weakhearted conformism. The laws of inherit-ance increase inequalities of wealth. Family love can be so particu-larist as to neglect the common good of society.

The Sixth and Ninth Commandments have enjoyed an inordin-ately large share of pastoral and doctrinal attention. We need to rethink the problems of love, marriage, and sex in relation to both the personal fulfillment of individuals and couples and the common good of humankind. Often the social norms imposed by state and church regard only the general harmony of society, tending to neglect the rights of individuals to a measure of happiness in this life. Here the state has sometimes been more liberating than the church. The church must emphasize genuine love and responsibility in all sexual relationships. It has tended to be too legalistic. This is an area where, in Catholicism, the male, clerical, celibate domi-nance has been paramount. The modern world is confronting the traditional, legalistic, male-dominated church with advances in science and rapidly changing values and structures. The global re-sponsibility of families and nations is another area in which ques-tions of family planning, consumerism, lifestyles, and social inequalities need to be reconsidered. The rights of persons of other religions should be more respected in the Christian teaching and law on marriage.

The Fifth, Seventh, Eighth, and Tenth Commandments have great social and cultural significance.

During the centuries when Christians were decimating peoples around the globe, theologians showed little concern about the Fifth Commandment, "You shall not kill." Today the ways and means of killing human beings have multiplied enormously. Problems of hunger, malnutrition, torture, and dictatorship have to be included in the Christian teaching derived from this commandment. Recent years have seen the development of materials for bacteriological, ecological, biological, and nuclear warfare. They have been used in Vietnam and Afghanistan. Vast numbers of Christians are engaged in the production of armaments. Yet these are not matters for wide-spread theological concern and action.

We have not yet begun to fathom the depths of the meaning and relevance of the Fifth Commandment. It can be related to the killing of peoples, cultures, and religions by diverse forms of invasion—ideological, commercial, cultural. Care of the environment and the safeguarding of life on earth have a special relevance here: to kill nature—lakes, rivers, seas, forests, the atmosphere—is also to kill human life now or in the future.

The Eighth Commandment, "You shall not bear false witness," can be applied to the cultural aspects of modern life. Minds are dulled by the sensational and the distorted, by artificial values and contrived needs—all bearing false witness to the real meaning of life and the fundamental problems that affect humanity today. Yet theological reflection and Christian education on this are scarcely developed. On the contrary, we find theologians co-opted into narrow concerns to the neglect of these wider issues. Thus it is that persons in countries where the communications media are most developed are among the most illiterate concerning the real condition of the world—and yet they are responsible for it.

Cultural subversion of poor nations by rich nations is a heinous crime. Multinational corporations create artificial wants when the masses lack basic essentials. The whole truth is not told about "contributions" or "aid" to "development," which so often fosters underdevelopment. Reflection on the Eighth Commandment can be an occasion for study and action on the myths, prejudices, and phobias that are rampant in society and thus help overcome racism, sexism, classism, and religionism.

Even the theology of secularization, which claims an autonomous area for temporal affairs, can be counterproductive—if it leaves the world free for the powerful and the rich to exploit. The Teilhardian view of the progress of science and human history can be deceptive, unless it is complemented by a realistic evaluation of the growing evil of human exploitation.

Reflection on the Tenth Commandment, "You shall not covet your neighbor's house . . . or anything that is his" is crucial for the planetary orientation of Christian theology. Today we are faced with the exploitation of whole peoples by a few affluent groups. Christian theology must make a serious study of the processes by which wealth and riches are taken or kept from the poor and given to the rich. Christian theology has not been fundamentally critical of the profit motive. Theologians should study commercial treaties signed between rich and poor countries and reflect on the world monetary system. Catechesis can help in the creation of world public opinion concerning the exploitation of natural resources and the need to defend human rights against unjust rulers and regimes.

The Tenth Commandment is particularly relevant to consumerism and lifestyles, for the misuse of resources and the excesses of consumerism result from coveting one's neighbors' goods. The entire range of ecological problems can also come under this commandment, including the obligation to leave resources for posterity.

RETHINKING THE SACRAMENTS

The sacramental ministry of the churches must shift emphasis from the external ritual to the internal spiritual meaning conveyed by it. The sacraments are outward signs of inward grace. Grace is their most important feature.

In the global perspective, it is also necessary to view the sacraments more in terms of humankind at large and the kingdom of God's justice and less in a church-centered manner. It is generally said in traditional theology that sacraments are for persons. We must now understand this in the worldwide context.*

Baptism should be understood as personal conversion to God and the kingdom of justice and love as announced by Jesus. We can understand St. Paul's saying that we are baptized in the death and resurrection of Jesus in the sense of the dying to self that is implied in this conversion, or passover from selfishness to unselfishness. This conversion should be expressed at baptism, or at least by the parents or sponsors in the case of infant baptism. In any case the reality of baptism is something much more than the external rite and the recording of names in a registry.

In the perspective of the cosmic dimension of Christ, we need to elaborate and give much greater practical value to baptism of desire. This is the main factor in any adult conversion. This is the baptism that is open to all human beings, universally, in time and space. It is entry into the concerns of the kingdom of God. It is the deciding factor for membership in the invisible church, and the way for all persons to be reunited in the cosmic Christ.

The invisible church, the mystical body of Christ, is a reality known by faith to which Christians must give much more concern and respect. It is the communion of all persons of good will. It is the consequence of the universal presence of God in everyone, the fruit

---

*For a thorough examination of the sacrament of the Eucharist, see Balasuryia, *Eucharist and Human Liberation* (Maryknoll, N.Y.: Orbis, 1979).

of the Spirit. It is the real beginning of the eternal kingdom of God on earth. We cannot easily define its doctrinal content or count its members. It is not subject to any other authority than the Spirit of God teaching everyone. The more we respect the invisible church, the more we are likely to respect other persons and be prepared for a dialogue of faith, life, and action with all persons of good will. As humanity goes deeper into planetary intercommunion, the theological meaning of the invisible church will dawn more on us. We may be able to comprehend it less than the visible churches, but why should such a deep spiritual reality be more comprehensible to us? Should we not leave room for faith and the mystery of God's relationship to other persons, each of whom is also a mystery unfathomable to any of us?

The sacrament of penance is meant to be an affirmation of the forgiveness of sins when there is repentance for them and a determination to change one's ways and make amends for one's sins. For real penance there has to be contrition, restitution—if applicable—and a firm purpose of amendment. We can hardly say that these factors are present when we consider the economic relationships that prevail in the world.

In the sacrament of penance there will have to be more concern for genuine reconciliation of persons and groups. The examination of conscience done by individuals and groups can have reference to our sins of omission and commission in relation to other persons, peoples, religions, cultures, and nature itself. For instance, the loss of arable land at the rate of twenty-seven square miles every day, or about six million acres every year, in the U.S.A. by soil erosion is a matter for the public examination of conscience of the hundred million or more American Christians.

Penance and reconciliation should extend also to the past and to churches. Can a spirit of reconciliation bring together the Vatican and China into communion after nearly three decades of estrangement? Ecumenism requires reconciliation, mutual respect, and pardon.

In the Catholic Church today, auricular confession to a priest is decreasing all over the world. Perhaps a serious public and general examination of conscience may be a way of giving the spirit of penance a more important place in Christian spirituality and community life.

In international relationships the forgiving of debts can have a particularly meaningful application today. The "forgive us our debts, as we have forgiven those who are in debt to us" was intended to be a sort of jubilee-year reconciliation, when lands return to their original owners. The question of national public debts is a matter for public examination of conscience. To what extent is the debt of a poor country to an oil-rich or industrial country due to unfair terms of trade? Does the public debt of poor countries lead to their being unable to provide food for their undernourished masses? How is a people to be repaid for the loss of its dignity, culture, and freedom? Should not exploited countries be compensated for long-term colonial robbery? Do debts of nations begin only after 1945 or the independence of poor countries? All these need somehow to be made a matter of penance, compensation, and reconciliation.

This sacrament can be closely linked to counseling, at both the personal and group levels. Persons today seek meaning in their interpersonal relationships. Whereas social norms, values, and structures often crush human personalities, the interrelationships and spiritual dynamics of reconciliation in penance can be an immense help and solace to many. Such a reinterpretation would also give a deeper meaning to the function of the minister of reconciliation. The sacrament of penance can thus be a vital help to radical conversion.

The sacrament of confirmation by which Christians are strengthened in spirit must also be rethought and ministered in such a way that a genuine commitment is brought out. As it is presently ministered, it is given before recipients are even aware of the basic problems that face them in the world. The sacramental ritual has very little significance to the major questions of culture, liberation, and justice. When the apostles received the Holy Spirit, they acted boldly to bring about a social transformation.

More than being a sacrament received once and for all, and that from the hands of a bishop, confirmation can be thought of as a continual reference to the Spirit within us. It can be a source of inspiration to individuals and groups to acquire and live the gifts and fruits of the Spirit. Wisdom, peace, fortitude, and joy are graces that every human person seeks. It is the Spirit of God universally present in humanity that peoples of all countries can encounter in mutual respect.

The charismatic movement too can contribute much to the deeper conversion of Christians if they combine community awareness and justice with their intense experience of the Spirit within each person and in small groups.

Confirmation can be an occasion for recipients to be made more aware of the type of demands the Spirit makes on convinced believers living in the real world of large-scale human exploitation. Unfortunately, Christianity has tended to ritualize the Spirit into a once-a-lifetime sacrament and neglect the vital reality of communion with the Absolute.

The concept of the indwelling of the Holy Spirit is basic to Hinduism and can teach Christians much. It is the normal atmosphere of Hindu meditation. The yoga tradition recognizes that there is an alienation in the very structure of human nature. Authenticity requires that persons be released from the bonds attaching them to the phenomenal world in order to attain perfect equilibrium. The experience of self-identity is a liberating power. The inner being can be brought into union with the Absolute, who is the innermost being of ourselves. Chinese religious traditions also teach that persons find their true identity in response to the Spirit active within them. Can we not incorporate these intuitions within our own theological tradition, our catechesis and ministry? They can help us understand the spiritual riches of other traditions and holy persons, and also discover the treasures of the Judeo-Christian tradition of revelation.

Matrimony needs to be reevaluated in a similar manner. Christianity has insisted far too much on the sanctity of Christian marriage to the relative discrediting of other forms of marriage. We need not downgrade one to upgrade the other. If we accept the presence of the Spirit of God in all persons, then a marriage of those who are not Christian is also a sacred reality. Respect for all forms of marriage is more important than comparing the sanctities of each, which is a temptation of religionism.

The attitude of the churches, especially the Catholic Church, to mixed marriages has often been heartrending. The shunning of mixed marriages led to the formation of Christian ghettos, especially in Asian and African countries. Social pressure was linked to ecclesiastical sanction. When we learn to truly respect the freedom and love of persons and the working of God within them, regardless of ecclesiastical communions, we shall be more Christlike in our attitude toward the marriages of persons who are not Christians.

Religion must help build genuine love and respect for one another and not create artificial barriers, thereby intensifying human suffering and bitterness.

Christian married life can be a lifelong service to the values of the kingdom of love and justice in the relationships of the sexes, of spouses, parents and children, the aged, through all the vicissitudes of life. The personal and social, the physical and psychological, are intertwined in marriage and family life. Because issues are more deeply experienced at this level, catechesis has to be more relevant.

Concerning the sacrament of Holy Orders, the acceptance of a theology in which priority is given to the kingdom of God rather that the institutional church will change our concepts of ministry. Service to the human community seeking understanding, justice, and sharing will require different methods of training and even criteria for the choice of candidates to ministerial and religious roles. Earlier the desire was to have docile subalterns who carried out the priorities and instructions of central church authorities in building local Christian communities. Now initiative, leadership, discernment, and a spirit of collaboration with local groups is required in the clerical, religious, and lay ministers of the churches.

Seminary formation will have to change in the content of theology, by a return to the sources in Scripture, and by a rereading of God's designs in human history. Much more attention will have to be given to the study of human movements for social transformation, their goals and methods, as well as to the study of the human psyche and the earth as our provident mother. The elaboration of a moral and spiritual approach to the cosmos needs more attention, along with ways and means of defending the treasures of the earth.

Christian ministry is a permanent need of the Christian community. Today the churches are called to open themselves to a more general, nonsexist, nonreligionist orientation of Christian ministry as genuine service to all in the footsteps of Jesus. "The servant," as he said, "is not greater than the master."

What was once called the sacrament of extreme unction is now called the anointing of the sick. It is an occasion for the church to be present to almost everyone at a particularly difficult moment in life. The very thought of our mortality can help us to have a more relaxed attitude toward the transitory values that we tend to cling to, without much wisdom. The other religions can help Christianity to adopt a more peaceful attitude toward death, and Christianity can communicate a clearer vision of the hope for future life.

Preparation for death in the longer term can be related to our return to mother earth to which our physical self will be reincorporated. Reflection on the cycle of life and death from time immemorial and our closeness to the stuff of the earth can teach us to respect the physical reality on which our psychic powers too depend. It can also give us a sense of continuity with the past, more closely with one's own people, its history and culture, but also with the whole human race and the cosmic whole. The hope of eternal life can be related to this ever recurring continuity, as can also the biblical promise of the new heaven and the new earth, and eternal union with God in Christ Jesus.

These are aspects of theology that a planetary perspective may help evolve; they too can contribute to our empathy with all human beings and the whole of nature, for we are but a moment—a spate of consciousness, freedom, and love—in a long, unbroken line from the timeless past stretching into the infinite future.

CATECHETICAL METHODOLOGY

In catechesis there should be an unending dialectic between action and reflection, between theory and practice, one challenging and motivating the other in a continual dynamic.

The impact of social dynamics on catechesis will inevitably change the relationship between teacher and student, between the one who expounds the gospel and the one who receives it. The impact of psychology has already led to some changes in catechesis. This has been further developed by an understanding of small-group dynamics. But when we take into account the dynamics of larger groups—social class, racial grouping, sex, religion, nation—there will be still further changes. The roles of teacher and pupil will interact and even reverse at times in a way that has seldom happened hitherto.

An action/reflection-based catechetical method has to adapt its social and psychological analysis to each new group. Keeping in mind the context, vision, goals, and means discussed earlier, religious reflection has to be integrated with the age, experience, and sensitivity of persons. Pedagogy has to be active and activating.

Groups must be able to think out lines of action that will lead participants to an encounter with the deeper problems of the mentalities and structures that oppress or liberate human beings in our societies. Traditional activities need to be evaluated one by one in depth. Students should be able, for example, to analyze the nature of a given village society, the structures of domination or liberation operating there, and their relationships to power blocs in the surrounding region, nearby cities, the nation, and the world itself. Or, if they intend to take up action relating to trade in milk products, they must be able to find out how production and distribution are organized at the local level and are perhaps related to international economic combines such as the Nestlé Corporation. The whole problematic of development/liberation can be pursued through such issues as consumer goods, transportation, electrification, minerals, oil, banking, insurance, education, defense systems, and so forth.

Development/liberation movements can help in such an understanding of issues by drawing up pedagogical methodologies for the young, tracing one rather obvious issue to its roots and its worldwide ramifications. If the search continues with openness and commitment to other issues, it can lead participants to a more global understanding of a local situation. On the other hand, because they begin with a rather simple experience, beginners can choose their level of involvement and commitment. Unfortunately, many radicals have little awareness of or sensitivity to the stages necessary in a radicalization process, especially when major issues are not immediately noticeable.

Each stage of life has its own pedagogy. The same is true for the pedagogy of liberation. In this there is a twofold process. On the one hand, the stages of the process of growth in awareness must be respected. This is a demand of justice: to respect the person or group at the stage at which they are and adopt suitable methods. This is not mere diplomacy; it contains an element of real love. Understanding the stage of conscientization does not necessarily mean approving it as final, however. Hence the second element in this pedagogy is to encourage participants to further commitment. The two processes have to be linked in a single ongoing process that has also to take into account the balance of risks involved and yields expected from action taken in society.

The opening up of catechesis to sociopolitical issues will help Christians to discover new meaning in the Scriptures. This can help and motivate church leadership to understand radical movements. In a country such as the U.S.A., where movements for structural change of society through specific struggles are quite pronounced, this approach is a necessity.

Such a development in catechesis will also have a deep impact on Christian liturgy and prayer. They will become more real, more related to explosive issues and to the ongoing risks of Christian living in society today—a drawing closer to the cross of Jesus Christ.

In sum, relevance to sociopolitical issues within nations and the world as a whole is a necessary phase of the contemporary evolution of the catechetical movement. If Christianity fails here, it will once again be a force for reactionary foot-dragging in the social sphere and will lose the allegiance of its more youthful and dynamic members. But if the catechetical movement responds favorably to this pressing challenge, it will be deeply transformed in the process.

Chapter 12

Worship in Word and Deed

During the centuries when Christianity was allied to the Roman empire and Western domination, the liturgy—especially the Latin liturgy—educated Christians to accept the prevailing social order. Today the rubrics of the Latin liturgy have been simplified, the texts altered to include the bulk of the New Testament; the role of the saints in the liturgy has been greatly reduced and the accent placed on the life of Christ. Thousands of songs have been composed that reflect the aspirations of the people. There is more spontaneity and room for different cultural expressions. In Africa and Asia there is a growth of indigenous religious music. The Indian rite mass that has been accepted by the Catholic bishops of India incorporates many aspects of Indian culture within the eucharistic liturgy. These all are positive gains, but a much deeper transformation is required if liturgy is to respond to contemporary and planetary needs.

The liturgy, which should be both inspiration and expression of the universal joy of salvation, must be impregnated with a concern for the task of humankind within temporal reality. At present the liturgy lacks this concern, and far-reaching reforms are required if it is to perform its true function.

THE EARLY LITURGICAL TRADITION

In the earliest centuries, liturgy bore a close relationship to life. The Old Testament tradition of God's special relationship with the ancient Hebrews, linked with the later history and struggles of the Jewish people, was remembered and celebrated. The exodus was a liberation from bondage and a pledge of the promised land flowing with milk and honey. The events of history, in victory and in defeat, carried within them the enlightening word of God to a chosen people.

The New Testament concept of the kingdom of God stressed its spiritual values, yet was not removed from humankind and history. The incarnation, the paschal mystery, and the new pentecost carried the central message of God's deliverance for all. The apostles understood the deep connection between liturgy and life: they gave themselves to prayer and the breaking of bread, they held all things in common, and there was no one in need among them. There was a direct link between worship and service, between prayer and witness to love. Christ and the Old Testament prophets continually referred to the vital necessity of this bond, which is also the gauge of the sincerity of religious rites and sacrifices.

The cycle of seasons, the needs and festivities of agricultural communities, and the rites and celebration of prevailing religions had a significant influence on the development of Christian liturgy, including the Roman rite. Ancient feasts and rites were "baptized," almost as if Christian mysteries were superimposed on them. The rogation days, the litanies, and even feasts such as Christmas bear witness to this process.

As the liturgy became organized and structured, and as the central authority of the Latin church grew stronger, there was little opportunity for further adaptation. Saints who reflected the rather monastic concepts of sanctity were added to the calendar: popes, bishops, priests, monks, virgins, and widows. Few persons who had lived an ordinary lay life in the world were thought of as saints.

NEW THEMES FOR THE LITURGY

The contemporary world requires radical changes in a church whose mission is to respond to the hopes and joys, the griefs and anxieties, of the peoples of this age. A consideration of these interests suggests certain themes that must form part of the modern Christian's instruction, reflection, mission, and witness. These themes should, therefore, find a place in the liturgy. They should form a point of departure for Christian reflection and a point of return for dedicated action. The liturgy, coupled with catechesis, can mediate between such reflection and action.

The liturgy should be reorganized to provide for personal and collective focalization on such themes as food: moderate eating and drinking, fasting, famine, malnutrition; shelter: slums and shanties, migrants, refugees; the family: parenting, children, teenagers, the aged; sex: marriage, divorce, single parents, women's rights; the environment: pollution, waste, care of nature; health: disease, medicine, social services, world health; education: illiteracy, schools, universities, mass media; work: employment, underemployment, unemployment, wages, work conditions; freedom: personality development, religious freedom, prison conditions, political prisoners; truth: honesty and sincerity in public and private life, respect for truth from whatever source; justice: within the nation and among nations, social justice, elimination of inequalities, racial harmony, human rights; religious harmony: cooperation among religions, ecumenism.

These new themes must be understood as being intimately connected with the mystery of Jesus Christ and the mission of the church in the world. They are not distractions from the core of the Christian message; they incarnate it in the very heart of human life.

Meditation on these themes would make the church a better sign of Jesus Christ's love for all humankind. Christians would be helped to move from the ghettos into which they may have retreated. The life of priests and religious would also find more meaning in such an orientation of the liturgy. The liturgy could be purified of any remaining irrelevant sentimentality and taken into the midst of the struggle between good and evil that is being waged within every person and every society.

The content of preaching is almost certain to become more relevant when such themes are consciously and explicitly incorporated in the liturgical cycle.

One function of the liturgy of old was instruction of catechumens. Today many missionaries are seeking better ways to bring catechumens to an understanding of the Christian mystery. A restructuring of the liturgy with more explicit recognition of some of these new themes would help catechumens to participate more profitably in the service of the word.

The liturgical year could be revised in such a way as to correspond better to the seasons and calendars of different countries and their national and local celebrations. The entire Christian church could initiate celebrations that might eventually lead to a universal reflection of these values and problems.

Far from stopping at the externals of liturgy, such a revision would naturally overflow into renewed motivations for relevant action within the context of daily life and responsibility. Thus the interrelatedness of proclaiming the word of God, celebrating the word in worship, and witnessing to the word in service and love would be accented and deepened.

If Christian communities are to participate in the ongoing struggles for a better world, their liturgy must be related to those struggles. Weekly gatherings for worship are the principal occasions for Christians to come together. The activities to which they are geared at present are largely church-centered projects: festivals, devotions, fund-raising, social services, and the activities of parish associations. What is needed is a conscientization to broader and deeper levels of human life and its problems.

Christians need a profound cultural revolution to transform them into a force that will subvert injustice and tyranny. The weekly meetings of Christians provide an excellent opportunity for both inner personal growth and social commitment—if these meetings are wisely and courageously utilized.

LITURGICAL RENEWAL AND NON-WESTERN CULTURES

Article 37 of the Vatican II Constitution on the Sacred Liturgy lays down a clear policy:

> Even in the liturgy, the Church has no wish to impose a rigid uniformity in matters which do not implicate the faith or the good of the whole community; rather does she respect and foster the genius and talents of the various races and peoples. Anything in these peoples' way of life which is not indissolubly bound up with superstition and error she studies with

sympathy, and, if possible, preserves intact. Sometimes in fact
she admits such things into the liturgy itself, so long as they
harmonize with its true and authentic spirit.

Theoretically, this is official policy; in fact it had been so for quite
some time, even prior to Vatican II. Yet its practical implementation
is still very restricted in Asia.

A major obstacle to liturgical reform in this direction is the way in
which Christians, including priests and bishops in Africa and Asia,
have been brought up. Due to a strictly disciplined training, which
regarded uniformity as a major value, and due also to a disregard of
ancient cultures even by native Christians, it has not been easy to
carry out the reform and adaptation called for by the council.
Church leadership must provide a greater impetus in this direction.

We can distinguish between the general culture of a country and
elements that derive specifically from its religious heritage. General
cultural elements can be considered for incorporation in the liturgy
without any serious theological difficulty. They include such rites as
those used in marriages, funerals, and certain festivals. At present
some of these festivals, such as New Year and the feast of lights, are
celebrated mainly by other faiths. In certain countries, such as
Thailand and Cambodia, Christians join in New Year celebrations.
Yet in other places, such as Sri Lanka, Christians by and large do
not join in. The commemoration of ancestors, as in Vietnam,
China, and Japan, may also be regarded as an event of cultural
significance, even though it may have some religious aspects.

Christians need to understand the significance of these festivities
and then try to participate in the expression of their fundamental
values. New Year's day, for instance, could be the occasion for a
renewal of family ties, for filial homage to parents, and for friendly
visits to relatives and neighbors. But it is regarded by many Christians as an alien celebration because of its origin in other religions.
And yet the values of family life are central to Christian practice.
The Hindu Deepavali, the feast of lights, offers an occasion for all
to reflect on the theme of enlightenment. Unfortunately, trends in
these directions are still slow and hesitant.

Another characteristic of oriental cultures is their emphasis on
simplicity, especially in religious services. Asians going to temples
wear simple white dress without any signs of distinction. Christians
go to worship in the "Sunday best." The church tends to be a place

for fashion-setting and ostentation. This also contributes to the alienation of the Christian community in Asia. Greater simplicity in dress and lifestyle can help in the cultural integration of Christians.

The whole field of art, theater, music, and dance offers a wide area of renewal and adaptation for the Christian liturgy in Asia and Africa. This will entail a liberation from the rather rigid ceremonial of the Roman and Western liturgy. The peoples of Asia and Africa are also accustomed to discussion and implementation of their cultural traditions within a family, village, or tribal group. Story-telling and epics of the past are very important in these traditions. China has rebuilt itself through this traditional approach, as is evidenced by the communes and the communal efforts of mass campaigns. Students of liturgical renewal would do well to study such methods.

LITURGICAL RENEWAL AND ASIAN RELIGIONS

The Vatican II Declaration on the Relation of the Church to Non-Christian Religions offers a starting point for consideration of liturgical renewal in reference to the ancient religions of Asia. Article 2 states:

> The Catholic Church rejects nothing that is true and holy in these religions. She regards with sincere reverence those ways of conduct and of life, those precepts and teachings which, though differing in many aspects from the ones she holds and sets forth, nonetheless often reflect a ray of that Truth which enlightens all men.

The council, although emphasizing the uniqueness of Christ as "the way, the truth, and the life," exhorts Christians to promote the values of the other religions. The same Article 2 continues:

> The Church, therefore, exhorts her sons, that through dialogue and collaboration with the followers of other religions, carried out with prudence and love and in witness to the Christian faith and life, they recognize, preserve and promote the good things, spiritual and moral, as well as the socio-cultural values found among these men.

The Decree on the Mission Activity of the Church (Article 9) also speaks of the good in other religions, and sees thereby a stepping stone to a discovery of Christ by others and a fulfillment of all in Christ:

> Whatever good is found to be sown in the minds and hearts of men, or in the rites and cultures peculiar to various peoples, not only is not lost, but is healed, uplifted, and perfected for the glory of God, the shame of the demon, and the bliss of men.

Some of the Protestant churches have been much more open in their attitude to other religions, especially under the inspiration of the World Council of Churches.

It is part of Christian mission to recognize the values in other religions, for they ultimately are of God, and through them the fullness of Christ can be realized on earth. Missionary methodology in this regard should be threefold: acceptance of such values; incorporation of them within the Christian way of life; witness to the other-centeredness of the Christian message in our work for human liberation in collaboration with others. This process also involves a transformation of, or breakaway from, what is not good in any religious tradition.

Such an approach implies an acceptance of the presence of Christ in those outside the visible dimensions of the Christian churches. From this acceptance it is our mission to work toward a recognition of the role of Christ in human history beyond the Christian churches. The acceptance of other religions means acceptance of their positive values and even some of their rites and symbols, though not of anything that would be superstitious.

NON-CHRISTIAN RELIGIOUS VALUES THAT CHRISTIANITY CAN SHARE

Among the principal values in Asian religions that Christianity can accept are detachment, fasting, meditation, resignation, selfless service, simplicity of life, temperance, and unselfishness in thought and action. Christianity already acknowledges these values, it is true, but does not truly appreciate them in their Asian context.

Consider, for example, meditation, the effect of self-purification through reflection. In Buddhism, which places great emphasis on meditation, it is an effort at self-liberation from the sorrowful cycle of birth and death. All countries in which Buddhism has a strong impact are marked by this approach: Burma, Cambodia, China, Korea, Japan, Sri Lanka, Thailand. Christian liturgy could benefit greatly from a serious consideration of the Buddhist type of meditation.

Through its sacraments Christianity could emphasize the necessity for meaningful personal response on the part of participants in the liturgy, starting with values common to both other religions and Christianity, and communicating through them what is specifically transcendent in Christian revelation. Christian liturgy would thus have meaning for followers of other religions who attend such Christian ceremonies as weddings or funerals.

Rites and Symbols

How can liturgical rites and symbols be made meaningful for the peoples of our time throughout the world? One line of reform proposes to make them relevant to our modern technological world with its secular preoccupations; another suggests rendering them intelligible to the different peoples of the world according to their sociocultural and religious traditions.

The second line of thought is the one we are dealing with here. The Roman liturgy, for example, has evolved according to the cultural traditions of the West. In its rites we can distinguish elements that are from Jesus and are therefore of more universal value, and other elements that are of church origin and hence conditioned by time and space. Vatican II advocated revision of liturgical rites in accordance with local customs. Indeed, as far back as the Council of Trent such adaptation was approved. Yet few Asian countries have so far availed themselves of this opportunity. It is now most opportune and important that liturgical rites be revised accordingly.

Symbolism and symbolic rites in other religions—ablutions, lights, simple white attire, flowers—are often more related to the sociocultural milieu than to religious beliefs as such and are easily adaptable to the Christian liturgy. Such an adaptation would be especially meaningful to Asians: it would unite their traditional social values with Christian values.

Asia's Spiritual Leaders and Sacred Writings

Christian dialogue with followers of other religions must acknowledge and respect their spiritual leaders and sacred writings.
Foremost among Asia's spiritual leaders are the Buddha and Confucius. Asian religious leaders have contributed more to the spiritual
formation of the peoples of Asian countries than have any saints of
the Christian religion. It is true that their teachings do not contain
some aspects of the revelation made in Jesus Christ, but Christian
theology itself allows us to hold that they could not have had such
deep spiritual insights and influence without the grace of God.
When Christians honor them, they honor the gifts of God in Christ
and the Holy Spirit as received and witnessed by them. To honor
them is also a way of winning the good will and sympathy of the
many Asians who revere them.

Christians are generally reluctant to honor Asian religious
leaders. But it should be remembered that the followers of Asian
religions do not regard the Buddha, Confucius, Muhammad, or
Gandhi as God, in the sense in which Christians think of God. Any
danger of scandal must be weighed against the Christian obligation
to give honor where it is due. Is not another kind of scandal given
when Christians are reluctant to recognize authentic goodness outside their own fold?

How can Christians honor these leaders of other religions and
what relationship will this have to the liturgy? Could not Christians
celebrate certain observances in honor of these saintly leaders? For
instance, why not join with Buddhists in public veneration of the
Buddha on Vesak Day when his birth, enlightenment, and death are
commemorated?

Further, within the context of the liturgy, Christians could recall
the virtuous doctrines of other religions. Could not Christians thank
God collectively and in public for the signal graces of the spiritual
leadership of the great Asian religious leaders? Do their lives not
have a relationship to the paschal mystery? Such an approach would
open great possibilities for interreligious cooperation. More good
will would be generated, and others would see the true universality
of Christianity, a faith that has come to fulfill what is good, not
destroy it.

There is also a great wealth of spiritual writings in the East. They
are part of the revelation of God to humankind in these countries.

Works such as the Vedas, the Dhammapada, the teachings of Confucius and Lao-tzu and the Koran have nourished the souls of Asians for countless generations. Christians can accept and incorporate what is good in these teachings into their teaching of religion—their catechesis—as also into their meditation and worship.

Reform of the liturgy of the word offers excellent opportunities for this approach. The liturgy of the word could be revised to include not only more relevant readings from the Bible, but also passages from the sacred writings of other religions. Such an approach would provide a link between Christianity and other religions. Converts would feel more at ease in the Christian community. Asian Christians, including clergy and religious, would be more integrated into the sacred tradition of their own culture and country. This would not mean a neglect of the essential values of Christianity; on the contrary, they would be seen in the context of God's revelation to others.

Vatican II, in the Constitution on the Sacred Liturgy, recalls the eschatological dimension of the liturgy, where the full realization of the kingdom of God is to be found: "In the earthly liturgy we take part in a foretaste of that heavenly liturgy which is celebrated in the holy city of Jerusalem toward which we journey as pilgrims" (Article 8).

In the heavenly liturgy all persons of good will take part. We must try, within our limits, to realize on earth the universal dimensions of the liturgy in Christ Jesus. Some know and acknowledge Christ, others do not even know him. We who know that Christ is at work in all, and that all persons of good will really honor God by their good lives, should try to bring together as many of these as possible in a universal hymn to God. A first step in this realization could be the recognition of values in other religions, sacred writings, and spiritual leaders. They too can be related in their own way to the paschal mystery that for us is the unique sacrifice of the new and eternal testament.

Interreligious Action/Reflection

A radical transformation of the world and of human mentalities is not likely to come about without the participation and cooperation of believers in the world religions. In such action, ongoing reflection in groups—large and small—is an essential element. No deep cultural revolution is possible without a profound reflection that changes values. Such a reflection can be made on the inspiration of the Christian Scriptures in the Western countries, including Latin America, and perhaps in the Philippines. But in most countries of Asia and Africa, Christians are intermingled with others. If we accept only the Christian Scriptures for reflection, the groups that can meet together will be narrow and self-defeating.

Social action takes place within groups where Christians share with others. Asian and African action/reflection groups should be interreligious. Exclusively Christian movements, many of them imported from the West—for example, lay apostolate movements and charismatic prayer groups—are inadequate.

The challenge of common reflection and prayer is even greater when Christians form action groups with humanists, socialists, and Marxists. In these encounters too it is the search for common values and the sacrifice for a cause that builds a group. The theology of the cosmic Christ and the indwelling of the Spirit in all are of immediate significance in such situations. Thus a planetary approach to prayer can lead to the universal cooperation required for global revolutionary strategy.

Contemplatives in different religious traditions can contribute toward the growth of such forms of reflective worship. Even if largely divorced from action, they can study the sacred writings and spirituality of different religions. They can try to see the common elements and the richness of diversity. Thomas Merton considered this an important mission of contemplatives. His visit to Sri Lanka, prior to his final trip to Bangkok, was linked to this quest. His last conference on the role of the monk in our revolutionary world is full of insights on the interrelationships between religious revolutionaries, world justice, and the worship of the Lord. It is to be hoped that the thousands of contemplatives in the Christian tradition will take up this contemporary challenge of the love of God.

Mystical Experience

Mystical experience is the deepest intuition of the divine that human beings have described. All the great religions have at their heart such a deep experience. The Buddha was a profound mystic, as were the great leaders of other religions throughout the ages. Islam, Hinduism, and Confucianism have their great spiritual heights. These are the penultimates of a human union with God in worship, a worship often linked to action. The Christian spiritual tradition must come to recognize and respect the mysticism of all traditions. At this level, theologies and definitions of faith do not count as much as do the quasi-immediate experiences of the Absolute. All believers can have a perception of this inner union within themselves at certain moments. This is the substance of our relationship to God, to the Absolute, to ultimate values. It is where our authenticity and our relationships are tested at the bar of conscience.

Nor should we exclude from this consideration the finer qualities of humanists and revolutionary traditions. A great scientist or artist has an element of the mystic. A Lenin or a Mao Tse-tung cannot be fully appreciated without seeing the mystical traits of their struggles and their characters. The classless, stateless society of Karl Marx and Friedrich Engels recalls Christians to their long-forgotten apocalyptic vision and vocation. The lifestyle of Ho Chi Minh was as attractive in its simplicity and daring as those of the great religious liberators. Humanity will be the richer if, as whole peoples, we can come to appreciate such peaks of human endeavor, as they consciously or unconsciously touch something of the divine. The grace of the Christian bids these signs to be recognized and praised for the marvels God has worked among us.

As humanity grows in its consciousness of its oneness and of the roots of liberation in all religions and persons, it will be possible for women and men to worship together both in spirit and in word and deed. Inspiration can be drawn from all the religions and cultures of the world. We shall thus join worship in the struggles for integral human liberation. We shall also be approaching the ultimate worship in which there will be no separation of churches, no priestly caste, no exclusion of women, no holy books and ceremonials, but God will be all in all in a new heaven and a new earth.

Chapter 13

Toward a Spirituality of Justice

"Spirituality" is a term used in traditional religious writings to designate the search for self-fulfillment and perfection. Members of religious orders understood it as a search for personal sanctification, for growth in virtue and liberation from sin, inspired by the desire for union with God by striving to live for certain transcendental values.

At one period in the modern scientific evolution led by the West, there was a disdain of the spiritual and the religious. It was argued that only that which could be felt by the senses was real; all else was a creation of the human mind. This view harmonized with capitalism, which had profit maximization as its ultimate value. Marxism also affirmed materialism and the primacy of economic factors in determining human values, thoughts, and actions. Today there is in the West a search for spirituality. Many persons, especially the young, feel the emptiness of the Western capitalist ethos. They turn to all types of solutions and alternatives—conservative fundamentalism, the charismatic movement, yoga, maharishis, and other Eastern traditions, as well as to the exhilarating experiences of drugs. Whether it be through the motivations of Eastern religions or the hallucinations of LSD, their search is for something different from the rat race of individualism and for new perceptions of self and the universe.

In the context of Marxism, the experience of the Chinese revolution also shows a new emphasis on the need of human motivation for carrying through a vast revolutionary transformation of society.

Chinese communism fostered the creative role of the human spirit in bringing about a change in social relationships and processes.

It is within a wide panorama of contemporary cultures and religious traditions that a spirituality of justice is emerging.

Expressions of values in terms of nationalism, individualism, and democracy have proved inadequate. Socialism must also continue its search to transcend socialist nationalism and the corruption of power elites. The human person seeks selfhood—self-expression and self-realization—in all societies. The young are asserting their rights. Women are discovering and affirming new potentialities for personhood. The suppressed peoples of the world are revolting against oppression.

In this vast and rapidly changing world, self-realization—at all levels—is a primary concern of all. What we are concerned with, then, is a spirituality of liberation, whereby persons free themselves, personally and societally, to become capable of genuine freedom, responsibility, and love.

WHY JUSTICE?

The question of justice is a question of basic values gnawing at the conscience of sensitive human beings. What is a person's responsibility in this context? What is it that can really fulfill one's personality, ennoble a person, and offer undiluted joy as far as it is possible on this earth? Can a person find satisfaction and self-realization in joining or belonging to the affluent elite and thus forgetting the masses? And can one be a truly human person while being a member of the weak, exploited, apathetic mass of marginalized humanity? Can solace be found for either of these in the consolations of religion, the distractions of a consumer culture, the hallucinations of drugs, or the ineffectiveness of dropping out?

True human fulfillment cannot come from a conscious participation in exploitation, from destroying the livelihood of others, from possessively grabbing the little that others have, from competitiveness that brings the law of the animal kingdom into the human sphere, from deceiving and miseducating ignorant peoples, from suppressing discontent and legitimate expressions of selfhood and freedom, from alienating persons from their true well-being by consumerist advertising and ostentation. Yet all these are daily features of the capitalist world system.

True human happiness can be found only in unselfishness, in an effort to live for others—according to one's possibilities and situations.

Can unselfishness generate mass enthusiasm for nation-building and for making this earth a habitable home for the human race? Nationalism has always been combined with a competitive selfishness vis-à-vis other nations. This can only lead to destruction of all. A universal approach is needed that can motivate all human beings to give of their best toward building a sound and just world order. A truly enlightening conscientization and a collective effort by all can liberate the creative energies of the masses everywhere.

Justice is the virtue by which we endeavor to give one's due to each. It requires a fair distribution of wealth, income, and opportunities in society and relationships in which everyone's human dignity is recognized and respected. Justice is a virtue that has to be acquired; its acquisition demands that we struggle against the contrary vices, which spring ultimately from selfishness. Justice is not the "charity" of social-service paternalism.

Growth in social justice requires a collective struggle against contrary vices. The virtue of social justice cannot be acquired or even studied individually, for social justice is concerned with the distribution of goods and services within a community and the relationships among its members. Hence it necessarily moves beyond the purely individual aspects of a person's life. To advance in justice we must have an understanding of the type of social situation within which we live and make our decisions.

Obstacles to social justice cannot be overcome by individual efforts, for they are entrenched within the power structures of a country. Only through group action can such obstacles be overcome.

Social justice is a dynamic virtue that has to be acquired through action within a given situation in relation to a particular place, time, and course of events. It is a virtue that directly affects our own use of material goods, their possession, distribution, and exchange in society. It affects our own lifestyle, because lifestyles are related to the use of resources. Lifestyles set value patterns that can bring about relationships of inferiority and superiority. Social justice is also directly related to one's political commitment, for in the present world a fair distribution of resources and the realization of human rights cannot be achieved without political action. Social justice necessitates, moreover, group self-criticism and the systematic, objective analysis of the de facto environment.

Cultic vs. Prophetic Spirituality

Unfortunately, religions have not generally regarded justice as central to the spiritual life. This is one of the deepest causes of the present crisis of religion. There is an increasing realization today that much of the thinking and action of so-called religious persons has, in fact, been contrary and harmful to the demands of social justice. The Old Testament prophetic tradition in religion has often been submerged by cultural adaptations of religion.

The means of spiritual advancement were thought to be of a cultic rather than prophetic nature. Prayer, meditation, and separation from the world were the traditional means of sanctification. Spiritual growth was thought of as attained through monasticism and monastic practices, not through concern with the problems of ordinary persons. Penances were of a personal nature, such as prayers and fasting, and had little to do with any struggle for justice.

For lay persons who could not devote a lifetime to the pursuit of this model of spirituality there was a proliferation of popular devotions, which tended to satisfy their need of religiosity and console them in the difficulties of life. Saints "specialized" in protection from sickness, plague, theft, loss of property, and in helping find a partner in marriage, resist evil influences, and the like. Such spirituality has little relationship to civil rights, women's rights, land reform, foreign exploitation, feudalism, equitable distribution of resources and GNP, just wages, and world peace.

Although such spirituality may have produced many saintly persons who were greatly dedicated to person-to-person service to the poor and the afflicted, it was not associated with any movement for radical change in the world. On the contrary, it was often an obstacle: it gave religious persons a high degree of complacency. They believed themselves to be on the road to sanctity and on the side of God. It is very important that this critique of traditional spirituality be clearly understood. For one of the main objections to commitment to social justice is that it is not "spiritual" or "supernatural" enough. Traditional spirituality has, in fact, been one of the main mental and cultural obstacles to the commitment of religious persons to social justice, because it did not help them understand the social radicalism of the gospel.

However, deep within each religious tradition there is a basis for social radicalism. For the religions, in their different ways, teach universal solidarity, equality, justice, compassion, and honesty. When understood this way, religions can be seen as an inexhaustible source of motivation for the cause of justice. Thus, religious reformers have been social reformers, especially on the Indian subcontinent.

Biblical Demand for Social Justice

Social justice is an essential virtue in Christian revelation and the Judeo-Christian tradition. The Old Testament reveals a God concerned with life and relationships among human beings. God wants not merely worship and honor, but the happiness of humanity in mutual love:

> I have seen the miserable state of my people in Egypt. I have heard their appeal to be free of their slave drivers. Yes, I am well aware of their sufferings. I mean to deliver them out of the hands of the Egyptians and bring them up out of that land to a land rich and broad, a land where milk and honey flow [Exod. 3:7–8].

The prophets of the Old Testament clearly reveal that God wants justice, not merely ritual sacrifices:

> I hate and despise your feasts,
> I take no pleasure in your solemn festivals.
> When you offer me holocausts, . . .
> I reject your oblations,
> and refuse to look at your sacrifices of fattened cattle.
> Let me have no more of the din of your chanting,
> no more of your strumming on harps.
> But let justice flow like water,
> and integrity like an unfailing stream [Amos 5:21–24].

"With what gift shall I come into Yahweh's presence
and bow down before God on high?
Shall I come with holocausts,
with calves one year old?
Will he be pleased with rams by the thousand,
with liberations of oil in torrents? . . ."
—What is good has been explained to you, man;
this is what Yahweh asks of you:
only this, to act justly,
to love tenderly
and to walk humbly with your God [Micah 6:6–8].

Yahweh Sabaoth, the God of Israel, says this: Amend your
behavior and your actions and I will stay with you here in this
place. Put no trust in delusive words like these: This is the
sanctuary of Yahweh, the sanctuary of Yahweh, the sanctuary
of Yahweh! But if you do amend your behavior and your
actions, if you treat each other fairly, if you do not exploit the
stranger, the orphan and the widow (if you do not shed inno-
cent blood in this place), and if you do not follow alien gods,
to your own ruin, then here in this place I will stay with
you. . . . Yet here you are, trusting in delusive words, to no
purpose! Steal, would you, murder, commit adultery, perjure
yourselves, burn incense to Baal, follow alien gods that you
do not know?—and then come presenting yourselves in this
Temple that bears my name, saying: Now we are safe—safe to
go on commiting all these abominations? [Jer. 7:3–10].

Many Old Testament texts make it clear that true religion is based
on justice to one's neighbor. Where there is no justice to one's
neighbor, religious ritual is not only meaningless but an insult to
God.

The New Testament clearly demands social justice. John the
Baptist preached a message not only of prayer and penance but also
of sharing:

When all the people asked him, "What must we do, then?" he
answered, "If anyone has two tunics he must share with the
man who has none, and the one with something to eat must do

the same." There were tax collectors too who came for baptism, and these said to him, "Master, what must we do?" He said to them, "Exact no more than your rate." Some soldiers asked him in their turn, "What about us? What must we do?" He said to them, "No intimidation! No extortion! Be content with your pay!" [Luke 3:10–14].

The teaching of Jesus Christ is perfectly clear, for he preached integral liberation, both personal and societal. In the parable on the final judgment he teaches that what counts is our work for the alleviation of human suffering and the liberation of the oppressed. He does not want meaningless ritual, but rather that the goods of the earth be available to all in justice and that love prevail in relationships among human beings. Christ identified himself with the oppressed and gave up his life in working for their liberation. "A man can have no greater love than to lay down his life for his friends" (John 15:13).

The apostles gave a similar lesson, both in their actions and in their writings. St. Paul says, "Pay every government official what he has a right to ask. . . . All the commandments . . . are summed up in this single command: You must love your neighbor as yourself" (Rom. 13:7, 9).

St. James says that if we discriminate among persons we cannot be followers of Jesus Christ. He has harsh language for the rich:

> Now an answer for the rich. Start crying, weep for the miseries that are coming to you. Your wealth is all rotting, your clothes are all eaten up by moths. All your gold and your silver are corroding away, and the same corrosion will be your own sentence, and eat into your body. It was a burning fire that you stored up as your treasure for the last days. Laborers mowed your fields, and you cheated them—listen to the wages that you kept back, calling out; realize that the cries of the reaper have reached the ears of the Lord of hosts. On earth you have had a life of comfort and luxury; in the time of slaughter you went on eating to your heart's content [James 5:1–5].

St. John tells us repeatedly that it is not possible to love God if we do not also love our neighbor (see 1 John 3:10; 4:4–21). The Book of Revelation also tells us that the final stage will be marked by love and justice, for every tear will be wiped away from every eye (21:4).

Mary, the mother of Jesus, epitomizes this concern of God for integral liberation of all persons. Her Magnificat is a revolutionary message, which has unfortunately been domesticated, so that its daily recitation has little radical impact. In it a threefold revolution is hymned—cultural: "he has routed the proud of heart"; political: "he has pulled down princes from their thrones and exalted the lowly"; and economic: "the hungry he has filled with good things, the rich sent empty away" (Luke 1:51-53).

Justice is the first demand of love of God and of neighbor. It is the sacrament of the love of God.

The Holy Spirit and Justice

When Jesus left this earth, he told his disciples that he would send the Holy Spirit to teach them many more things. The followers of Jesus are therefore to learn much as they go through their lives and continue in history until the end of the world.

The Spirit inspires persons to work toward the kingdom of God, the rule of righteousness, and live its values of truth, love, justice, and peace. The Spirit is present within the vast changes taking place in the whole world and can be understood as inspiring what is good in the revolutionary struggles of our time.

Conscientization can be understood as a process of listening to the Spirit in our societies and within ourselves, an effort to respond to the call of God in continuing the work of the humanization (and hence divinization) of the world. Correspondingly, reluctance and refusal to take this seriously and to question one's explicit or implicit social options may be seen as a closing of oneself to the grace of the Holy Spirit. In this sense many persons who claim to be saintly, because they are traditional, conservative, and almost wholly cultic in their spirituality, may in fact be hardening their hearts against the voice of God speaking to them through persons, events, and movements of our age.

Among the gifts or graces of the Holy Spirit must be included discernment of social reality, courage to work for justice, the evaluation of relationships within a group, the choice of employment and lifestyles, the facing of risks, the timing of action, decisions on strategies, and polarization when necessary.

Such an understanding of Jesus, God the Father, and the Holy Spirit is an authentically trinitarian interpretation of the task of human liberation in the world. Relationships within the Trinity can also be articulated in terms of creative, redemptive, and inspirational roles in the continuing evolution of humanity and of the universe toward the ultimate kingdom planned by God for humankind.

RETHINKING FAITH, HOPE, AND LOVE

Our relationship to God is said to be articulated basically in terms of the three theological virtues of faith, hope, and love. These virtues must be rethought in terms of the understanding of the Trinity and integral human liberation.

Faith in the Promises of God

The faith of Christian believers is like that of pilgrims on a journey. They have to face many obstacles both within themselves and from society. Faith in God, therefore, calls for a deep conviction in the march of history, in which we can improve personal, social, and planetary relationships. Faith believes that God is present in our efforts, and he wishes the fulfillment and self-realization of each person, group, and community. Faith accepts the basic message of the Scriptures, the God of loving justice.

Hope, the Forgotten Theological Virtue

Hope is the unshakable certainty in the realization of the promises of God in Jesus Christ, based on Jesus' life, death, and resurrection. In Christian revelation there is a clear promise that "creation still retains the hope of being freed, like us, from its slavery to decadence, to enjoy the same freedom and glory as the children of God" (Rom. 8:21). Humanity is even now undergoing the labor pains of its new birth: "we groan inwardly as we wait for our bodies to be set free" (Rom. 8:23).

This is the ultimate and total liberation promised and being realized now in our present sufferings and efforts. These efforts to realize the kingdom of truth, freedom, justice, love, and peace are therefore worthwhile and endurable because of the certainty of the splendor of the future of humankind and the universe (see Rom. 8:18).

Christian hope is therefore an unquenchable, optimistic thrust into the building of our future. It is never satisfied with the status quo. It does not canonize the present establishment as if it were the kingdom already achieved. Christian hope is not presumptive in its present achievement but ever tends to fulfill what is deficient in existing reality by the measure of the promise of ultimate human liberation. Hope is meaningful only if the strategies we adopt are realistic and adequate to reach the goals desired.

Love Growing out of Justice

Christian thought generally identifies love as the central and highest virtue in human relationships. However, the relationship between love and justice is seldom presented adequately. We cannot say that we truly love others if they are being hurt, exploited, deprived of their basic rights, and we do nothing about it. Love cannot be practiced without justice. Love cannot be built on injustice, for injustice is lovelessness. Love is not an alternative to justice. There is no substitute for justice. Justice is the beginning of love.

ACQUIRING THE VIRTUE OF SOCIAL JUSTICE

We must be prepared to accept the consequences of the option for social justice—that is, we must engage in action for justice. We must identify the persons, groups, and forces that are allies of social justice and those that are its enemies. This includes, of course, the forces at work within ourselves.

In order to deal with the obstacles to justice we must first identify them. We may see them around us, but we shall also find most of them within ourselves:
- self-complacency
- love of material security
- disinclination to let one's daily routine be upset
- insensitivity to the many injustices around one
- superficiality (seeing social issues in relation to values emphasized by the mass media, distorted educational objectives, etc.)
- work and family demands absorbing all of one's time and energies

- complacency with palliatives and minor changes that do not touch the substance of problems
- crusades for issues of little relevance (anticommunism, overconcern with sexual morality)
- ignorance of the real issues and unwillingness to learn
- unawareness of being confined to the limits of one's own social, cultural, racial, and religious groupings, and thereby overlooking their wider implications
- overconcern with structures; infighting within groups
- fatalism ("I can't do anything about it")
- uncritical acceptance of educational systems, the mass media, the promises of those in charge
- fear of being misunderstood by the majority
- fear of punishment for nonconformity
- failure to acknowledge and heed prophetic voices
- unwillingness to exert oneself
- overconcern with money, security
- belief that the poor are lazy, selfish, unwilling to help themselves
- political neutrality (which usually favors the status quo)
- belief that all change must be violent, and is therefore to be avoided
- providing for one's posterity for a century ahead, but not providing for those who suffer due to today's social structures.

All these are important issues to which an individual or group concerned about growth in the virtue of justice must give serious and sincere attention. Far too often the spirit of justice within us is silenced and not permitted to relate critically to such issues.

The process of overcoming these obstacles shows us the way to our own personal liberation. Being bound by our internal fears and selfishness is a chief cause of the continuance of injustice in the world. Overcoming self and living for others is extremely difficult, because of our social conditioning. Both societal liberation and personal liberation involve a struggle against the selfishness embedded within us and in society in general.

Conflicts are inevitable in the struggle for justice. Our choices are bound to be ambiguous, for we deal in an area in which there is no absolute certainty.

It is within these situations that we must articulate a spirituality in which love is the motivation. It is precisely love for the oppressed that can make us strong in our action against oppression without engendering bitterness for anyone. Conflict does not occur for its own sake, but in order to ensure justice and peace without the violence of exploitation and war.

In this process, it is likely that we shall have to rethink our alliances, friendships, and social relationships. We may find that groups and persons with whom we have worked for many years are, in fact, obstacles to social justice. We may even come to the conclusion that persons and institutions that claim to represent God and religion are actually defenders of social injustice. Sometimes conflict may come closer to home: family relationships may be strained, and so cause tensions. We may feel alienated from former friends, from entire institutions, perhaps from an entire social class. The oppressed themselves sometimes do not support persons who want change, for they are heavily influenced by the thought-conditioning to which they have been subjected for long periods.

We may also find that the forces of law and order, be they the police and military or religious agencies and moral discipline, are marshaled against our efforts. Our morality may be challenged. Our own sanity may be questioned. We are likely to be isolated, mistrusted, misunderstood, calumniated, and alienated by others who believe themselves to be normal, sane, law-abiding, and holy.

Nevertheless we must set ourselves to the task of developing a spirituality in which conflict and contestation are seen as part of the process of growth in self-realization to service of neighbor and love of God.

A spirituality of justice can help us achieve deep interior peace in the midst of conflict and tension, but this requires much reflection and group evaluation in the midst of action. Hence a spirituality of social justice must evolve radical forms of reflection and meditation, prayer and retreats. These will have to include an awareness of the social environment and of the options available to a group or person. Prayerful reflection will require self-criticism and evaluation by the individual and the group, for there is always a temptation to make compromises with existing power structures rather than to keep moving forward toward the kingdom. Evaluation, self-criticism, and reflection may themselves contribute to tension and conflict, for there may be differences of opinion even among similarly motivated groups. It is not one's sincerity alone that gives meaning to one's commitment: it has to be tested within a given social context.

In this connection, the methodology of spiritual retreats needs to be recast. Traditional retreats, emphasizing interiority and totally a stranger to sociopolitical analysis, cannot meet the demands of the more radically committed or even socially critical persons and groups. The group in retreat will have to emerge from the exercise with a clearer understanding of social issues and trends, of its own options, fears, and inhibitions, and, if possible, with a consensus on goals, short-term objectives, strategies, and even tactics. Traditional religious life and spiritual retreats have not responded to this need.

COURAGE, PRUDENCE, AND MODERATION

The spirituality of social justice requires that the virtues of courage, prudence, and moderation be rethought within the framework of tensions and conflicts.

Courage

We need courage to make our options, to decide in favor of justice for the oppressed—the courage, as Rabindranath Tagore says, "never to bend the knee before insolent might"—to continue when we do not see immediate results, to form new relationships with those who are fighting on our side, to go forward in the midst of uncertainty, to endure misunderstandings and repression, to hope for the future of humankind here on earth and to undertake the risks involved, to suffer in ourselves and in others. We need the courage to persevere day by day, month by month, year by year, renewing commitment, forming strategies, and trying always to be faithful to the cause of justice despite the many temptations of an unjust system.

Courage also requires careful strategy, for justice is not the result of good luck. The road to peace with justice is long and arduous. Victories have a great price and must be safeguarded with vigilance.

Prudence

The virtue of prudence will have to be understood in a different context.Earlier spirituality thought of prudence in terms of personal relationships; in the struggle for social justice, prudence has a role within the framework of the social conflicts of our time. It includes an understanding of each one's own personality and abilities, and also of the forces that are operative in a given society. Prudence requires that we not waste our time and energies in unnecessary battles and secondary issues, for this will dissipate the effort even of the well intentioned. Prudence will decide on the issues that are worth fighting for, as well as the means to be used in the struggle. Prudence tells us when it is necessary to bypass an issue or pursue it to the extent of polarization.

Prudence will help us calculate risks so that the risks taken will yield results. Prudence decides when to give oneself for a cause, even if it means such extreme sacrifices as imprisonment or life itself. The action of Che Guevara in joining guerrillas may have seemed imprudent in the short term. But in the long term it has made an inestimable contribution to the cause. A spirituality of liberation therefore involves an understanding of risk-bearing and disappointment.

Moderation

The virtue of moderation can be understood as a balancing of patience and impatience, action and reflection, haste and caution, compromise and polarization. It will also teach us to respect others and challenge them to social justice. Moderation requires that we respect persons at the stage at which they actually are, while inviting them to transcend their self-interest. Temperance counters the danger of arrogance, which can easily separate radical leadership from the masses.

Freedom and discipline must be combined in a radical struggle. The freedom of each person is to be respected. Discipline can prevent fragmentation among those who want a just society. The virtue of moderation can unite freedom and discipline.

Prudence and moderation will also tell us what means are possible in the struggle for justice. It will always be suicidal to resort to means that are found to fail. At other times, a long armed struggle may be required, as happened in the case of Mozambique.

IDENTIFICATION WITH THE OPPRESSED

Work for social justice requires some form of identification with the oppressed. This has been the example set by the great revolutionary and social leaders of our century—Mao Tse-tung, Ho Chi Minh, Mahatma Gandhi, Lenin.

The forms of such identification are varied: (1) service to the oppressed—helping the needy personally, sharing one's resources and talents with them; (2) joining in mind and heart—understanding the suffering of the oppressed and the deeper causes of their affliction; (3) identification in their struggle—by helping build awareness and creating public opinion, by forming action groups and bringing pressure to bear for change, by supporting the cause of social revolution from one's own social and class position, by suffering misunderstanding and alienation from one's own friends and family; (4) identification in lifestyle—in being poor physically, in esthetic values in social life, in community relationships.

Suffering with the poor is possible for the affluent by identifying with them in thought. But it is when one feels physically in one's own body the pressures of poverty—in food, transportation, clothing, the difficulties of obtaining acceptance in a public office— that one understands a little better the difficult condition of the poor: their inability to move out of their situation; their narrowness of outlook; their very limited range of options; their limited staying power; their vulnerability to all types of calamities; the vicious circle of misery and powerlessness. For the person of affluent circumstances, there can be an identification only from without.

The demands of loving one's neighbor as oneself can be very exacting—if this call of Christ is taken seriously. It can lead to an ongoing process of self-denudation, of giving up things that cushion the hard knocks of life.

Our usual reaction is to build up defenses for ourselves against the calamities of life. However, the call of Christ is a call to give up our securities. "Foxes have holes and the birds of the air have nests, but the Son of Man has nowhere to lay his head" (Matt. 8:20).

Following Jesus means accepting one's daily cross. Even more difficult than dying once and for all is the acceptance of a daily death to oneself in identification with the suffering of others.

This voluntary and individual acceptance of the cross of social justice can vary, depending on social situations. For the poor it may mean not giving up their companions, even if they themselves rise up the social ladder. It means a refusal to be integrated within a higher social level at the expense of another who remains oppressed. For the affluent it may mean giving up privileges to which they have grown accustomed, thinking them to be theirs as a matter of right due to education or inheritance or hard work.

When we understand the real relationships of rich and poor in our world today, we begin to see that an identification with the oppressed is not something extra that the affluent may do out of kindness and generosity; it is a necessity for the realization of social justice.

However, it is not enough to be poor externally. One more poor person is not the route to global liberation. There must be a deliberate and active joining in the struggle against oppression.

LIFESTYLES

The spiritual growth of persons is intimately linked to the problem of lifestyles, for that is where the option for social justice comes home to a person, a family, a group.

Social justice requires a rethinking of the lifestyles of families, especially of the affluent. Action for justice can lead persons to situations in which they may have to suffer loss of employment, imprisonment, or other dire consequences. Then the whole family is affected. Action for justice thus requires a common reflection among the members of a family. This brings to the fore a dimension of social concern that may be generally absent from or neglected by families. Groups of families may have to pool their resources in order to cope with the calamities that affect them. Such sharing of risks and securities will bring families closer to each other. Individual families alone can hardly solve the problems of social justice, hence the necessity for some form of association of families as action for justice deepens. This is the lesson of radical movements in many countries. Reflection on the Asian joint family system can be a help in such situations.

In all this, what is important is not the category a person belongs to—employee or employer, male or female, adult or youth, cleric or lay person, rural or urban dweller. It is their unity in the option for social justice that can lead persons to participate in the liberative cause. The evolution of new lifestyles often means a regrouping of persons on the basis of socio-political options. The older divisions according to religion, class, racial group, and sex are less relevant than divisions according to social goals, strategies, and tactics. This is also a new form of ecumenism. Intraecclesiastical struggles and interchurch conflicts are simply less important today. Radicals, on the other hand, must appreciate that fragmentation into small, mutually exclusive groups is counterproductive.

Change in lifestyle requires awareness, conviction, and courage. It is as difficult to opt for a simpler, poorer, and more authentic way of life as it is to give up other areas of personal selfishness. A person, family, or group going through the process will therefore need the help of friends and associates. For a certain period of time, individuals may have to be supported by others financially and psychologically.

RISKS AND YIELDS

The two processes of respect—for persons and groups—and challenge are linked in a single, ongoing pedagogy. We provoke because we respect. We truly respect others when we challenge them to keep going further.

An orientation of goals and methods toward a fundamental restructuring of personal values and societal structures implies many risks at each stage of the process. There must, therefore, be preparatory reflection on risk-bearing. There has to be a balancing of risks: the more radical the action, the greater the risk of isolation, suppression, imprisonment, and even death itself.

Options within the sociopolitical field seldom are absolutely clear, but we must have the courage to choose with an awareness of predictable consequences.

The analysis of means can be judged or categorized according to the difficulties or risks to be faced. A fourfold delineation suggests itself, as follows.

Low Risk/Low Yield

- informing groups, educating elites; study groups, seminars, research papers, documentation
- cooperation with elites for bringing about change, such as supporting their political candidates
- pressure within the sociopolitical system: petitions, declarations, lobbying, legal mass demonstrations, symbolic public fasts, theater, song, liturgies

- action of politically neutral agencies such as the Red Cross, Boy Scouts, UNESCO

These methods have the advantage of being least costly in energy and manpower. Many can participate in them. The extent of confrontation is low, and they may be tolerated for quite a while by the power system.

The disadvantage is that the power system may ignore them or sometimes co-opt them within a scheme of minor reforms. Such methods are reformist: they do not lead to fundamental changes in mentalities or structures. They seem to be based on the presumption that ignorance is the only, or main, barrier to justice, and that awareness will bring about change.

However, these are means that can be part of a wider strategy. For without the creation of awareness and the engendering of good will, changes are unlikely.

High Risk/High Yield

Some such types of activities were popularized by Mahatma Gandhi in the struggle for Indian independence. He called it satyagraha, the passive struggle for truth. It is nonviolent civil resistance.

The advantage of these methods is a degree of pressure and escalation that the previous methods do not attain. These methods require a certain mass participation. Deliberate choice is required. They permit time for issues to be clarified, and hence the public is not so easily confused, as it is when more radical measures are taken.

These methods can maximize the moral force of a people. They can cause a breakthrough in awareness and lead to commitment. They are likely to provoke reaction from power structures, and thus participants must be prepared to suffer the consequences.

A disadvantage is that such measures can be crushed by a strong power system. Usually such methods will not be resorted to unless convictions are very deep.

Very High Risk/Uncertain Yield

These are do-or-die methods directly related to the physical overthrow of an existing regime: systematic sabotage, insurrection, guerrilla warfare, terrorism. The result is victory or elimination. They leave little opportunity for intermediate goals. Control over what is happening is difficult and depends on the flow of events. This type of action is seldom undertaken by a massive segment of a society.

The advantage of such methods is that if they succeed they can bring about a reshaping of society. They maximize the commitment of a few. What form of society will emerge after a successful effort depends very much on the readiness of the leadership to work for real justice.

The disadvantage of these methods is that violence is a domain generally well controlled by a power system. Modern states are resourceful in putting down insurrections and are united in supporting each other's regimes.

But the important issue is the likelihood of success in changing society. The Chinese revolution led by Mao succeeded with such methods carried out over a long period of time. The cultural revolution of 1967, however, ended in the overthrow of those who led it for nearly a decade.

No Risk/No Yield

Here issues of a sociopolitical nature are not present at all: youth groups that organize picnics, socials, and dances, or even engage in activities that are indifferent to social goals, such as personality development and debating; likewise, purely religion-related activities, such as novenas and pilgrimages.

GROUP EVALUATION

The evaluation of one's activities is an important stage in the spirituality of social justice. This is quite different from the modes of spiritual direction and personal examination of conscience in traditional spirituality.

Group evaluation, within a renewed form of spirituality, can be a safeguard against individualism, compromise due to fear, insularity, personal worries, and the like. It can also contribute to the acceptance of diversities and the pooling of talents, skills, age groups, and strategies, as well as give practicality to prophecy.

Group evaluation calls for openness to criticism, both in giving and receiving it. This is a more exacting humility than even that of personal confession. Fidelity to regular evaluation is important for the continued existence of a group as a meaningful agent of social justice. When a group is not prepared to evaluate itself, it may be a sign that the group has ceased to be a meaningful entity ready to work together for social justice. It is then time to question the very existence of the group.

Group cohesiveness is particularly challenged when a member of the group is publicly attacked. Reactionary repression is sophisticated and powerful today. Psychological warfare is a weapon that the social establishment uses with great skill. A group that wishes to struggle together for social justice must prepare itself to face such attacks and endure the consequent external and internal tensions. It may otherwise fall apart under the weight of public criticism, derision, or attack.

When a group joins together in a single cause, each one's individuality and specificity must be accepted. There must be room for spontaneity, imagination, creativity, and dynamism. No group should seek consensus for its own sake, but should provide for each one's self-fulfillment within the struggle. Ultimately, a group or a family is best held together by the fidelity of members to their own informed consciences.

The effort to live a new lifestyle of social liberation has its joys and its consolations. A simpler lifestyle may be physically healthier, psychologically more liberating and fulfilling. It can generate more authentic interpersonal relationships and a deeper level of happiness. One can experience the joy of children growing up in an atmosphere of unselfishness, sharing, and dedication. This is a happiness often denied to families whose primary motivation is the maximization of their personal and family wealth or power.

SOCIAL JUSTICE AND SANCTITY

Social commitment, with its risks, tensions, conflicts, and ruptures, is not likely to take place without deep reflection. It requires a more thoughtful decision for persons to commit themselves to the defense of civil rights at a time of political repression than to remain hidden from the world, meditating in a convent chapel or attending weekly novenas. Profound reflection is required for motivation, action, and evaluation. Marx, Lenin, Mao Tse-tung, and Mahatma Gandhi were all men of deep reflection—*and* passionately committed to action for justice.

For the Christian, the prayer of social justice finds substance in the Scriptures, especially in the life and teaching of Christ. The Our Father is intimately connected with social justice. "Give us today our daily bread" and "your kingdom come, your will be done, on earth as in heaven" are eminently related to the concerns of justice. To call God "Father of all" is to take an option against all forms of social discrimination based on color, class, caste, and sex.

In the pattern of Christ's teaching, a work such as Daniel Berrigan's *Dark Night of Resistance* can help us rediscover the radical meaning of the gospel in our times.

When religions come to understand the radical and revolutionary demands of their basic message, they will cease to be obstacles to justice. It will then be seen how close the love of God is to the dedicated service of others and the struggle for a better world.

Action for justice implies a dying to self. In the world today, especially where repression is on the increase, a person committed to social justice will have to expect to suffer. It may result in loss of status and employment, even imprisonment and separation from one's dearest companions in life. Ultimately, in the moment of deepest suffering, one is alone. On the cross, Jesus was alone. Yet this was his supreme moment of self-giving in love. The quest for justice can lead to a self-donation in which love existentially experiences the price and joy of love. This is not the love of sentiment or paternalism. It is love purchased with flesh and blood.

All persons seek happiness. Religions purport to show the way to human happiness and fulfillment. Those who accept a religion as a guide in life choose holiness or sanctity as a goal for themselves. Spirituality is the understanding of the path to such sanctity.

In Christian spirituality we can discern three levels or ways of understanding holiness:

(1) Sanctity as individual persons think of it within themselves in response to their consciences. This is the area known best by a person, the ultimate criterion of personal decision-making.

(2) Sanctity as mediated through an institution that claims the right to indicate God's will for us—that is, a community or church.

Sometimes the nation-state too claims this authority—for example, when it demands that citizens conform to its norms, even to the point of laying down their lives for it.

(3) Sanctity as the search for the kingdom of God, the rule of righteousness, for all persons, women and men, nations, racial groupings, religions. This is a more general norm that has to be discerned as we go through history, and in given conjunctures of events.

The planetary age requires an integrated spirituality in which all three norms converge in the direction of a personal conscience and a community (authority) urging us toward the common good of humanity.

A crisis of spirituality emerges when we perceive a conflict among these norms or levels. Thus when an American religious sister thinks of her position in relation to the U.S. involvement in the Vietnam war and her own cardinal archbishop says that anything less than complete victory is unacceptable to the U.S.A., if in her own heart she feels that so many bombs—more than all the bombs of World War II—should not be dropped by her government on the poor people of North Vietnam, what is she to think of obedience to the church, and the loyalty ingrained in her to the American flag? If she does not speak against the war, she is counted as part of the silent majority supporting the military, industrial establishment. But if she speaks out, will her religious congregation understand it? What of the church as a whole, which seemed to bless the war effort against North Vietnam? What of the anticommunism she has absorbed for so many years?

These are examples of the inner tensions of spiritual growth within a global society. War and peace are not the only issues. The economic relationships of countries, racial tensions, sexism, the self-righteous attitude toward other religions, the rape of nature— all these bring their problems to the individual person and cause inner turmoil, uncertainty, and worry about whether one is doing the right thing in continuing in a given line of spirituality and a given lifestyle.

The spirituality that is needed in our planetary interrelatedness is one that integrates all the three levels mentioned above. The small action group, neighborhood association, house-church, or commune may perhaps be pointers in the direction of the future. Their

coalescence into networks for relevant public impact should give
them more meaning than isolation can bring. Their participation
in the still wider human search beyond religions, ideologies, and
national frontiers may be the type of communions required for
pressing toward the values of human rights, food, environmental
protection, peace, and women's liberation, all of which are far
more relevant kingdom issues than many of the parochial concerns of local churches that continue the traditional emphases
on church building, parish schools, Sunday mass, and bingo.

In the Christian understanding of mission there has to be a spirituality that integrates different dimensions in a wholistic vision.
Proclamation, witness, dialogue with other faiths and ideologies,
inculturation, struggles for societal justice and personal purification
need to be correlated in one spiritual thrust within us. The planetary
theology of the kingdom of God, the gospel of Jesus of Nazareth,
the presence of the cosmic Christ, the indwelling of the Holy Spirit
within each and all of us, and the return of all beings to the Creator
God can inspire such a wholistic integration in us, in the churches
and among peoples.

In this total mission we meet Jesus the Christ more fully. The
more deeply we are committed to the human cause and the care of
nature, the more truly we are identified with Jesus the Christ, who
gave his life in service to others. The churches too will grow to ma-
turity insofar as they die to themselves in service to all.

This is the same spirituality of the emptying of ourselves as persons and groups in courageous service to others in today's world
situation, but always beginning with our local context. The churches
and their institutions will live only in dying to self for others—for
this is the law of the gospel. It is the poor, the weak, the marginalized, and defenseless nature that may point the churches to the
way of the cross—the unique path to the resurrection.

Index